CONSTRUCTS OF PROPHECY IN THE FORMER AND
LATTER PROPHETS AND OTHER TEXTS

Society of Biblical Literature

Ancient Near East Monographs

General Editors
Ehud Ben Zvi
Roxana Flammini

Editorial Board
Michael H. Floyd
Jose Galan
Erhard S. Gerstenberger
Steven W. Holloway
Alan Lenzi
Santiago Rostom Maderna
Martti Nissinen
Graciela Gestoso Singer
Juan Manuel Tebes

Number 4
CONSTRUCTS OF PROPHECY IN THE FORMER AND
LATTER PROPHETS AND OTHER TEXTS

CONSTRUCTS OF PROPHECY IN THE FORMER AND LATTER PROPHETS AND OTHER TEXTS

Edited by
Lester L. Grabbe
Martti Nissinen

Society of Biblical Literature
Atlanta

Copyright © 2011 by the Society of Biblical Literature

All rights reserved. No part of this work may be reproduced or published in print form except with permission from the publisher. Individuals are free to copy, distribute, and transmit the work in whole or in part by electronic means or by means of any information or retrieval system under the following conditions: (1) they must include with the work notice of ownership of the copyright by the Society of Biblical Literature; (2) they may not use the work for commercial purposes; and (3) they may not alter, transform, or build upon the work. Requests for permission should be addressed in writing to the Rights and Permissions Office, Society of Biblical Literature, 825 Houston Mill Road, Atlanta, GA 30329, USA.

Library of Congress Cataloging-in-Publication Data

Constructs of prophecy in the former and latter prophets and other texts / edited by Lester L. Grabbe and Martti Nissinen.
   p. cm. — (Society of Biblical Literature ancient Near East monographs ; v. 4)
   Proceedings of meetings of the Prophetic Texts and Their Ancient Contexts Group of the Society of Biblical Literature held in 2007 in Washington, D.C. and in 2008 in Boston, Mass.
   Includes bibliographical references (p.   ) and indexes.
   ISBN 978-1-58983-600-6 (paper binding : alk. paper)— ISBN 978-1-58983-599-3 (electronic format)
   1. Bible. O.T.—Prophecies—Congresses. 2. Bible. O.T.--Criticism, interpretation, etc.—Congresses. 3. Bible. O.T. Prophets—Criticism, interpretation, etc.—Congresses. I. Grabbe, Lester L. II. Nissinen, Martti. III. Society of Biblical Literature. Prophetic Texts and Their Ancient Contexts Group.
   BS1198.C66 2011
   224'.066—dc23
                    2011031964

Dedicated to

EHUD BEN ZVI

Founder of the Prophetic Texts and Their Ancient Contexts Society of Biblical Literature Group

CONTENTS

Contributors ix
Abbreviations xi

Introduction
    Lester L. Grabbe 1

Constructs of Prophets and Prophecy in the Book of Chronicles
    Pancratius C. Beentjes 21

Some Precedents for the Religion of the Book: Josiah's Book and Ancient Revelatory Literature
    Jonathan Ben-Dov 43

The Weberian Construct of Prophecy and Womanist and Feminist Recuperative Criticism
    Steve Cook 65

1 Samuel 1–8 The Prophet as Agent Povocateur
    Serge Frolov 77

Daniel: Sage, Seer . . . and Prophet?
    Lester L. Grabbe 87

Cult of Personality The Eclipse of Pre-exilic Judahite Cultic Structures in the Book of Jeremiah
    Mark Leuchter 95

Zephaniah How this Book Became Prophecy
    Christoph Levin 117

The Shape of Things to Come Redaction and the Early Second Temple Period Prophetic Tradition
    Jill Middlemas 141

Israel and the Nations in the Later Latter Prophets
    David L. Petersen 157

Samuel's Institutional Identity in the Deuteronomistic History
   Marvin A. Sweeney 165

Ezekiel: A Compromised Prophet in Reduced Circumstances
   Lena-Sofia Tiemeyer 175

The Qur'anic David
   Peter Matthews Wright 197

Bibliography 207
Author Index 229
Index of Scripture Citations 235

CONTRIBUTORS

Pancratius Beentjes is Professor Emeritus of Old Testament and Hebrew in the Faculty of Catholic Theology, Tilburg University.

Jonathan Ben-Dov is Senior Lecturer in the Department of Bible, Haifa University.

Steve Cook is an Adjunct Faculty Member of Louisville Presbyterian Theological Seminary.

Serge Frolov is Associate Professor and Nate and Ann Levine Endowed Chair in Jewish Studies at Southern Methodist University.

Lester L. Grabbe is Professor of Hebrew Bible and Early Judaism at the University of Hull.

Mark Leuchter is Director of Jewish Studies at Temple University in Philadelphia.

Christoph Levin is Professor of Old Testament at the Ludwig-Maximilians-Universität, Munich.

Jill Middlemas is Research Associate at the Theology Faculty, University of Zürich.

Martti Nissinen is Professor of Old Testament Studies at the University of Helsinki.

David L. Petersen is the Franklin Nutting Parker Professor of Old Testament in the Candler School of Theology at Emory University.

Marvin A. Sweeney is Professor of Hebrew Bible, Claremont School of Theology, and Professor of Religion, Claremont Graduate University.

Lena-Sofia Tiemeyer is Lecturer in Old Testament/Hebrew Bible at the University of Aberdeen.

Peter Matthews Wright is Assistant Professor, Department of Religion, Colorado College, Colorado Springs.

ABBREVIATIONS

AASF	Annales Academiae Scientiarum Fennicae
AASOR	Annual of the American Schools of Oriental Research
AB	Anchor Bible
ABD	David Noel Freedman (ed.), *Anchor Bible Dictionary* (6 vols.; Garden City, NY: Doubleday, 1992)
ADPV	Abhandlungen des Deutschen Palästina-Vereins
AfO	*Archiv für Orientforschung*
AGAJU	Arbeiten zur Geschichte des antiken Judentums und des Urchristentums
ALGHJ	Arbeiten zur Literatur und Geschichte des hellenistischen Judentums
AnBib	Analecta biblica
ANET	James B. Pritchard, *Ancient Near Eastern Texts Relating to the Old Testament* (3rd ed. with Supplement; Princeton: Princeton University Press, 1969)
AOAT	Alter Orient und Altes Testament
ASOR	American Schools of Oriental Research
ASR	*American Sociological Review*
ATD	Das Alte Testament Deutsch
BA	*Biblical Archeologist*
BAR	*Biblical Archaeology Review*
BASOR	Bulletin of the American Schools of Oriental Research
BBB	Bonner biblische Beiträge
BBR	*Bulletin for Biblical Research*
BCE	Before the Common Era (= BC)
BEATAJ	Beiträge zur Erforschung des Alten Testaments und des antiken Judentums
BETL	Bibliotheca Ephemeridum Theologicarum Lovaniensium
BHS	*Biblia Hebraica Stuttgartensia*
BJRL	*Bulletin of the John Rylands Library*
Bib	*Biblica*
BibOr	Biblica et orientalia
BN	*Biblische Notizen*
BO	*Bibliotheca Orientalis*

BWANT	Beiträge zur Wissenschaft vom Alten und Neuen Testament
BZ	*Biblische Zeitschrift*
BZAW	Beihefte zur *ZAW*
CBC	Century Bible Commentary
CBET	Contributions to Biblical Exegesis and Theology
CBQ	*Catholic Biblical Quarterly*
CBQMS	*Catholic Biblical Quarterly* Monograph Series
ConBOT	Conjectanea biblica, Old Testament
CRAIBL	Comptes rendus de l'Academie des inscriptions et belles-lettres
CR: BS	*Currents in Research: Biblical Studies*
CT	Cuneiform Texts in the Collections of the British Museum
DtrH	Deuteronomistic History
EncJud	*Encyclopedia Judaica*
EsIr	*Eretz-Israel*
ESHM	European Seminar in Historical Methodology
ET	English translation
ETL	Ephemeridae Theologicae Lovaniensis
EvT	*Evangelische Theologie*
FAT	Forschungen zum Alten Testament
FOTL	Forms of Old Testament Literature
FRLANT	Forschungen zur Religion und Literatur des Alten und Neuen Testaments
HAR	*Hebrew Annual Review*
HAT	Handbuch zum Alten Testament
HBM	Hebrew Bible Monographs
HK	Handkommentar zum Alten Testament
HSM	Harvard Semitic Monographs
HSS	Harvard Semitic Studies
HTR	*Harvard Theological Review*
HUCA	*Hebrew Union College Annual*
ICC	International Critical Commentary
IEJ	*Israel Exploration Journal*
JAAR	*Journal of the American Academy of Religion*
JANES	*Journal of the Ancient Near Eastern Society of Columbia University*
JAOS	*Journal of the American Oriental Society*
JBL	*Journal of Biblical Literature*
JCS	*Journal of Cuneiform Studies*

JEA	*Journal of Egyptian Archaeology*
JETS	*Journal of the Evangelical Theological Society*
JJS	*Journal of Jewish Studies*
JPSTC	Jewish Publication Society Torah Commentary
JQR	*Jewish Quarterly Review*
JNES	*Journal of Near Eastern Studies*
JNSL	*Journal of Northwest Semitic Languages*
JSOT	*Journal for the Study of the Old Testament*
JSOTSup	Supplements to *Journal for the Study of the Old Testament*
JSPSup	Supplements to *Journal for the Study of Pseudepigrapha*
JSRC	Jerusalem Studies in Religion and Culture
JSS	*Journal of Semitic Studies*
JTS	*Journal of Theological Studies*
KAT	Kommentar zum Alten Testament
KHC	Kurzer Hand-Commentar zum Alten Testament
LHBOTS	Library of Hebrew Bible/Old Testament Studies
LAS	Simo Parpola, *Letters from Assyrian Scholars to the Kings Esarhaddon and Assurbanipal*, 2 vols; AOAT 5/1–2, 1970–1983.
LS	Louvain Studies
LXX	Septuagint version of the Old Testament
MT	Masoretic text
NABU	Nouvelles assyriologiques brèves et utilitaires
NCB	New Century Bible
NEB	Neue Echter Bibel
NICOT	New International Commentary of the Old Testament
NJPS	*The New Jewish Publication Society Jewish Study Bible*
OBO	Orbis biblicus et orientalis
OBT	Overtures to Biblical Theology
Or	*Orientalia*
OTL	Old Testament Library
OTS	*Oudtestamentische Studiën*
PEQ	*Palestine Exploration Quarterly*
RB	*Revue Biblique*
R&T	*Religion & Theology*
SAA	State Archives of Assyria
SAAS	State Archives of Assyria Studies

SANE	Studies on the Ancient Near East
SBL	Society of Biblical Literature
SBLBMI	SBL Bible and its Modern Interpreters
SBLDS	SBL Dissertation Series
SBLMS	SBL Monograph Series
SBLSBL	SBL Studies in Biblical Literature
SBLSBS	SBL Sources for Biblical Study
SBLSCS	SBL Septuagint and Cognate Studies
SBLSymS	SBL Symposium Series
SBLWAW	SBL Writings from the Ancient World
SBS	Stuttgarter Bibelstudien
SBT	Studies in Biblical Theology
SEL	*Studi epigrafici e linguistici*
SHANE	Studies in the History of the Ancient Near East
SHCANE	Studies in the History and Culture of the Ancient Near East
SHR	Studies in the History of Religions
SJOT	*Scandinavian Journal of the Old Testament*
SSN	Studia Semitica Neerlandica
SWBA	Social World of Biblical Antiquity
TA	*Tel Aviv*
THAT	*Theologisches Handwörterbuch zum Alten Testament* (2 vols.; ed. Ernst Jenni and Claus Westermann; Munich: Kaiser, 1967)
ThTo	*Theology Today*
TRE	*Theologische Realenzyklopädie*
TRu	*Theologische Rundshau*
TynBul	*Tyndale Bulletin*
TZ	*Theologische Zeitschrift*
UF	*Ugarit-Forschungen*
VT	*Vetus Testamentum*
VTSup	Supplements to *Vetus Testamentum*
WBC	Word Bible Commentary
WMANT	Wissenschaftliche Monographien zum Alten und Neuen Testament
ZA	*Zeitschrift für Assyrologie und vorderasiatische Archäologie*
ZABR	*Zeitschrift für altorientalische und biblische Rechtsgeschichte*
ZAH	*Zeitschrift für Althebräistik*

ZAR	*Zeitschrift für altorientalische und biblische Rechtsgeschichte*
ZAW	*Zeitschrift für die attestamentliche Wissenschaft*
ZDPV	*Zeitschrift des Deutschen Palästina-Vereins*
ZTK	*Zeitschrift für Theologie und Kirche*

INTRODUCTION

Lester L. Grabbe

The Prophetic Texts and their Ancient Contexts Group (PTAC), one of the many groups within the Society of Biblical Literature, was founded by Ehud Ben Zvi in 1998. He chaired the steering committee and was the driving force behind PTAC for almost a decade, until he relinquished the chair at the end of 2006, as required by regulations. Since January 1, 2007, Martti Nissinen and Lester Grabbe have served as co-chairs of PTAC, though Ehud Ben Zvi continues on the steering committee and is also available to offer advice from his experience. In tribute to his vision and work we have dedicated this volume to the PTAC founder, Ehud Ben Zvi.

The contents of the present volume come from the PTAC meetings in Washington, D.C. in 2007 ("Constructs of Prophecy in the Former Prophets and Daniel") and in Boston in 2008 ("Constructs of Prophecy in the Latter Prophets"). As indicated by the overall theme of each session, the emphasis was on the "constructs of prophecy" as found in both the Former and Latter Prophets, but more controversially, the question of prophecy in some other literature (such as Chronicles and the Quran) is also addressed. There is a good reason for broadening the scope of the volume in this way.

When the steering committee chose the themes of the Former and the Latter Prophets for two separate sessions, the main reason was to see how different sections of the Bible may have differed in how prophecy was constructed. But it was recognized that the different types of biblical literature and the different approaches to them were not exhausted by drawing on these two main prophetic sections of the biblical text. Hence, essays on Daniel, Chronicles, and the Qur'an were also accepted for the volume to give this additional perspective.

By "constructs of prophecy" is meant potentially two separate issues. There is the way that the various biblical books construct prophecy, and there is the way in which modern scholars go about constructing prophecy in ancient Israel. Both approaches are valid and important, and both are addressed by the various essays in this volume. This leads to a number of themes cutting through the essays, which are spelled out later in this Introduction. Each contributor was given scope to develop his or her essay as seemed best to the author. This means that there are a variety of methods and a variety of approaches, a plurality that demonstrates the earnest quest for understanding that still goes on in a field so frequently plowed over the past decades.

The rest of this Introduction will be devoted to the papers offered on those two occasions. The first part gives a summary of the individual articles. Part two integrates the articles by addressing common themes and also some of the main points arising from the individual studies.

The reader may wonder why the volume lacks a contribution by one of the editors, Martti Nissinen. The reason for this is that his essay on the very topic of the volume will appear in another context.[1]

SUMMARY OF PAPERS

In one of the essays on prophecy outside the Former and Latter Prophets **Pancratius Beentjes** examines "Constructs of Prophets and Prophecy in the Book of Chronicles." Because of differences from the books of Samuel and Kings and the small number of addresses adopted from those books, it appears that the Chronicler had a particular view of prophets and prophecy. The "classical prophets" are presented in a completely different way from other parts of the Hebrew Bible: seldom if ever are the classical prophets central characters and many prophets in the Chronicles not found elsewhere in the Bible (these are probably the Chronicler's invention, but it is suggested that here is the place to look for the Chronicler's own theological conventions and accents). There is a distinction between speakers with a prophetic title and those introduced by "possession formulae" but not title. The former normally speaks to the king; the latter, to the people. The former gives the interpretation of events; the latter, inspired interpretation of authoritative texts. The Chronicler's view should be apparent in prophetic passages with no parallel elsewhere in the Hebrew Bible, as follows: 2 Chr 12:5–8 introduces the theme of abandoning the Torah and also

---

[1] Martti Nissinen, "Prophecy as Construct: Ancient and Modern," forthcoming in *"Thus Speaks Ishtar of Arbela": Prophecy in Israel, Assyria and Egypt in the Neo-Assyrian Period* (ed. Robert P. Gordon and Hans M. Barstad; Winona Lake, Ind.: Eisenbrauns, 2012).

uses the words "treachery" (מעל) and "humble themselves" (נכנע). Second Chronicles 15:1–7 employs the "possession formula" to show the divine authority of the prophet. A mosaic of prophetic texts is placed in Azariah's mouth. The notions of "seeking" YHWH and "being found" occur, though also "forsaking" YHWH. Azariah (as the Chronicler's spokesman) makes a number of statements from the Latter Prophets but almost entirely without verbal quotation. In 2 Chr 20:14–17 is a quotation from Exod 14:13–14 in which both display a similar narrative structure. In Chronicles the prophets are also characterized as keepers of the royal archives, with many references to prophets in connection with documents (2 Chr 9:29 uses "prophecy" with reference to a written document). Thus, the Chronicler does not use explicit quotes from the Former and Latter Prophets, refuses to make classical prophets central characters, and uses the verb "to prophesy" in a special way to refer to liturgical functions (1 Chr 25:1–3 should be read as having the verb rather than the noun).

In "Some Precedents for the Religion of the Book: Josiah's Book and Ancient Revelatory Literature," **Jonathan Ben-Dov** explores the mutual relationship between prophecy, law, and authoritative books. Moshe Weinfeld argued that Josiah initiated a new "religion of the book." Deuteronomy combines two key concepts of the later monotheistic religions: writtenness and revelation. The Josiah narrative uses the same building blocks that were later used to construct canonical awareness: the concepts of prophecy, law, and divine authority of the written word. Yet these concepts existed long before in the book culture of the ancient Near East. As argued in an earlier article, Josiah's reform takes place in two distinctive settings: the oracular process of the court that supported the king's religious reform and the legal-canonical setting in which Deuteronomy became part of the legal document that made up the Torah. The composition of the narrative of Josiah's reform has been much debated, but the assumption that a book find must be Deuteronomistic needs to be contested. In the original story the book was not Deuteronomy or the book of the law. The story in its original form intended to legitimate Josiah's religious reforms. It reaffirmed the divine instructions to the king by providing a cross check in another divinatory medium. A number of examples are known from the ancient Near East in which texts are used as oracular media. In the passage the book sometimes referred to as *sēper hattôrāh* and sometimes as *sēper habbĕrit*. The latter is used when specifically Deuteronomic concepts (e.g., the reading of the law; a centralized Passover) are referred to, but in the former the word *tôrāh* has the prophetic-divinatory meaning of "instruction, oracle" (a similar meaning to its Akkadian cognate *tērtum*). The finding of a text is exemplified in Second Plague Prayer of Mursili, in which two old tablets with religious messages were found. He tested their messages by means of oracular queries and then implemented their messages. The two different modes by which Assyrian prophetic texts have come down to us are the short format for notes, reports, and the like to record oral utterances but not meant for preservation, and a more formal multi-column format for long term storage. It may be that Josiah's book was a short report (only short sections of Deuteronomy) in its original form but was later expanded to a more extensive and permanent form. Precedents for a "religion of the book" can be found in Ashurbanipal and Nabonidus, both of whom had the astrological series *Enūma Anu Enlil* copied onto ivory writing boards so that they could consult them (cf. Deut 17:18). This was revealed authoritative literature that occasioned reflection, devotion, and even kingly attention to be understood. It served as an early laboratory for developing a "religion of the book"; indeed, *Enūma Anu Enlil* was authored "by the mouth of (the god) Ea" and was transmitted to humanity through the sage Enmeduranki. To conclude, reflection on the concepts of writtenness, revelation, and scribal authority reached its peak in Mesopotamia in the Neo-Assyrian and Neo-Babylonian periods. These illustrate a parallel (though not necessarily a borrowing) with the acculturation of writing and scholarly habits in ancient Judah. Religion under the monarchy was not a "religion of the book," but Josiah's book created a transition point rather than a revolution.

Steve Cook ("The Weberian Construct of Prophecy and Womanist and Feminist Recuperative Criticism") notes that scholars have constructed ancient Israel according to various paradigms. The purpose of this essay is to interact with womanist and feminist recuperative critics' points of contact with a Weberian model of prophecy, recognizing the value of this model for promoting women in religious leadership. Like Weber, recuperative scholars have operated with ideas that prophets achieve their status on the basis of charisma, preach or articulate religious doctrine, and have enduring social importance. This essay draws upon recuperative criticism from the nineteenth century (Jarena Lee, Maria Stewart, and Elizabeth Cady Stanton) to the present (Phyllis Bird, Lisa Davison, and Wilda Gafney). Recuperative hermeneutics has been appreciated and critiqued in the *Postmodern Bible*. This essay concludes by providing further thoughts on the gains derived from recuperative attention to women prophets in the Hebrew Bible and exploring possible "blind spots" in this work.

Serge Frolov's "1 Samuel 1–8: The Prophet as Agent Provocateur" argues that there is substantial tension between the concepts of prophecy and the prophet's role emerging from Deut 18, which contains the only block of prophecy-related commandments in the Torah, and the first few chapters of 1 Samuel, which feature the first biblical character consistently referred to as a prophet. In Samuel's first prophetic experience (1 Sam 3), he receives a message that is entirely redundant, because it does not go beyond what is already known to both Eli and the audience; accordingly, the main purpose of the theophany is to lay the foundation of his prophetic reputation. This ensures that the people heed Samuel's call to confront Philistine rule (1 Sam 4:1a); yet, the oracle leads to two defeats and loss of the ark. He consequently acts here as *agent provocateur*, making it possible for YHWH to settle scores with Eli and his wayward sons. A similar pattern is found in 1 Sam 8. In this case, God warns Samuel of the disaster that will follow the appointment of a human king, but tells Samuel to heed the people's wishes, nevertheless. God's command to attack the Philistines in 1 Sam 4 and to appoint a king in 1 Sam 8 can be seen as real-life tests of the Deuteronomic model of prophecy in Deut 18. There are the sinister aspects to this model: first, it may land the people in a Catch-22 situation, with obedience failing to bring the rewards promised in Deut 28; second, Deuteronomy's identification of true and false prophecy (18:22) would make Samuel seem a false prophet, even though he faithfully spoke God's words. First Sam 1–8 may thus be offering an alternative to the Deuteronomic concept of prophecy. Two lines of investigation appear promising. One sees 1 Sam 1–8 as an extension and refinement of Deuteronomic thought: the people suffer for their own sins, even if it is the result of following the prophet's instructions. Another approach is to see 1 Sam 1–8 as directed polemically against the Deuteronomic concept of prophecy. It could be an anti-Deuteronomic addition to a largely Deuteronomistic base narrative of the Former Prophets (the views on the cult, priesthood, monarchy, and ark in this section are also anti-Deuteronomic). The clash between Deut 18 and 1 Sam 1–8 may exemplify the change that developed historically in which God's communication ceased to be the word of the prophet and became the written Torah.

Lester L. Grabbe asks, "Daniel: Sage, Seer … and *Prophet*?" He begins by making the point that there is a difference between prophetic literature and the persona of a prophet. He then examines Amos and compares the book with the book of Daniel. They both contain oracles against other nations ("oracles against the nations" in Amos and prophecies against Near Eastern empires in Daniel). Both contain symbolic visions that indicate God's plans for the future. Daniel seems to embody the statement in Amos 3:7: "For the Lord YHWH will do nothing except that he reveals his purpose to his servants the prophets." Of course, there are differences between Amos and Daniel—some very large differences—but there are also big differences between Amos and Nahum and between Daniel and the apocalypse *4 Ezra*. Similarly, there are some fundamental parallels between Jeremiah and Daniel, and many of the characteristics of Jeremiah's life are paralleled in Daniel's. Daniel looks as much like a prophet as Jeremiah. Apocalypses are often put in the mouth of an ancient patriarch, but the material in prophetic books may be as pseudonymous, with much material that did not stem from the prophet named in the title. On the other hand, the content of both prophecies and apocalypses may be the result of visions or ecstatic experiences. In most cases, we do not know for sure, but the possibility is there. Much can be explained if we accept that prophecy is a form of divination (spirit or possession divination) and that apocalyptic is a subdivision of prophecy.

In looking at the "Cult of Personality: The Eclipse of Pre-Exilic Judahite Cultic Structures in the Book of Jeremiah," **Mark Leuchter** notes the "antonymic" character of Jeremiah: it makes statements and undertakes activities that are mutually contradictory. This makes it difficult to place him within a specific social or religious context. Yet this is the key to its survival, because the book's authors created a model for survival that placed the prophetic personality above and beyond the cult. Three major themes within the book of Jeremiah lay the foundations for this authorial strategy. The first theme is the Levitical cult. Jeremiah came from the Mushite Levites of Anathoth, and there are Levitical motifs in his call narrative, including the important Levitical figures of Moses and Samuel. Jeremiah 34 represents a Levite proclaiming *torah*. Yet several passages also go against this Levitical heritage. One is 11:21–23, against the men of Anathoth; the imagery of the Song of Moses (Deut 32) is used against the Levites, as also in Jer 2–6. The message is that this Levitical cult and lineage are to be cut off, i.e., that the Mushite Levites in Anathoth would no longer compete with the prevailing Deuteronomic ideology. In another passage, Jeremiah is forbidden to marry and have offspring, which symbolizes the debilitation of the Levitical cult. A further passage concerns the "new covenant" oracle in Jer 31:31–34, which to a significant degree empowers the laity with regard to sacral knowledge. The traditional duties of the Levite to teach (Deut 33:8–11) are negated, since all will know the *torah*. In the context of Jer 30–31 the passage affirms covenantal blessings on the Levites but redirects their role to supporting the new Josianic theological enterprise. The second theme is royal and family cults. The attitude to these in Jeremiah is largely negative. Only two kings receive sympathy: Josiah and Jehoiachin. A major reason seems to be that both are separated from the royal cult in Jerusalem. This is part of the Deuteronomic assault on family religion, and many Jeremiah oracles critique family (e.g., 7:16–20). The cult of "the Queen of Heaven" is a good example of a practice condemned by Deuteronomy, though not mentioned by name there. The term in Jeremiah has a deliberate ambiguity, to condemn any numinous female concept. Similarly, "Baal" in Jeremiah represents any religious practices condemned in Deuteronomy. Jehoiakim and Zedekiah are condemned by the prophetic word because of the royal family cult. Regional shrines and family-based religious structures throughout the country imitated the royal cult; hence, the oracle of 8:1–3, in which the practice of the family cult leads to being cut off from the family in the afterlife. The third theme is the Deuteronomic cult. Surprisingly, Jeremiah subjects the Deuteronomic cult to the same critique as the Levitical and family cults, especially the temple sermon of 7:(1–2)3–5. The temple is regarded as legitimate (28:6), especially as Jeremiah supports Deut 12 which is central to the Josianic reform. But instead of a dwelling place for God, it is a dwelling place for the people (7:3), a symbolic locus of social and ethical values. Unlike the one Mosaic prophet (Deut 18:15–18), Jeremiah (and Kings) mentions several prophets as Deuteronomic advocates. Jeremiah is mostly unsupportive of these prophets (Hananiah being a prime example). In conclusion, Jeremiah promotes an alternative cult, the prophetic literary *persona*, of which Jeremiah is the outstanding example. Jeremiah's rhetoric dismantles all dominant cultic and theological traditions from pre-exilic times. The personality of Jeremiah became the symbol to which exiled Judahites could look as a model of faith.

Christoph Levin ("Zephaniah: How this Book Became Prophecy") argues, contrary to long scholarly tradition, that prophetic books came into being by *Fortschreibung*. That is, they did not begin with the preaching of an individual prophet but developed by literary growth of a non-prophetic writing. In Zephaniah individual sayings are mostly closely linked, with few independent sayings. *Fortschreibung* requires a nucleus: in Zephaniah this is found in ch. 1. An analysis of 1:1–2:3 indicates seven main layers. The superscription (1:1) is editorial, probably composed by interbiblical combination. A sort of motto follows in 1:2–3, alluding to Gen 6–8, and seems to be a later insertion. The "sin of Manasseh" (1:4–6) draws on language and detail from the book of Ezekiel, Jer 19, and 2 Kgs 23; the language of v. 6 is that of late piety, no earlier than the Persian period. The theophany of 1:7 is couched as a cultic proclamation and is not a part of the original prophetic saying. Zephaniah 1:8–13, which explains the coming of the catastrophe, is often ascribed to the prophet. From the literary form and syntax, this is probably an insertion. It constitutes a threat, expanded by the futility curse of v. 13, while the topographical details in v. 10 are those of Persian-Period Jerusalem. The Day of YHWH (1:14–16a) seems to have been originally a positive celebration: a comparison with Ps 97 shows the cultic origin of the terminology here. But the allusion to Amos 5 in v. 15 changes it into a prophecy of doom. In 1:16b–2:3 the eschatological focus of the motto (1:2–3) is applied to the Day of YHWH, expanding it to a cosmic catastrophe, using the idea of late eschatology as found in the Isaiah Apocalypse and the book of Joel. In sum, the first step in the growth of the book was a cultic proclamation relating to the Day of YHWH in 1:7, 14, and 15.

In the "Shape of Things to Come: Redaction and the Early Second Temple Period Prophetic Tradition," **Jill Middlemas** investigates the form of editorial additions to prophetic states, using Haggai and Zechariah 1–8 as a test case. Much of the discussion has followed the lead of Peter Ackroyd who distinguished editorial additions from the words of the prophet and Willem Beuken who assessed the circles that gave rise to the editorial additions, arguing that the framing material has linguistic characteristics in common with

Chronicles. Middlemas finds that the editorial material in Haggai and Zech 1–8 falls into four different categories. First, an intermediary formula in which an individual is represented as one conveying a divine message. This may be the prophet himself but, as in Zechariah, may be an interpeting angel. Second, a formula with historical information, such as a dating formula. Third, a formula in which the two are combined, as in Hag 2:1. The combination of intermediary, dating, and historical information is sometimes referred to as the *Wortereignisformel* ("word-event formula"), as in Hag 1:1–2 and Zech 7:1–3. Fourth, the editorial formula provides interpretative detail. Large blocks of editorially added interpretative material appear alongside the visions in Zechariah (e.g., Zech 3:6–10). This editorial activity has a variety of functions: to preserve historical context, to give legitimacy to the prophet and authority to his tradition, to link books, to clarify and explain, and to indicate the immediacy of the words transmitted. Reassessments of the rhetoric of Haggai and Zech 1–8 suggest different approaches to understanding the nature of the prophetic book than by separating out the editorial material, however. Michael Floyd has argued, for example, that much regarded as editorial activity is actually an integral part of the oracles themselves, sharing language and viewpoint with the oracles. The framework and speeches in Haggai are inextricably intertwined, forming a unified composition in outlook and purpose. Moreover, Carol and Eric Meyers have identified a concentric structure in Zech 1–8, in which the fourth and fifth visions form the core (and focus attention on the temple and leadership in the community), with the first three parallelling the last three. Middlemas builds on this suggestion by noting that a concentric structure is found more widely than the night visions and encompasses the whole of Zech 1–8. A concentric structure is identifiable elsewhere in the Hebrew Bible. For instance, the prophecies of Isa 56–66 (Trito-Isaiah) are thought to have a concentric shape, in which a series of explanatory details gather around a core of Isa 60–62. This core links to Deutero-Isaiah by recapitulating the main prophecies of Isa 40–55, which makes it function like an attributive or chronological framework. It allows the editor to comment on the core text by the editorial additions arranged concentrically around it. A similar arrangement has been suggested for Amos, Lamentations, Proverbs, and Job. An examination of the editorial strategies in Haggai and Zechariah (along with a brief look at Trito-Isaiah) suggests limitations as well as the importance of literary shaping as an editorial strategy. Greater attention to the rhetorics of the prophetic books indicates new ways of analyzing the editorial material, especially highlighting how further work needs to be done on concentric composition and editing.

David L. Petersen ("Israel and the Nations in the Later Latter Prophets") examines the oracles against the nations in the last six books of the Twelve (Nahum, Habakkuk, Zephaniah, Haggai, Zechariah, and Malachi) to ask how the context affected the nature of prophecy and literature. In the first half of the

Minor Prophets, the oracles against the nations are specific but there are also general comments on "the nations" (probably redactional). The oracles against the specific nations are not like those in Amos and the major prophets, except in Zephaniah and Zechariah. They tend to be vague, and the oracles against specific nations are clearly less prominent in the latter half of the Twelve. The language of references to "peoples" or "nations" is different from that used of individual nations. In the last six books are references to (1) YHWH fighting against the nations and (2) to the nations venerating YHWH (found in Zephaniah, Zechariah, and Malachi but not used in reference to individual nations) in various modes: (a) from a distance, (b) by pilgrimage to Jerusalem, (c) by other means of veneration. How is one to explain this new language and views with regard to the nations? The oracles against the nations were rooted in the theo-political world of Jerusalem, with YHWH's rule of Zion and the prophetic utterances in the David court and chapel (i.e., the temple). In the Persian period, however, there was no longer a royal court in Jerusalem, but foreign nations were still important because of the diaspora of Judahites. Also, even though the court had disappeared, the temple still existed, and prophecy was associated with temple ritual in this period (e.g., the Levitical singers). The Psalms have some of the themes known from prophetic literature, supporting the view that the language of late prophetic literature comes from the sphere of worship. This leads to several conclusions: (1) The oracles against the nations are primarily phenomena of the monarchic period (the David court), with little positive comment; (2) The oracles against the nations become less important in prophetic literature at the end of Judah as a state and are replaced by more general references to "the nations"; (3) Post-exilic prophetic discourse about the nations includes diverse traditions: judgment, pilgrimage, and veneration; (4) Veneration of YHWH is a new element in the later Latter Prophets, with the closest literary parallels in the Psalms, suggesting connections with the ritual world. International discourse is "de-historicized" and becomes more general; (5) Further study is needed on the Major Prophets and first half of the Twelve to confirm or qualify this perspective.

Marvin A. Sweeney considers "Samuel's Institutional Identity in the Deuteronomistic History." His institutional identity is unclear in that he functions as a visionary prophet, a cultic priest, and a judge in the narratives. It is true that 1 Samuel always refers to Samuel as a prophet and never as priest or judge. A key passage for the prophetic identity is 1 Sam 3:20–21 in which Samuel is referred to as a "prophet" (*nābî'*), he experiences a vision to inaugurate his career, and his visionary experiences overcomes the dearth of prophecy in Israel at the time. In the context of anointing Saul as king, he is referred to as "seer" (*rô'ēh*) and "man of G-d" (1 Sam 9–10). A number of other passages also make him a prophet. Although he is never referred to by the noun "judge," the verbal form ("he judged") is used in 1 Sam 7:6, 15, 17, and he also appoints his sons as "judges" (1 Sam 8:1–3). His role as judge also has priestly overtones, as when he sacrifices and calls on YHWH before battle but does not actually lead troops into battle. Thus, his functions as a judge coincide with those of priest. As with "judge," the term "priest" or "Levite" is never used of him, but he frequently functions as a priest. He presides over several sorts of sacrifice, including the "whole burnt offering" (*'ōlâ*), the "sacrifice" (*zevaʿ*), and the "well-being offering" (*šĕlāmîm*). Saul, on the other hand, is condemned for offering some of these same offerings. But Samuel's role as visionary is also an indication of his priestly status. Visionary experiences were not exclusively associated with prophets but often occurred in a temple context. The high priest entered the Holy of Holies once a year, where he might have a vision of God, and his garments contained the ephod. Samuel's initial visionary experience took place in Shiloh where he had access to the temple and the ark of the covenant. The Chronicler resolves the potential conflict by making Samuel's father Elkanah a Levite. So why does 1 Samuel label Samuel only as a prophet but not priest? There are three considerations: (1) Northern traditions often give leading figures, such as Abraham and Jacob, prophetic features; (2) Numbers 3 shows awareness that the first-born functioned as priests before the tribe of Levi was designated in this role, as do other passages requiring the first-born to be redeemed; (3) The DtrH seems to have taken an earlier Samuel narrative in which he functions as a priest and edited it to characterize him as a prophet. To sum up, Samuel follows the model of priest in Northern Israel, where the first-born still functioned in this pre-Levitical role.

Lena-Sofia Tiemeyer ("Ezekiel—A Compromised Prophet in Reduced Circumstances") looks at the literary persona of Ezekiel in the MT of the book (without addressing historical questions). First, Ezekiel appears as "God's appointed marionette." Ezekiel seems to be God's ultimate tool, yet there are hints that he is uncomfortable with this role. In contrast to many other prophets, Ezekiel speaks little with YHWH in the vision reports but instead falls to the ground, seems to have no control over his body or outward show of feelings, and is described as more like a robot. Although described as without initiative or independence, here and there are references to Ezekiel's feelings, suggesting his reluctance to be so controlled by God. Second, Ezekiel appears as God's appointed spokesman. With Ezekiel the prophetic office is redefined: previous prophets commonly had the task of intercession, even those of the sixth century BCE, and Ezekiel was modelled on Moses for whom intercession was a key duty. But Ezekiel is not an intercessor. Two key themes contribute to this redefinition: first is his call to be a watchman, which entails conveying God's will verbatim. The second is Ezekiel's being rendered mute: he is not permitted to speak beyond what God tells him. He is reduced to a one-sided signpost. There are hints that Ezekiel understands this and is frustrated that he cannot speak or intercede for Israel. Ezekiel is willing to intercede for his people but is not allowed to (9:8). God's mind is made up (ch. 11) and attempts for Ezekiel to intercede are rejected. Although God calls for an intercessor (22:30), he does not allow Ezekiel to fulfill that function. Indeed, the lack of reference to prophetic language in 40–48 suggests that Ezekiel gave up the prophetic office. Who gains from this change of the prophetic role? It can be argued that all lose: God, the people, and Ezekiel himself. Ezekiel's persona is one of mute protest. Is the "I" of the book of Ezekiel a protest by its author against God, against the theodicy of the book?

In the second paper going outside the Former and Latter Prophets, **Peter Matthews Wright** considers "The Qur'anic David." A current dispute concerns the Qur'anic appropriation and "correction" of prior sacred revelations and how to evaluate them. Muslims usually see this as evidence that the Qur'an has superseded earlier writings. Yet the Qur'an states in several places that it "confirms" prior scriptures. To "correct" is not the same as to supersede. The original context is very important. This shows that the Qur'anic corrections of biblical material is only an example of a wider Near Eastern rhetorical mode that is also attested in the Bible. The Qur'an is part of a religious literary tradition beginning perhaps as early as the twelfth century BCE and draws not only on Old Testament and New Testament prophecy but also that from the wider ancient Near East. It belongs to a "super-canon" that includes Zoroastrian literature and the Tanakh. The Qur'anic David illustrates how the Qur'an corrects prior sacred traditions but also confirms them. David appears as a prophetic figure. He also appears as a penitent, though the nature of his sin is not spelled out. But 1 Chronicles is also silent on David's sin. Thus, both 1 Chr 20 and the Qur'an use allusion to show that they are aware of the tradition but are passing on an existing tradition while also revising it. The revisionist interpretation of 1 Chronicles was only the beginning of a long process. The rabbis of the Babylonian Talmud continued to sanitize the Davidic tradition and the Qur'an brought it to a state of "prophetic impeccability." Indeed, the interpretation of early prophecy is a post-exilic prophetic mode. This "rehabilitation" of David is part of a larger literary activity in the ancient Near East ("the rehabilitation of kings"?), as is illustrated by the development of the Alexander legend.

THEMES AND TOPICS

This section discusses various major themes and topics that arise from the essays. In some cases, an important topic is confined to one essay, whereas sometimes a theme cuts across several essays. In either case, though, the topic or theme is an important one to which attention needs to be drawn. Please note that reference to essays in the present volume are referred to by citing the AUTHOR'S NAME IN SMALL CAPS.

Prophets and Books

We tend to think of prophecy as an oral phenomenon, but most of what we know about prophets is related to the written word: much of our knowledge is from prophetic books, including the record of possible prophetic words themselves; communication in writing rather than orally is a feature of many prophetic pronouncements (cf. Jer 29; 30:1–2; 36). A number of the contributors brought up issues relating to books and written prophecies.

A continuing issue of discussion is how the prophetic books originated. Was a collection of originally oral sayings collected as the core, which was later developed and expanded to give the final prophetic book? As pointed out by BEN-DOV, Martti Nissinen has discussed a phenomenon in Mesopotamian literature that may serve as a useful analogy to the recording of prophecies in writing. Nissinen describes the two methods of recording Assyrian prophecies: the *u'iltu* was an initial note or memorandum that was not regarded as permanent and was not usually retained; however, the temporary text of the prophecy might be recorded on an archival tablet (usually with other prophecies) and preserved in a longer format. The prophetic book may have begun in such a way, with a very small amount of text initially but with a later increase as other material was added over time.

While this might explain the origin of some books, the historical situation is likely to have been more complicated. With regard to the book of Zephaniah, LEVIN argues that the process was *Fortschreibung*, which carries the idea of a nucleus that was then developed (often by drawing on other written texts); however, the book did not begin with a collection of "prophetic words" but a non-prophetic writing—in the case of Zephaniah a cultic proclamation (relating to the Day of YHWH). The idea that the core of present prophetic books was not an oral prophecy or collection of such prophecies but another sort of writing is an intriguing one—indeed, a radical one. In Chronicles BEENTJES found a mosaic of earlier prophetic texts placed in Azariah's mouth. There was seldom explicit quotation, but the author had drawn on previously existing prophetic texts, without doubt. This suggests a particular composition technique.

PETERSEN also looks at the growth of prophetic literature, the last books of the Minor Prophets in his case (Nahum, Habakkuk, Zephaniah, Haggai, Zechariah, and Malachi). He looks specifically at the Oracles against the Nations. These are directed mainly against specific nations in the Major Prophets and Amos. In the last six books of the Twelve, though, the Oracles against the Nations are more general, against "nations" rather than a particular nation; also, the statements have become more diverse, not only about YHWH fighting against or punishing but also veneration of YHWH by the nations, including pilgrimage to Jerusalem. The difference seems to be due to historical development: the original Oracles against the Nations had their origins in the monarchic period, with the background of the royal court, whereas the six books investigated here are post-exilic and reflect that situation (including influence from the Psalms).

Using Haggai and Zech 1–8, MIDDLEMAS discusses how scribes may have worked in their editorial activity. It has been conventional to make a sharp distinction between (original) prophetic material and editorial additions that provide a variety of interpretative material. Yet Michael Floyd has argued that much of the supposed editorial additions are actually integral to the oracles (including shared language and viewpoint). Floyd's argument that the editorial material in Haggai shares the viewpoint of the prophetic oracles draws attention to the variability of editorial strategies among the prophetic books. MIDDLEMAS, drawing on the theory of concentric construction of Carol and Eric Meyers, argues that the same sort of construction is found in Isa 56–66. In both prophetic collections visions are surrounded by material of a more regulatory nature directed to the community. Concentric structuring has also been suggested for Amos, Lamentations, Proverbs, and Job. The question is of course whether this concentric construction is an indication of an original composition or whether it has been created editorially by additions and the importation of material from elsewhere. The latter seems to be the case with regard to Third Isaiah. If it is persuasive that shaping is an editorial strategy akin to the use of framing material to clarify and explain, the analysis of concentric shapes throughout biblical literature would require more attention in assessments of scribal activity.

FROLOV suggests that the differing concepts of prophecy in Deut 18 and 28 versus 1 Sam 1–8 may be in part a redactional question. He suggests that the largely Deuteronomic base narrative of 1 Samuel has a particular view of prophecy, the cult, priesthood, monarch, and ark. Yet 1 Sam 1–8 give a different perspective on all these topics. One explanation would see an expansion of Deuteronomic thought in these chapters, with the people suffering for their own sins, even if following the guidance of a prophet. Another suggestion is rather more radical but entrancing. This is the proposal that this section may be not just a later addition but even a deliberate anti-Deuteronomic addition, meant to present the prophet as an *agent provocateur* who deliberately misleads the people.

If FROLOV is correct, 1 Sam 1–8 offers a different concept of the prophet from that in Deuteronomy (especially 18 and 28), primarily in the importance assigned to the written word in Deuteronomy, whereas obedience to the oral prophetic word is the main reaction expected in 1 Sam 1–8. The movement from prophecy as mainly an oral phenomenon to the primary medium of the written book is an interesting development that is often forgotten. The early prophets were mostly preachers, but when we talk about prophecy today, we usually think of books of the Bible. When scholars discuss the phenomenon of prophecy or the prophet, this basic fact is sometimes forgotten. Most of our discussion around prophecy is based on the written word; the oral utterances of prophets are by and large theoretical rather than a part of the actual data.

Prophetic books also seem to have contributed to Judaism's becoming a "religion of the book" (BEN-DOV). According to the present form of the story, a book was found in the temple in the reign of Josiah and became the basis of his reform. The context suggests that this was a form of the book of Deuteronomy. Yet the Josiah story was not the only one which made the discovery of an ancient book an important impetus for new royal measures: parallels from Mesopotamia suggest that the book originally functioned as a means of confirming Josiah's measures by another form of divination. Revealed authoritative literature was a phenomenon for reflection on revelation, writtenness, and scribal authority in Mesopotamia. Reflection on literature and the scribal process is paralleled in Judah, and this helped to develop a sense of authoritative writings and, eventually, canon. The temple was not abandoned, and the Torah did not become the center of worship until much later.[2] Yet it seems clear that the focus on a holy book is first manifest in diaspora Judaism, perhaps as a substitute or surrogate for the temple. The proximity of the large Jewish community in Babylonia to the ancient Mesopotamian centers may have contributed to this development, however. Also, it can be said that the "religion of the book" had its beginnings under Josiah.

BEENTJES draws attention to the fact that Chronicles associates prophets with archives and documents in a number of passages (1 Chr 29:29; 2 Chr 9:29; 12:15; 13:22; 21:12; 32:32). These passages suggest a number of writings composed by or preserved in the name of various prophets and seers of antiquity, such as the "chronicles [words] of Iddo the seer." We may doubt whether we can take these statements as historically trustworthy descriptions of prophetic figures from the distant past, but they illustrate how the Chronicler saw prophets in his own time and context. Rather than just being preachers and sources of oral statements, they are pictured as scribes and authors.

The importance of writing as a prophetic medium was already noted by Max Weber who emphasized the *sine qua non* (in his opinion) of "emotive

---

[2] Cf. Lester L. Grabbe, *Judaic Religion in the Second Temple Period: Belief and Practice from the Exile to Yavneh* (London: Routledge, 2000), 178–82.

preaching" (*emotionale Predigt*), regardless of whether it was "oral or by pamphlet or revelations spread by written means like the suras of Mohammed."[3]

Prophets and the Cult

Traditionally, prophets have been interpreted as anti-cultic. More recently, this has been seen as a caricature, but some of the old attitude still seems to linger. Several of the essays impinged on the cult in one way or another, but usually it was to describe a more positive relationship between prophet and cult.

With regard to the book of Jeremiah, LEUCHTER is of the opinion that a sustained cultic critique is found in the book: a critique of the Levites (in Jer 11:21–23 Deuteronomy 32 is used to show that the Levitical cult and lineage are to be cut off, specifically the Mushite Levites in Anathoth), a critique of the royal and family cult (a part of the Deuteronomic assault on family religion, including the cult of "the Queen of Heaven" and "Baal," which in Jeremiah represents any religious practices condemned in Deuteronomy), and a critique of even the Deuteronomic cult (the temple becomes the dwelling of the people rather than God). This does not make the book entirely negative to cult as such, however, since the author instead imposes his own alternative cult: this is the cult of the prophetic literary persona.

As BEENTJES points out, Chronicles uses the term "prophesy" in reference to liturgical functions (1 Chr 25:1–3 [to read *nb'* as a verb rather than a noun]). The sons of Asaph, Heman, and Jeduthan "prophesied" to the sound of various musical instruments. They did so at the king's direction. The content of their prophesying seems to have been the glorifying of God (1 Chr 25:3–6), not what is normally understood as prophecy. The liturgical intent of *nb'* in this context seems clear. We might compare the use of *nb'* in some passages of 1 Samuel in which "prophesy" is used in reference to ecstatic utterances that might be interpreted as praise (1 Sam 10:5–6, 10–11, 13; 18:10; 19:20–21, 23–24).

Prophets, Divination, and Apocalyptic

In my opinion, prophecy can be classified as a form of divination.[4] Many would no doubt disagree, but the main function of divination is to ascertain the will of

---

[3] Max Weber, "Religionssoziologie," in *Wirtschaft und Gesellschaft* (2d ed; Tübingen: Mohr Siebeck, 1925), 254: "durch Rede oder Pamphlete oder schriftlich verbreitete Offenbarungen nach Art der Suren Muhammeds"; cf. *The Sociology of Religion*. Boston: Beacon, 2003.

God/the gods. This might well be information on future events but may rather be finding the basis for making a decision or determining the right direction among several alternatives. The subject is complicated, but many prophets induce a "prophetic ecstasy" by various means, such as singing and music, dance, drugs, physical stress or trauma. The prophetic figure might well respond to requests for information from "clients." Again, there has been a tendency in Old Testament scholarship to disassociate the "classical" prophets from trance or ecstasy, but there is no good reason to do so.[5] Some recents studies bear this out.[6]

In Chronicles there is a distinction between speakers who are called "prophet" or "seer" and those introduced by the "possession formula" who are not given a title (BEENTJES). Some prophets are explicitly described as "possessed." By "possession formula" is meant expressions such as "the spirit of God was upon" or "the spirit enveloped." He draws attention to five "inspired messengers," including Amasai (1 Chr 12:19), Azariah (2 Chr 15:1), Jahaziel (2 Chr 20:14), Zechariah (2 Chr 24:20), and Necho (2 Chr 35:21). The speaker with a prophetic title ("prophet" or "seer") normally has the king for an addressee, but those who are characterized by the possession formula, the "inspired messengers," normally speak to the people. The former is the usage of the Chronicler, whereas the "possession formula" is also found in other writings relating to the prophets (e.g., 1 Sam 19:20; Ezek 11:5).

Ezekiel is a puppet in God's hands, as TIEMEYER emphasizes, but this is a phenomenon normal in those experiencing spirit possession. They are taken over by the spirit and cease to have their own will or control of their actions. They

---

[4] Evan M. Zuesse, "Divination," in *The Encyclopedia of Religion*, vol. 4 (ed. Mircea Eliade et al.; New York: Macmillan, 1987), 376–78; Lester L. Grabbe, *Priests, Prophets, Diviners, Sages: A Socio-historical Study of Religious Specialists in Ancient Israel* (Valley Forge, Pa.: Trinity, 1995), 139–41; idem, "Prophetic and Apocalyptic: Time for New Definitions—and New Thinking," in *Knowing the End from the Beginning: The Prophetic, the Apocalyptic, and their Relationships* (ed. Lester L. Grabbe and Robert D. Haak; JSPSup 46; London: T&T Clark, 2003), 107–33.

[5] Grabbe, *Priests, Prophets, Diviners, Sages*, 108–12.

[6] I. M. Lewis, *Ecstatic Religion: A Study of Shamanism and Spirit Possession* (2d ed. London: Routledge, 1989), 32–58; Nils G. Holm, "Ecstasy Research in the 20th Century—An Introduction," in *Religious Ecstasy: Based on Papers Read at the Symposium on Religious Ecstasy Held at Åbo, Finland, on the 26th-28th of August 1981.* (ed. N. G. Holm; Stockholm: Almqvist and Wiksell, 1982), 7–26; Martti Nissinen, "Prophetic Madness: Prophecy and Ecstasy in the Ancient Near East and in Greece," in *Raising Up a Faithful Exegete: Essays in Honor of Richard D. Nelson* (ed. K. L. Noll and Brooks Schramm; Winona Lake, Ind.: Eisenbrauns, 2010), 3–29.

also do not usually remember what they did or said when under the spirit.[7] Ezekiel is certainly taken over by the spirit at various times (Ezek 2:2; 3:12, 14, 22, 24; 11:1, 5, 24; 37:1; 40:1). TIEMEYER's contention is a bit different from this, however. She makes the point that Ezekiel is God's ultimate tool in that he lacks a distinct personality. In the vision reports he says little but instead falls to the ground and appears to have no control over his body. Whether Ezekiel is unconscious of his actions and words while under the power of the spirit is not clear, but a protest against the operation of the spirit would be unusual.

One of the issues that many have regarded as settled a long time ago is the clear distinction between prophecy and apocalyptic. Unfortunately, some scholars do not seem to recognize that the matter is dead and continue to irritate sensible folk by claiming that Daniel is prophecy—as I do in this volume (GRABBE). The argument does not deny a genre of apocalyptic literature or a phenomenon of apocalyptic, but it makes this a subdivision of prophecy (which itself is a sub-division of divination). The many important parallels between a book like Amos or a prophet like Jeremiah support this view of Daniel. There are also major differences between these entities, but major differences also exist between prophetic books and, likewise, between apocalypses. By this classification the important resemblances between types of divination, prophecy and prophetic books, and apocalyptic literature can be better understood.

The Prophetic Persona

A number of the essays draw attention to the variety of ways in which the prophetic persona is constructed in different prophetic contexts, and a variety of prophetic personae issue from the essays here:

Max Weber has some important things to say about prophets (though it is interesting that COOK was the only contributor who mentioned Weber). Yet Weber's lack of specialist knowledge sometimes led to unsupportable statements. For example, he distinguished prophets from priests, which is not surprising, but he then commented, "It is no accident that, with minor exceptions, almost no prophets have emerged from the priestly class,"[8] which is an absurd statement, at least as far as ancient Israel is concerned. This required him to make the further rather silly statement, "Ezekiel ... can hardly be called a

---

[7] Lewis, *Ecstatic Religion*, 32–58.
[8] Weber,"Religionssoziologie," 250: "Es ist kein Zufall, daß mit verschwindenden Ausnahmen, kein Prophet aus der Priesterschaft auch nur hervorgegangen ist"; cf. Weber, *The Sociology of Religion*, 46.

prophet."⁹ He does not seem to comment on such individuals as Jeremiah and Samuel nor the whole question of cultic prophecy.¹⁰ A number of his other statements could be challenged.

Yet Weber recognized the importance of the personal call for all prophets, which some have denied.¹¹ He had further emphasized the importance of charisma as an essential feature of prophetic individuals. This of course tied in with his wider perspective on charisma in relation to individuals in positions of authority and leadership.¹² COOK treated the subject of prophetic charisma in the context of feminist recuperative scholars. In this case, the expression of prophetic charisma as "emotive preaching" was seen as a particularly useful model for this section of scholarship. That preaching could come by various media, including literary compositions.¹³

Another possible persona is the prophet as *agent provocateur* (FROLOV). By this is meant that the prophet says things that cause Israel to sin or omits to mention things that might deter them from sinning. For example, in 1 Sam 4 the prophet Samuel encourages the people to fight the Philistines for the first time in a long time. The implication is that there was a divine promise of victory. In actual fact, God was planning to use this occasion to punish Eli's sons, but Israel had to be defeated to bring this about. The prophet had, in effect, misled the people. Similarly, in 1 Sam 8 YHWH tells Samuel that for the people to ask for a king is rejection of his own divine kingship (1 Sam 8:7); nevertheless, his message to the people omits this fact. The reason is that God wants the people to go astray so he can punish them for their acts of requesting a human king.

In discussing cultic criticism, LEUCHTER puts forward the view that in the book of Jeremiah the prophet is presented as a cultic alternative. Instead of the cults critiqued in the book (the Levitical cult, the family and royal cult, and even the Deuteronomic cult) the author of the book cultivates the cult of the literary

---

⁹ Weber,"Religionssoziologie," 253: "Hesekiel ... kaum noch Prophet zu nennen"; cf. Weber, *The Sociology of Religion*, 51.

¹⁰ On this last, see Grabbe, *Priests, Prophets, Diviners, Sages*, 112–13 and references there, especially Sigmund Mowinckel, "III. Kultprophetie und prophetische Psalmen," Volume 3, pages 4–29 in *Psalmenstudien*, Parts 1–6. Skrifter utgit av Videnskapsselskapets i Kristiania II: Hist.-Filos. Klasse. Oslo: Dybwad, 1921–24 (1922).

¹¹ Weber, "Religionssoziologie," 250; cf. idem, *The Sociology of Religion*, 46.

¹² Weber, "Charismatismus," in *Wirtschaft und Gesellschaft* (2d ed. Tübingen: Mohr Siebeck, 1925); cf. idem, "Charisma and its Transformation," in *Economy and Society*. (ed. G. Roth and C. Wittich; Berkeley: University of California, 1978).

¹³ Cf. Weber, *The Sociology of Religion*, 53.

persona of the prophet. LEUCHTER argues that this created a model for survival by placing the prophetic personality above the cult of exterior objects, rituals, and social structures. It promotes an alternative cult where this literary persona forms the authoritative basis for devotion different from the old standards. The figure of Jeremiah stands in isolation from and in opposition to all previous categories of religious practice and experience, even as he draws from these categories in offering the oracles that take them to task. This must be seen in distinction from other major prophets such as Isaiah and Ezekiel who maintain the unwavering legitimacy of particular ancient traditions (the Zion tradition for Isaiah; the Zadokite tradition for Ezekiel). By contrast, Jeremiah's rhetoric dismantles all dominant cultic and theological traditions from the pre-exilic period, orchestrating the remnants of these thought structures into an ideology and foundation for belief in which the sanctity of older institutions are affirmed as the basis for discourse and yet persistently challenged.

It has long been pointed out that Samuel appears to occupy several roles, but SWEENEY examines the question in deliberate detail. Samuel is explicitly labelled a prophet (1 Sam 9:9), but the text implies that he also functions as a judge (in the sense of the ruler figures in the book of Judges) and as a priest. SWEENEY argues that, although Samuel is never explicitly referred to as judge, he does "judge" (use of the verbal form in 1 Sam 7:6, 15, 17) and appoints his sons as judges (1 Sam 8:1–3). Even more emphasis falls on the priestly activities of Samuel. He regularly offers sacrifices, which is one of the main traditional activities of a priest. Yet he seems to be a priest in the tradition of northern Israel where the first-born son had the job of carrying out priestly duties, a model that was later superseded by the Levitical tradition in which only members from a particular tribe could be priests (Samuel was an Ephraimite). A further priestly indication is Samuel's role as a visionary. Although this is seen as a prophetic activity (including in the Samuel tradition of the DtrH), priests in fact had a number of visionary functions, including control of the ephod which was a priestly form of communication with God.

More than any other prophet, Ezekiel fulfils the role of "God's appointed marionette" (TIEMEYER), though there are indications that he is not comfortable in this role. The "I" of the book of Ezekiel may be a protest by its author against God; if so, this has the intriguing effect of making him both puppet and divine passive resister. Previous prophets commonly had the task of intercession, but Ezekiel is not an intercessor. He is willing to interecede for the people but is not allowed to (9:8). Instead, he is mute: he is not permitted to speak beyond what God tells him. It can be argued that this new role causes all to lose something, whether God, the people, or Ezekiel himself. But this is an image of the prophet that sets Ezekiel apart in many ways from other prophets.

Prophets in Hermeneutical Perspective

The hermeneutical side is one that interests many people who are engaged with the prophets, yet most of the contributors here did not deal with that specific issue. One essay addressing the hermeneutical issue was that of COOK. The question of women and prophecy was raised by COOK who discussed the use of Weber's model by feminist recuperative critics. These scholars drew on the Weberian construct of charisma as the main characteristic of prophecy, in order to argue for women's contribution to the religious community as preachers. As with all hermeneutic encounters with the text, there is the question of what one does with aspects of the text that would be seen as problematic by modern readers (e.g., slavery).

In discussing the "Qur'anic David," WRIGHT draws attention to how the Israelite king was progressively "sanitized" to remove his sins and weaknesses. This is readily apparent in the Islamic tradition (which includes many characters from the Hebrew Bible). This "sanitizing" was a process known earlier, however, not only in the Babylonian Talmud but even in the Bible itself. The David of Chronicles has omitted some of the less desirable characteristics described in 2 Samuel, a prime example being the episode relating to Bathsheba and his subsequent murder of Uriah the Hittite.

CONSTRUCTS OF PROPHETS AND PROPHECY IN THE BOOK OF CHRONICLES

Pancratius C. Beentjes

INTRODUCTION

Within the Hebrew Bible, the book of Chronicles in many respects is a kind of a "lonely planet," since the book has many peculiarities that are found nowhere else in the Old Testament. Reading the book of Chronicles, one undoubtedly will be surprised that classical prophets such as Samuel, Isaiah, Jeremiah, and Ezekiel are hardly mentioned, if at all. Instead, the Chronicler presents prophets and inspired messengers who in the rest of the Bible are completely unknown and are often introduced and typified in a special way. In this contribution we will specifically investigate in what manner prophets, prophecy, and prophetical activities are presented in this document that most probably originates from the Persian period. The outcome of this investigation will be that the book of Chronicles has a specific theological view of prophets, prophecy, and inspired messengers.

SOME CHARACTERISTICS

A cursory reading of the book of Chronicles reveals quite a few characteristics that immediately strike the eye. The first to be emphasized is that the Chronicler never uses marked formulae to introduce quotations from prophetic literature.

Even in those occurrences such as 2 Chr 36:21–22, where he seems to use introductory formulae (למלאות דבר־יהוה בפי ירמיהו ... /... לכלות דבר־יהוה בפי ירמיהו), the subsequent phrases cannot be coined as straight quotations being adopted from one specific text. Here the Chronicler has constructed a mixture of Jer 25:11–12 and 29:10–14 with Lev 26:34–35, 43.

Second, whereas the book of Chronicles in several domains contains texts that in one way or another have a bearing on the books of Samuel and Kings, it appears that just a remarkably small number of *prophetic addresses* have been adopted from that source(s):

1 Chr 17:1–15 / 2 Sam 7:1–17 (Nathan)[1]
1 Chr 21:9–13 / 2 Sam 24:11–14 (Gad)[2]
2 Chr 11:2–4 / 1 Kgs 12:22–24 (Shemaiah)
2 Chr 18:5–27 / 1 Kgs 22:6–28 (Micah)
2 Chr 34:23–28 / 2 Kgs 22:15–20 (Hulda)[3]

As, however, many more prophets and inspired messengers are introduced in the book of Chronicles, the question presents itself whether this might be an indication that the Chronicler had a particular concept of prophets, prophecy, and divine messengers. That this could be the case indeed can, among other things, be inferred from some features that are rather specific to the book of Chronicles. For, in the first place, it catches the eye that in comparison to the Hebrew Bible, the Chronicler has presented the so-called "classical prophets" of Israel, such as Samuel, Gad, Isaiah, and Jeremiah, in a completely different way.[4] They hardly act as central narrative characters, nor as the main character of their eponymous books, but have another important role to which we will refer later on. Secondly, it can be no coincidence that the book of Chronicles presents quite a few prophets and inspired messengers which are met only here in the Hebrew Bible.

---

[1] See Pancratius C. Beentjes, *Tradition and Transformation in the Book of Chronicles* (SSN 52; Leiden: Brill 2008), 31–44.

[2] See Beentjes, *Tradition and Transformation*, 45–59.

[3] This pair of texts is not mentioned by Claus Westermann, *Grundformen prophetischer Rede* (BEvT 31; Munich: Chr. Kaiser, 1968), 116.

[4] "...the literary prophets play no part in the Chronicler's narrative"; Sara Japhet, *The Ideology of the Book of Chronicles and Its Place in Biblical Thought* (BEATAJ 9; Frankfurt a.M.: Peter Lang, 1989), 181.

Pancratius Beentjes 23

DIFFERENT CATEGORIES: PROPHETS AND INSPIRED MESSENGERS

William Schniedewind has convincingly demonstrated that, as far as the book of Chronicles is concerned, one has to differentiate between speeches by speakers with prophetic titles (איש־האלהים, חזה, ראה, נביא) and speeches by speakers without prophetic titles, but being introduced by "possession formulas" ("the spirit of God was upon ...", "the spirit enveloped ...").[5] Speakers with prophetic titles usually address themselves only to the king, whereas so-called "inspired messengers" generally address themselves to the people.[6]

After a careful investigation, Schniedewind concludes that individuals with prophetic titles "often give explanations for past or future events, functioning as *interpreters of events*" [my italics].[7] In the speeches of the "inspired messengers," emphasis is put on another aspect, viz. "the *inspired interpretation of authoritative texts* which revitalized the word of God anew for the post-exilic community" [my italics].[8]

In my view, it therefore can hardly be an accident that precisely in the final chapter of the book, the Chronicler mentions both "messengers" and "prophets":

> And YHWH the God of their fathers sent to them his messengers continually, because he had compassion on his people and his dwelling place. However, they were mocking the messengers of God, despising his words, and taunting his prophets until the anger of YHWH built up and there was no remedy (2 Chr 36:15–16).

This passage has given rise to a couple of questions and therefore some comments are in order here.

(1) Since with regard of King Zedekiah only "the prophet Jeremiah" is explicitly mentioned (36:12b), the lines in 36:15–16 can hardly be an evaluation

---

[5] These possession formulas "are atypical of classical prophecy"; William M. Schniedewind, "Prophets and Prophecy in the Book of Chronicles," in *The Chronicler as Historian* (ed. Matt Patrick Graham, Kenneth G. Hoglund and Steven L. McKenzie; JSOTSup 238; Sheffield: Sheffield Academic, 1997), 217.

[6] There are five "inspired messengers": Amasai (1 Chr 12:19), Azariah (2 Chr 15:1), Jahaziel (2 Chr 20:14), Zechariah (2 Chr 24:20), and Neco (2 Chr 35:21).

[7] William M. Schniedewind, *The Word of God in Transition: From Prophet to Exegete in the Second Temple Period* (JSOTSup 197; Sheffield: Sheffield Academic, 1995), 127.

[8] Schniedewind, *The Word of God*, 127.

that should be confined to the reign of King Zedekiah proper, as is the contention of some scholars.⁹ On the contrary, it must serve as a theological retrospective of a longer period of Israel's history, viz. the post-Solomonic era.¹⁰ That this view stands a good chance is expressed, first, in the collocation השכם ושלוח ("over and over again").¹¹ Second, the use of participles in v. 16 (... מלעבים ובוזים ... ומתעתעים) undoubtedly is an expression of Israel's continuous abhorrent behavior. Third, the collocation "anger of YHWH" (v. 16b) is also found in 2 Chr 12:7; 28:9; 34:21, 25, i.e. in narratives subsequent to King Solomon's reign, and should therefore be considered a generic term for that entire period. Fourth, the formula "YHWH, the God of *their* fathers" (v. 15a) would be rather odd if it should not have a bearing on a longer period. Fifth, the twofold עד ("until") in v. 16b has such a climactic force that it hardly can refer just to the period of Zedekiah's reign. Moreover, the phrase "until there was no remedy" (מרפא) to my mind is a direct referral to 2 Chr 7:14 that is part of King Solomon's prayer.

(2) Some scholars hold the view that "messengers" and "prophets" in 2 Chr 36:16 are part of a "parallelistic syntax."¹² Having read the book of Chronicles from beginning to end, in my view one can hardly maintain that point of view. The structure of the verse cries out for another interpretation, viz. that two different groups are meant: "they were

(a) mocking the messengers of God,
(x) despising his words,
(b) and taunting his prophets."

THE CHRONICLER'S VIEW OF PROPHETS AND INSPIRED MESSENGERS

Whereas in the book of Kings the narratives on Ahijah, Elijah, Elisha, and others commonly included miraculous elements and were concerned with efficacy of the prophetic pronouncements, in the book of Chronicles the ministry of the prophets is nowhere described in terms of ecstasy, miracles, or political

---

⁹ E.g., Japhet, *I & II Chronicles*, 1069.
¹⁰ William Riley, *King and Cultus in Chronicles: Worship and the Reinterpretation of History* (JSOTSup 160; Sheffield: JSOT, 1993), 146 n 3.
¹¹ Jer 7:25; 25:4; 29:19; 35:15.
¹² Japhet, *I & II Chronicles*, 1071. See also Reinhold Then, *"Gibt es denn keinen mehr unter den Propheten?": Zum Fortgang der alttestamentlichen Prophetie in frühjüdischer Zeit* (BEATAJ 22; Frankfurt a.M.: Peter Lang, 1990), 159.

dimensions,[13] such as, e.g., the exhortation to rebellion by Ahija of Silo (1 Kgs 11:29–39) or the anointing of Jehu by one of Elisha's disciples (2 Kgs 9).[14]

---

[13] Yairah Amit, "The Role of Prophecy and Prophets in the Theology of the Book of Chronicles," *Beth Mikra* 93 (1983), 3–23 (Hebrew); Christopher Begg, "The Classical Prophets in the Chronistic History," *BZ* 32 (1988), 100–107; Eusebio Hernando, "El Profetismo en los libros de las Crónicas," *Scriptorium Victoriense* 34 (1987), 45–66; Jürgen Kegler, "Prophetengestalten im Deuteronomistischen Geschichtswerk und in den Chronikbüchern: Ein Beitrag zur Kompositions- und Redaktionsgeschichte der Chronikbücher," *ZAW* 105 (1993), 481–97; Raymond Kuntzmann, "La fonction prophétique en 1–2 Chroniques: Du ministère de la parole au Service de l'institution communautaire" in *Ich bewirke das Heil und erschaffe das Unheil (Jesaja 45,7): Studien zur Botschaft der Propheten* (ed. Friedrich Diedrich and Bernd Willmes; FzB 88; Würzburg: Echter, 1998), 245–58; Rex Mason, "The Prophets of the Restoration," in *Israel's Prophetic Tradition: Essays in Honor of Peter Ackroyd* (ed. Richard Coggins, Anthony Phillips and Michael Knibb; Cambridge: Cambridge University, 1982), 137–54; idem, *Preaching the Tradition: Homily and Hermeneutics after the Exile* (Cambridge: Cambridge University, 1990); Rosemarie Micheel, *Die Seher- und Prophetenüberlieferungen in der Chronik* (BET 18; Frankfurt a.M.: Peter Lang 1983); David L. Petersen, *Late Israelite Prophecy: Studies in Deutero–Prophetic Literature and in Chronicles* (SBLMS 23; Missoula: Scholars Press, 1977); Herculaas Van Rooy, "Prophet and Society in the Persian Period According to Chronicles" in *Second Temple Studies 2: Temple and Community in the Persian Period* (ed. Tamara Cohn Eskenazi and Kent H. Richards; JSOTSup 175; Sheffield: Sheffield Academic, 1994), 163–79; Schniedewind, *The Word of God in Transition*; Isac Leo Seeligman, "Die Auffassung von der Prophetie in der deuteronomistischen und chronistischen Geschichtsschreibung," in *Congress Volume: Göttingen 1977* (ed. John A. Emerton et al.; VTSup 29; Leiden: Brill, 1978), 254–79; Kim Strübind, *Tradition als Interpretation in der Chronik: König Josaphat als Paradigma chronistischer Hermeneutik und Theologie* (BZAW 201; Berlin: De Gruyter, 1991), esp. 155–64; Then, *"Gibt es denn keinen mehr unter den Propheten?"*; Simon de Vries, "The Forms of Prophetic Address in Chronicles," *HAR* 10 (1986), 15–36; Joel P. Weinberg, "'Die Ausserkanonischen Prophezeiungen' in den Chronikbüchern," *Acta Antiqua* 26 (1978), 387–404; Thomas Willi, *Die Chronik als Auslegung* (FRLANT 106; Göttingen: Vandenhoeck & Ruprecht, 1972). The doctoral dissertation by James D. Newsome, *The Chronicler's View of Prophecy* (Vanderbilt University, 1973) was not available to me.

These prophets no longer make their appearance in narratives. According to William Schniedewind,

> The obvious reason for this is that the prophetic narratives in Samuel-Kings mostly concern the *northern* kingdom ... Since the Chronicler wrote a history of the *southern* kingdom, there was little for the Chronicler to borrow. There must have been stories of Judaean prophets, but we do not have them in the book of Kings. What then was the source of the Chronicler's prophetic narratives? Did the Chronicler freely compose or borrow from a prophetic source? There is scant evidence to prove that the Chronicler used any written collection of prophetic stories for his prophetic narratives. The prophetic speeches reflect the Chronicler's own language and theology. In this respect, the prophetic narratives are a first-hand reflection of the Chronicler's view of prophets, prophecy and inspiration.[15]

This view, however, cannot be substantiated as a comprehensive solution. Did Schniedewind, for instance, forget that Elijah plays a very special part in the book of Chronicles (2 Chr 21:12–15) and that prophets such as Isaiah and Jeremiah are actually present in the book of Chronicles, be it in a way that is completely different from the presentation as they used to be found elsewhere in the Hebrew Bible?

It can be taken for granted that the Chronicler's view of prophets and inspired messengers is especially to be found in those passages of his book which have no parallel in the remainder of the Hebrew Bible and therefore are classified as *Sondergut*. Among this category are the narratives relating to the following characters: the prophet Shemaiah (2 Chr 12:5–8), the inspired messenger Azariah (2 Chr 15:1–7), the seer Hanani (2 Chr 16:7–10), the visionary Jehu (2 Chr 19:1–3), the inspired Levite Jahaziel (2 Chr 20:14–17), the prophet Eliezer (2 Chr 20:37), the inspired messenger Zechariah (2 Chr 24:20–21), a man of God (2 Chr 25:7–9), a nameless prophet (2 Chr 25:15–16), the prophet Oded (2 Chr 28:9–11).[16] Let us now investigate some of these texts in order to see in what way the Chronicler has brought his intentions to light.

---

[14] Raymond Bryan Dillard, *2 Chronicles* (WBC 15; Waco: Word Books, 1987), 92–3; Kegler, "Prophetengestalten," 491.

[15] Schniedewind, *The Word of God*, 23–4.

[16] For an exhaustive inventory of all prophetic titles ("prophet," "seer," "visionary," "man of God") and "inspiration formulas" ("the spirit of YHWH came upon ...") that are used in the book of Chronicles, see Schniedewind, *The Word of God*, 31–79.

2 CHRONICLES 12:5–8

Right from the start, this pericope presents an interesting view, since here the Chronicler for the *second* time puts Shemaiah on the stage. The first time Shemaiah was presented (2 Chr 11:2–4), the Chronicler more or less adopted the text from his source (1 Kgs 12:22–24).[17] This time, however, both Shemaiah's appearance and the context in which he is presented are completely modeled according to the Chronicler's view. As compared to his source text, the Chronicler not only has separated 1 Kgs 14:25 from 14:26ff and between these verses *inserted* a new section of his own, he also has *added* an introduction (2 Chr 12:1) that bears his own stamp:

2 Chr 12:1		———
2 Chr 12:2a	//	1 Kgs 14:25
2 Chr 12:2b–8		———
2 Chr 12:9–11	//	1 Kgs 14:26–28

The verb חזק ("to be strong") which is a thread that in a *positive* way connected the first three years of Rehoboam's reign (2 Chr 11:11–12, 17), now is the upbeat to this king's decline: "When the rule of Rehoboam was established (כון) and he grew strong (חזק), he abandoned (עזב) the torah of YHWH ..." (2 Chr 12:1). The verb עזב ("to abandon") is one of the Chronicler's most favorite themes, since this verb is found remarkably often in the Chronicler's own material and with no exception refers to a *negative* attitude that people adopt vis-à-vis YHWH.[18]

Due to the composition of this narrative, the Chronicler unequivocally suggests that Shishak's campaign against Rehoboam is the *direct consequence* of abandoning the torah by the king and all Israel. That this causal connection was the Chronicler's intention indeed is unmistakably shown by the phrase "because they had been unfaithful to YHWH" (2 Chr 12:2b). Here we come across the verb מעל which is one of the book's favorite themes too and, moreover, is exclusively found in the chronicler's *Sondergut*.[19]

---

[17] There is, however, an interesting change. Whereas 1 Kgs 12:24 reads as follows: כל בית יהודה, the Chronicler's text (2 Chr 11:3) has כל ישראל ביהודה.

[18] 1 Chr 28:9, 20; 2 Chr 7:19; 12:1, 5; 13:10–11; 15:2; 21:10; 24:18, 20, 24; 28:6; 29:6; 32:31.

[19] 1 Chr 2:7; 5:25–26; 10:13; 2 Chr 12:2; 26:16, 18; 28:19, 22; 29:6; 30:7; 36:14. The noun is found in 1 Chr 9:1; 10:13; 2 Chr 28:19; 29:19; 33:19; 36:14.

Meanwhile a subtle change has taken place. Whereas the Chronicler in 2 Chr 11:2 has used the title "man of God" which was adopted from his source text, now in the passage that he has created himself Shemaiah is characterized as "the prophet." Shemaiah indeed starts acting as a prophet; his message—which by the way consists of exactly twelve words—is structured according to the basic form of prophetic speech (messenger formula, reproach, and announcement). The Chronicler makes Shemaiah play along with the verb עזב that he used in the introduction: "... he abandoned the torah of YHWH ..." (12:1). So doing he created a chiastic statement אתם עזבתם אתי / ואף־אני עזבתי אתכם which with slight alterations will recur in 2 Chr 15:2 and 24:20.[20] Adding the collocation "in the hand of Shishak" (12:5b), the second occurrence of the verb עזב gets the meaning "to deliver in the hand of ...".

Twelve Hebrew words are sufficient to get the officers of Israel (!) and the king to humble themselves (כנע *niph*.).[21] With the help of this verb, the Chronicler presents another of his favorite themes (12:6–7 [3 x], 12).[22]

AZARIAH'S ADDRESS IN 2 CHRONICLES 15:1–7

The Chronicler used the narrative of 1 Kgs 15:9–24 as the framework for a completely new composition dealing with Asa, king of Judah. Whereas 1 Kgs 15:9–24 includes sixteen verses, the Chronicler's narrative on Asa covers no less than forty-seven verses, so that the majority of it (esp. 2 Chr 14:2–15:15; 16:7–10) is peculiar to the book of Chronicles.[23]

After the victory over the Cushites, which according to the Chronicler's theology has entirely described as a divine act (2 Chr 14:11–12), Asa and his men returned to Jerusalem (14:15). Then with the help of the "possession formula" היתה עליו רוח אלהים, which in the Hebrew Bible is never used with respect to classical prophets, a literary character called Azarjahu son of Oded is introduced (15:1). Schniedewind, who offers a fine analysis of the two possession formulas being used in the Hebrew Bible,[24] viz., ותהי / היתה רוח ...

---

[20] It hardly can be coincidence that these two passages are found in the Chronicler's *Sondergut* too.

[21] See David A. Glatt-Gilead, "The Root *knʻ* and Historiographic Periodization in Chronicles," *CBQ* 64 (2002): 248–57.

[22] He really treasured this verb; out of twenty-five times that the Hebrew Bible has it in *niphʻal*, it is found sixteen times in the book of Chronicles.

[23] For a detailed synoptic overview, see Abba Bendavid, *Parallels in the Bible* (Jerusalem: Carta, 1972), 100–2.

[24] Schniedewind, *The Word of God*, 66–74.

על on the one hand[25] and לבשה את ... רוח on the other hand,[26] reaches at the conclusion: "In Chronicles, the possession formulas represent a claim to divine authority. They are used in cases of *ad hoc* prophetic inspiration of non-professional prophets."[27]

The Chronicler, not being hampered by an existing canonical text referring to Azariah, feels free to compose a prophetic address of his own.[28] By creating the literary character of Azariah, who with the help of a possession formula speaks with divine authority, the Chronicler puts himself into a position to select and transform canonical prophetic texts for his own purpose. Azariah is used as a vehicle to present "a mosaic of longer or shorter citations from existing prophetic texts, slightly altered and sophistically interwoven, to serve the new context and form a coherent statement of the Chronicler's view."[29]

Though it is said that Azariah "went out to meet Asa" (15:2a), it is not by chance that Azariah's address from the very beginning is in the plural (שמעוני). His exhortation—being an excellent summary of the Chronicler's theology—is not only meant for Asa's ears, but for "Asa and all Judah and Benjamin." It is the basic attitude all people need in their relationship with God.

Azariah's address, which opens with a call to attention (שמעוני, v. 2) and is concluded with a strong exhortation (ואתם חזקו ואל־ירפו ידיכם, v. 7), consists of two blocks. The first one (v. 2b) has been formulated as "an axiom, which for the Chronicler is the underlying principle of all history."[30] The second, major part of Azariah's address (vv. 3–6) is a sort of historical review.

---

[25] See Num 24:2b (Balaam); Judg 3:10 (Othniel); 11:29 (Jephthah); 1 Sam 19:20 (the messengers of Saul); 19:23b (Saul).

[26] Judg 6:34 (Gideon); 1 Chr 12:19 (Amasai); 2 Chr 24:20 (Zechariah).

[27] Schniedewind, *The Word of God*, 74.

[28] Raymond Dillard, "The Reign of Asa (2 Chronicles 14–16): An Example of the Chronicler's Theological Method," *JETS* 23 (1980): 207–18; Michael Fishbane, *Biblical Interpretation in Ancient Israel* (Oxford: Clarendon, 1985), 388–92; idem, *The Garments of Torah* (Bloomington: Indiana University, 1988), 14–16; Wilhelm Rudolph, "Der Aufbau der Asa-Geschichte," *VT* 2 (1952): 367–71; Gerrie Snyman, "'Tis a Vice to Know Him': Reader's Response-Ability and Responsibility in 2 Chronicles 14–16," *Semeia* 77 (1997): 91–113.

[29] Japhet, *I & II Chronicles*, 716.

[30] Ibid., 718.

AZARIAH'S AXIOMATICAL STATEMENT (2 CHR 15:2)

(1) "YHWH is with you when you are with him;
(2) if you seek him, he will let himself be found,
(3) but if you forsake him, he will forsake you."

Needless to say that a strong echo of Deuteronomistic theology, in particular from Deut 4:29–30 and Jer 29:13–14, is heard in the opening lines of Azariah's statement.[31] Almost every single element of this poetic and prophetic statement can be considered as repeating and recalling other passages in Chronicles.[32]

The first part of line (1) is found only twice in the book of Chronicles. The first time, in 1 Chr 22:18, it is phrased as a rhetorical question in David's address to his son Solomon to seek YHWH, in order to set about building his sanctuary (הלא יהוה אלהים עמכם).[33] The second time the phrase יהוה עמכם shows up is in the prophetic address by Jahaziel to "all Judah, and the inhabitants of Jerusalem and King Jehoshaphat" (2 Chr 20:17). It can hardly be an accident that this prophetic address is introduced in 2 Chr 20:14 by exactly the same possession formula as in 2 Chr 15:1 and is found in the book of Chronicles in these two texts only.

The closest parallel to line (2) is to be found in 1 Chr 28:9, where it—also being phrased conditionally (אם)—is part of the conclusion in King David's personal address to Solomon. Both addresses hold the key phrase "to seek YHWH,"[34] which is one of the most important theological notions of the book of Chronicles.[35] "'Seeking Yahweh' is frequently used to typify commitment to Yahweh and his worship according to legitimate norms."[36]

---

[31] This is confirmed by the repetition of specific vocabulary, e.g., בצר לו in 2 Chr 15:4 (cf. Deut 4:30), קבץ in 2 Chr 15:9 (cf. Jer 29:14), and "to seek YHWH ... with all their heart and soul" in 2 Chr 15:12.

[32] Some poetic features are the fourfold ending כם, the twofold opening ואם, and the twofold rhyme -*uhu*.

[33] The phrase "Is not the LORD your God with you?" (1 Chr 22:18) is immediately followed by another rhetorical question: "Will he not give you peace on every side?" The notion of God giving peace on every side is a theological notion governing the overall structure of 2 Chr 14–15.

[34] Expressed with either דרש (2 Chr 15:2, 12–13) or בקש (2 Chr 15:4, 15).

[35] Without dispute, the verb מעל is another major theological motif in the book of Chronicles. See, for example, William Johnstone, "Guilt and Atonement: The Theme of 1 and 2 Chronicles" in *A Word in Season: Essays in*

It can hardly be a coincidence, of course, that this important theological notion of "seeking YHWH" had already been incorporated in the preceding chapter (2 Chr 14:3, 6). In fact, it is this notion of "seeking YHWH" together with the phrase "He/YHWH had given ... security on every side" (2 Chr 14:5–6; 15:15) that creates a kind of an *envelope structure* for the first part of the Chronicler's narrative on King Asa.

Whereas the key notion "seeking YHWH" in 2 Chr 15:2 forms part of an *overall* structure to the Asa narrative as a whole, it is the verb נמצא *niph'al* (2 Chr 15:2, 4, 15) that appears to be the leading principle structuring Azariah's address. The conditionally phrased opening statement of the prophet ("If you seek him, he will let himself be found," v. 2) and its realization in v. 15 ("they had sought YHWH earnestly; he had let himself be found by them") are linked with the help of an appeal to history: "But when, in their distress, they turned to YHWH the God of Israel and sought him, he let himself be found by them" (v. 4).

Before paying further attention to this appeal to history in 2 Chr 15:3–6, let us quickly dwell on line (3) of Azariah's opening statement: "But if you forsake him, he will forsake you." We already discussed this statement in Shemaiah's address to Rehoboam and the leading men of Judah on the occasion of Shishak's attack on Jerusalem. And in 2 Chr 24:20 the spirit of God takes possession of Zechariah who reproaches the people with their forsakening YHWH. It is, however, again 1 Chr 28:9—the conclusion of King David's personal address to Solomon—where we find a conditionally (אם) phrased parallel to line (3) of Azariah's address. This is on a par with a characteristic feature of the book of Chronicles noticed by James Newsome: "...that, under the Chronicler's pen, the Davidic king himself received the divine word and, on several occasions, passed it on to others, thus assuming the prophetic role."[37]

Honour of William McKane (ed. J. D. Martin and P. R. Davies; JSOTSup 42; Sheffield: Sheffield Academic, 1986), 113–38.

[36] Brian E. Kelly, *Retribution and Eschatology in Chronicles* (JSOTSup 211; Sheffield: Sheffield Academic, 1996), 46–53 (52); see also Christopher Begg, "'Seeking Yahweh' and the Purpose of Chronicles," *LS* 9 (1982), 128–41. The dissertation of G. E. Schaeffer, *The Significance of Seeking God in the Purpose of the Chronicler* (Southern Baptist Theological Seminary, 1972) was not available to me.

[37] James D. Newsome, "Toward a New Understanding of the Chronicler and his Purposes," *JBL* 94 (1975), 201–17. In his synopsis (203–4), Newsome

Azariah's Appeal To History (2 Chr 15:3–6)

In 2 Chr 15:3–6, Azariah impresses upon his audience that the principle as brought out in v. 2 is crucial for Israel's welfare. In other words: vv. 3–6 serve as documentary evidence to the axiomatical statement of v. 2. Since v. 3, however, contains no verb, the phrase may just as well refer to the past as to the future.[38] Both the Septuagint and the Vulgate have taken Azariah's words as a prophecy of the future. Though modern scholarship almost unanimously assumes that the pericope refers to the past, more specifically to the time of the Judges, some authors presume that the Chronicler is referring either to the (end of the) exile[39] or to his own days.[40]

During the last thirty years or so, scholars have investigated a lot of aspects dealing with the Chronicler's view of prophets and prophecy. In my view there is at least one aspect, however, which appears to be neglected. Looking at the impressive list of publications on prophets and prophecy, one could get the impression that the Chronicler did not make use of what we term "the Latter Prophets." It is this particular aspect that we will pay attention to in this paragraph.

The Chronicler, as Azariah's ghostwriter, presents a speech which undeniably is scripture-oriented. There are a lot of references to passages in the Hebrew Bible, especially from the "Latter Prophets." An inventory of these instances reveals an intriguing pattern; the Chronicler appears to design his own manner of using authoritative words from tradition:

2 Chr 15:3	וימים רבים ... ללא ...ללא ...וללא
Hos 3:4	ימים רבים ... אין ... אין ... אין ... אין
2 Chr 15:5	אין שלום ליוצא ולבא
Zech 8:10	וליוצא ולבא אין־שלום

---

however does not mention 2 Chr 8:14, where David is called "man of God"... "daß bei unserem Autor die Könige und ihre Reden nicht selten prophetische Züge tragen" (Seeligman, "Die Auffassung von der Prophetie," 271).

[38] An extensive list of various interpretations is given by Edward L. Curtis and Albert A. Madsen, *A Critical and Exegetical Commentary on the Books of Chronicles* (ICC; Edinburgh: T&T Clark, 1910), 384.

[39] Fishbane, *Biblical Interpretation in Ancient Israel*, 389.

[40] Hugh G. M. Williamson, *1 and 2 Chronicles* (NCB; Grand Rapids: Eerdmans, 1987), 268; Peter R. Ackroyd, *I & II Chronicles, Ezra, Nehemiah* (Torch Bible; London: SCM, 1973), 138.

2 Chr 15:5	מהומת רבות
Amos 3:9	מהומת רבות
2 Chr 15:7	ואל־ירפו ידיכם
Zeph 3:16	אל־ירפו ידיך
2 Chr 15:7	כי יש שכר לפעלתכם
Jer 31:16[41]	כי יש שכר לפעלתך

With the exception of the idiomatic expression (מהומת רבות 2 Chr 15:5), Azariah's historical review contains not a single *verbal quotation* from the Hebrew Bible. Words from tradition are handled on different levels. In 2 Chr 15:3, it is mainly the *pattern* that is unmistakably adopted from Hos 3:4. Hosea's prophecy, however, refers to a situation in the future, whereas the Chronicler's focus is on some event(s) in the past. [42]

With respect to 2 Chr 15:5//Zech 8:10, a special comment is appropriate. Wim Beuken in his excellent doctoral thesis has circumstantially argued that, in spite of striking similarities, a direct literary dependence on Zech 8:10 cannot be assumed for 2 Chr 15:5.[43] I like to resist my *Doktorvater* at this particular point, since in my opinion the Chronicler uses a literary device, which the present author has coined *inverted quotation*.[44] Within an existing formulation from tradition (a sentence, a colon, a set phrase, or a rare or unique combination of words) an author sometimes reverses the sequence. By such a deviating model he attains a moment of extra attention in the listener or the reader, because they hear or read something other than the traditional words: the reversed order is a sign that there is something special going on.

Since Zech 8:10 and 2 Chr 15:5 are the only two instances within the entire Hebrew Bible where the participles תוצא and בא have been constructed with a preposition, and, moreover, since we have here the only occurrence within the book of Chronicles where the noun שלום is found in a negative context, a direct link is obvious. And since 2 Chr 15:3–7 as a whole holds so many resemblances

---

[41] Not Jer 31:6 as indicated by Japhet, *I & II Chronicles*, 721.

[42] Maybe the Chronicler in 2 Chr 15:4 has deliberately used the verbs בקש and שוב as an echo from Hos 3:5.

[43] Willem A. M. Beuken, *Haggai–Sacharja 1–8: Studien zur Überlieferungsgeschichte der frühnachexilischen Prophetie* (SSN 10; Assen: Van Gorcum, 1967), 162–3.

[44] Pancratius C. Beentjes, "Discovering a New Path of Intertextuality: Inverted Quotations and Their Dynamics" in *Literary Structure and Rhetorical Strategies in the Hebrew Bible* (ed. Leonard J. de Regt, Jan de Waard and Jan P. Fokkelman; Assen: Van Gorcum, 1996), 31–50.

to Biblical texts, the most plausible inference must be that Zech 8:10 is the parent text.

With respect to the last two couples of texts (2 Chr 15:7a//Zeph 3:16; 2 Chr 15:7b//Jer 31:16), the Chronicler makes only one small alteration in each of the two prophetic texts, changing the suffix of the second person singular (ך-) into a plural one (כם-). This is done in order to emphasize again that Azariah is not just addressing King Asa, but "all Judah and Benjamin" (v. 2).

JAHAZIEL'S ADDRESS IN 2 CHR 20:14–17

In an unusually extensive genealogy which traces him back to King David's time, a person called Jahaziel is introduced.[45] With the help of the apposition "a Levite of the line of Asaph," liturgical-cultic aspects are brought to the fore. Because of some classical formulas his appearance, nevertheless, must be characterized as a prophetical activity: "The spirit of YHWH came upon Jahaziel ..." (v. 14);[46] "Thus says YHWH to you ..." (v. 15).[47] One therefore should disagree with the designation "Levitical sermon" which was introduced in 1934 by Gerhard von Rad and to this day is still used by many scholars.[48] One would expect 2 Chr 20:14–17 to play an important role as a witness to such a theory on the "Levitical sermon" as a genre of its own. For within the book of Chronicles, this passage is the only text in which a Levite is actually speaking. Curiously enough, in von Rad's argumentation 2 Chr 20:14–17 hardly plays a part; all in all, he has devoted only eleven lines to this passage.[49]

---

[45] See Hartmut Gese, "Zur Geschichte der Kultsänger am zweiten Tempel" in *Abraham unser Vater: Juden und Christen im Gespräch über die Bibel. Festschrift für Otto Michel* (ed. Otto Betz, Martin Hengel, and Peter Schmidt; Arbeiten zur Geschichte des Spätjudentums und Urchristentums 5; Leiden: Brill, 1963), 230 n. 2.

[46] Cf. 1 Chr 12:19; 2 Chr 15:1; 24:20.

[47] Micheel, *Die Seher- und Prophetenüberlieferungen*, 50–53; Rimon Kasher, "The Saving of Jehosaphat; Extent, Parallels, Significance," *Beth Mikra* 31 (1985), 242–51 (Hebrew). Strübind does not analyse 2 Chr 20:14–17, as he is occupying himself with material exclusively dealing with Jehoshaphat ("das Josaphat–relevante Material"); Strübind, *Tradition als Interpretation*, 179.

[48] Gerhard von Rad, "Die levitische Predigt in den Büchern der Chronik" in idem, *Gesammelte Studien zum Alten Testament* (ThB 8; Munich: Chr. Kaiser, 1965), 248–61; repr. of *Festschrift für Otto Procksch* (ed. Albrecht Alt et al.; Leipzig: Deichert & Hinrich, 1934), 113–24.

[49] Von Rad, *Gesammelte Studien*, 254. Von Rad's hypothesis is more and more criticized, e.g., by Dietman Mathias, "'Levitische Predigt' und

In 2 Chr 20:14–17, the question is raised to what extent the author is using older traditions; and in what way he is dealing with them. For it makes a difference whether such traditions are just adopted, or are attributed new (or even different) accents and senses.

One can fully agree with Schmitt's conclusion that the Chronicler in 20:14–17 has imitated the general pattern of the *Gottesbescheid*, which is found in extra-biblical texts and biblical texts as well.[50] The *form critical* provenance Schmitt has offered with respect to 2 Chr 20:14–17, however, should have been accompanied with a more specific "traditionsgeschichtliche" analysis of this passage. Therefore, it is necessary to make some comments in that direction.

If one reads 2 Chr 20:14–17 aloud, one will encounter two highly alliterative phrases in which—no wonder—the essence of this episode has been exactly concentrated:

(v. 15b) לא לכם המלחמה כי לאלהים
(v. 17a) לא לכם להלחם

Each of these two utterances plays an important part within this passage. The first one (v. 15b) functions as the motivation of the prophet's summons not to be dismayed: Israel will be out of harm's way. The second one (v. 17a) not by

---

Deuteronomismus," *ZAW* 96 (1984), 23–49, as well as by Mason, *Preaching the Tradition*, and by Kent Sparks, "The Prophetic Speeches in Chronicles: Speculation, Revelation, and Ancient Historiography," *BBR* 9 (1999), 233–45, esp. 241–3.

[50] Judg 4:1–9; 2 Kgs 19:1–7 = Isa 37:1–7. Armin Schmitt: "Das prophetische Sondergut in 2 Chr 20,14-17," in *Künder des Wortes: Festschrift Josef Schreiner* (ed. Lothar Ruppert et al.; Würzburg: Echter, 1982), 273–85. Letters from Mari ARM 26 213 and ARM 26 237; see Martti Nissinen, *Prophets and Prophecy in the Ancient Near East* (SBLWAW 12; Atlanta: SBL, 2003), 47–48, 67–69. It is interesting that Schmitt is rather reticent to trace back the formula אל־תיראו to the priestly oracle of salvation. For this see Manfred Weippert, "Assyrische Prophetien der Zeit Asarhaddons und Assurbanipals" in *Assyrian Royal Inscriptions: New Horizons in Literary, Ideological, and Historical Analysis* (Orientis Antiqui Collectio 17; ed. Frederick Mario Fales; Rome: Istituto per l'Oriente, 1981), 71–115; Martti Nissinen, "Fear Not: A Study on an Ancient Near Eastern Phrase," in *The Changing Faces of Form Criticism for the Twenty-First Century* (ed. Ehud Ben Zvi and Marvin A. Sweeney; Grand Rapids, Mich. and Cambridge, U.K.: Eerdmans 2003), 122–61.

chance is found in the heart of the lines which hold the instructions, a section which takes clear shape with the help of a striking inclusio:

"Tomorrow ... go down"   (v. 16a)
"Tomorrow ... go out"   (v. 17b).

A impressive crowd of commentators is somehow convinced that the phrase לא לכם המלחמה כי לאלהים (v. 15b) is indeed such a plain parallel to 1 Sam 17:47 (כי ליהוה המלחמה). I would like to throw doubts on that conviction.[51] The wording of 2 Chr 20:15b—just as that of v. 17a—is set in a *negative* structure which is very rare; it is found nowhere else in the entire Old Testament. The striking alliterative form of both phrases helps to accentuate their unique character. By them we come across a theme which is constantly occupying the Chronicler.[52] In a very special way this aspect is shown by the instructions of v. 17. With the exception of the word עמדו—which must surely have been added by the Chronicler in order to fill up v. 21 surprisingly with a rather massive liturgical content—the entire wording of v. 17 corresponds literally with phrases uttered by Moses in Exod 14:13–14:

אל־תיראו התיצבו וראו את־ישועת יהוה
....
יהוה ילחם לכם

This verbal parallel, right up to its conjugations, is too striking to be merely a coincidence. Whereas every commentator lists this reference, the reader's attention is seldom drawn to stipulate that the resemblance is far beyond the quotation alone. Both 2 Chr 20 and Exod 14 display a similar narrative structure. In both texts, a situation of distress is found caused by a hostile attack. This brings about a lament by the people, which is answered by an encouraging speech and clear instructions about how to react. From a distance, Israel is therefore a witness of the enemy's defeat by the hand of God. From this parallel

---

[51] E.g., von Rad, *Gesammelte Studien*, 254; Willi, *Die Chronik als Auslegung*, 108 n. 129; Williamson, *1 and 2 Chronicles*, 298; Micheel, *Die Seher- und Prophetenüberlieferungen*, 52; Petersen, *Late Israelite Prophecy*, 74; De Vries, *1 and 2 Chronicles*, 325; Curtis and Madsen, *A Critical and Exegetical Commentary*, 408. Schmitt is more careful: "Möglicherweise liegt hier eine Anlehnung an 1 Sam 17,47b vor"; Schmitt, "Das prophetische Sondergut," 283 n. 24.

[52] In the Hebrew Bible, מלחמה is found 319 times. By far the most occurences, 64 to be exact, are found in 1–2 Chronicles; see Adam S. van der Woude, "ṣābā'/ Heer," *THAT* 2 (1967): 502.

structure, one can infer that the frame of 2 Chr 20 is determined to a high degree by Exod 14.[53]

A SPECIAL FUNCTION OF PROPHETS IN THE BOOK OF CHRONICLES

In the Introduction, it has already been mentioned that in the book of Chronicles one perceives a tenor to play down a lot of narratives in which prophets are central characters. Twenty years ago, Christopher Begg tried to find a solution for this phenomenon. He, however, confined himself to the category of the "Latter Prophets," which is only part of the problem, since the question relates to the "Former Prophets" as well. This latter category, therefore, should also be taken into account.

In the book of Chronicles, the noun "prophet" is found at least seven times in connection with a *document* that is attributed to a specific prophet: "The records of the prophet Nathan" (1 Chr 29:29; 2 Chr 9:29); "The records of the prophet Shemaiah" (2 Chr 12:15); "The 'midrash' of the prophet Iddo" (2 Chr 13:22); "A letter from Elijah the prophet" (2 Chr 21:12); "Isaiah the prophet wrote the rest of the acts of Uzzah" (2 Chr 26:22); "The rest of the acts of Hezekiah ... are written in the vision of the prophet Isaiah" (2 Chr 32:32). This is a major clue to the Chronicler's view of how to determine the function of quite a few prophets known from the collection that was later known as *Nebi'im*.

In the Chronicler's presentation, these prophets do not act as messengers, but rather hold the position of keepers of the royal archives; they are characterized as responsible for the records of a specific king. This observation can be strengthened with the help of 2 Chr 9:29, a passage in which the noun נבואה ("prophecy") undoubtedly refers to a *written document*, since it is part of a collocation within a threefold parallelism: "the records of the prophet Nathan // the prophecy of Ahijah the Shilonite // and the visions of the seer Iddo."[54]

---

[53] It seems rather striking that Schmitt in his analysis of Jahaziel's address is actually describing the parallel to Exod 14:13–14, but in his conclusion has completely left aside this aspect; Schmitt, "Das prophetische Sondergut," 278–9. The close textual and structural relationship between 2 Chr 20:14–17 and Exod 14:13–14 should therefore also be connected with the interpretation of King Jehoshaphat's address (2 Chr 20:20). See Beentjes, *Tradition and Transformation*, 61–77.

[54] The noun נבואה ("prophecy") is found only two more times in the Hebrew Bible: 2 Chr 15:8, and Neh 6:12, where it has a bearing on the words spoken by someone.

To my mind, this must be the reason why the Chronicler, on the one hand, nowhere in his document has used explicit quotations from the Former and Latter Prophets and, on the other hand, is reserved to make the classical prophets act as central narrative characters. In the third place, the activity of prophesying in the Chronicler's mind has a crucial bearing on a specific field, as can be inferred from the way he made use of the verb "to prophesy."

THE VERB "TO PROPHESY" (נבא) *IN THE BOOK OF CHRONICLES*

In the book of Chronicles, the verb "to prophesy" (נבא) is used eight times. Four occurrences are found in 2 Chr 18, a chapter that without changes has been adopted from 1 Kgs 22, being its parent text.[55] In 1 Chr 25:1–3, however, the Chronicler has given the verb נבא a highly personal interpretation, since it is connected with the activity of a special group of *liturgical* functionaries.[56] At the text critical level, it must be emphasized that in 1 Chr 25:1–3 the verb נבא ("to prophesy") should be preferred to the noun נביא ("prophet"), since there are some valid arguments in favor of the verb: (*a*) The verbal form is a *lectio difficilior*; (*b*) In 1 Chr 25:1, the verbal form is confirmed by the majority of the Hebrew manuscripts, the Septuagint, the Targum, and the Vulgate; (*c*) In 1 Chr 25:2, the verbal form is confirmed by the majority of the Hebrew manuscripts, the Targum, and the Vulgate; (*d*) In 1 Chr 25:5, Heman is called "seer" חזה. It would be quite odd to characterize the same person some lines before (25:3) with a different title (prophet). Moreover, it can hardly be an accident that the Chronicler has also used the qualification חזה "seer" for both Asaph (2 Chr 29:30) and Jeduthun (2 Chr 35:15).

The purport of 1 Chr 25:1–6 undoubtedly is that

> [t]he author wanted to trace the institution of temple music back to David. Since in actual fact this profession was the province of the "sons of Asaph, Heman and Jeduthun," it was those whom David had to appoint. The author made the connection between David and these three groups by having the three eponymous fathers function as prophets at David's court....

---

[55] 2 Chr 18:7, 9, 11, 17 // 2 Kgs 22:8, 10, 12, 18.

[56] For a detailed analysis of 1 Chr 25:1–6, see John W. Kleinig, *The LORD's Song: The Basis, Function and Significance of Choral Music in Chronicles* (JSOTSup 156; Sheffield: Sheffield Academic, 1993), 148–57; Piet B. Dirksen, "Prophecy and Temple Music: 1 Chron. 25,1–7," *Henoch* 19 (1997), 259–66; Schniedewind, *The Word of God*, 174–82; Gary N. Knoppers, *1 Chronicles 10–29* (AB 12A; New York: Doubleday, 2004), 843–60.

In the second place the writer could make use of the profession of the three fathers as prophets by attributing to them the use of the same instruments as in the future temple service and the know-how with regard to "thanking and praising the Lord". For this the author could take advantage of the ancient tradition which connected the prophetic profession (*nb'*) with music.[57]

The fact that the profession and activities of Asaph, Heman, and Jeduthun are directly related to David creates an atmosphere of authenticity and sacrosanct esteem. These three temple functionaries are so to say the bridge between King David, who from the very beginning is presented as the organizer of the Jerusalem Temple cult, and the institute of the temple singers in the Chronicler's days. That is why these three functionaries elsewhere in the book of Chronicles are prominently brought to the fore at moments that are so crucial to the pre-history of the temple (e.g., 1 Chr 15:16–17; 16:4–6, 37–42; 2 Chr 5:12).[58]

Apart from three occurrences in 1 Chr 25:1–3, in the Chronicler's *Sondergut* the verb נבא "to prophesy" is found one more time, viz., in 2 Chr 20:37, a passage in which an unknown Eliezer is presented.[59]

CONCLUSION

The majority of the prophets and inspired messengers we met in the book of Chronicles have been "invented" by the Chronicler and should therefore be characterized as "literary personages" rather than historical persons.

---

[57] Dirksen, "Prophecy and Temple Music," 263.

[58] Kleinig, *The LORD's Song*, 156: "[T]he Chronicler explains the significance of the choral service by treating it as a species of prophecy. All the singers exercised a prophetic role in their singing at the temple. Even though the singers did not usually act as prophets by communicating divine oracles to the people, their regular musical performance was regarded by the Chronicler as a 'kind of ritualized prophecy … in which God spoke to his people.'" The final words are a quotation from Newsome, *The Chronicler's View of Prophecy*, 224–5.

[59] See, e.g., Schniedewind, *The Word of God*, 76–77; Mason, *Preaching the Tradition*, 71–73; Strübind, *Tradition als Interpretation*, 195–7.

Consequently, the speeches delivered by these literary personages are the most appropriate place to look for the Chronicler's own theological convictions and accents. One will hardly wonder that it is just these prophetic addresses where fundamental theological notions of 1–2 Chronicles are to be found.

As far as so-called "classical prophets" are met in the Chronicler's text, they do not act as inspired messengers, but rather hold the position of keepers of the royal archives, being responsible for the records of a king's reign.

SOME PRECEDENTS FOR THE RELIGION OF THE BOOK
Josiah's Book and Ancient Revelatory Literature

Jonathan Ben-Dov

The Josiah Narrative, one of the most often discussed passages of the Bible, refuses to let go of the scholarly imagination. In a recent article I called attention to some new aspects of the story of Josiah's book-find, mainly with regard to the role of Josiah's book in a wider ancient Near Eastern context.[1] The present paper will continue my earlier reflection, focusing attention on the relevance of the Josiah narrative for the crystallization of what is now called "the Religion of the Book."[2] This matter has received considerable attention lately, with the rise of interest in such concepts as authorship, revelation, and canonization.[3] The tools

---

[1] Jonathan Ben-Dov, "Writing as Oracle and as Law: New Contexts for the Book-Find of King Josiah," *JBL* 127 (2008): 223–39.

[2] For an expanded discussion of this concept see mainly Moshe Halbertal, *People of the Book: Canon, Meaning, and Authority* (Cambridge: Harvard University, 1997).

[3] See Arie van der Kooij and Karel van der Toorn (ed.), *Canonization and Decanonization: Papers Presented to the International Conference of the Leiden Institute for the Study of Religions* (SHR 82; Leiden: Brill, 1997); Margalit Finkelberg and Guy G. Stroumsa (ed.), *Homer, the Bible and Beyond: Literary and Religious Canons in the Ancient World* (JSRC 2; Leiden: Brill, 2003); important recent studies which focus on writing and authorship rather than on the notion of Canon are: David M. Carr, *Writing on the Tablet of the Heart: Origins of Scripture and Literature* (New York: Oxford University, 2005); Karel

developed by the group "Prophetic Texts in their Ancient Context" over the years are particularly relevant for the study of this topic since they shed light on written texts as the revealed word of god and as an object for reflection and study. Previous work done in the PTAC group on prophecy, orality, and literacy will serve as a basis for the present exploration of the mutual relationship between prophecy, law, and authoritative books.[4]

As a trigger for the discussion, I will summarize the argument by the late Moshe Weinfeld, a radical proponent of the view that Josiah initiated a new religion of the Book:[5] a) Josiah's reform brought about a new religious situation in which prayers and Torah readings (2 Kgs 23:1–2, 21–23), being purely textual rituals, were no longer related to Temple and Sacrifice, but rather existed as an essential religious element by themselves; b) The acts of Josiah "began the process of the canonization of Scripture, a concept which penetrated also Christianity and Islam." It was Josiah who initiated the urge to write and canonize the national religious traditions, an urge that continued later in writing the law, history, prophecy, wisdom, and other Israelite essentials. "The first motive for the crystallization of Scripture was the sanctification of Deuteronomy, an act which transformed the religion of Israel into the Religion of the Book."

Admittedly, it is not entirely clear whether Weinfeld refers to the actual Josiah narrative or to a reconstructed historical scenario of the composition of Deuteronomy in the late seventh century BCE. More recently van der Toorn claimed that "The biblical narrative about this event [i.e., the Josiah Reform,

---

van der Toorn, *Scribal Culture and the Making of the Hebrew Bible* (Cambridge: Harvard University, 2007). The recently published monograph by van der Toorn is an especially convenient point of departure and will thus be referred to quite often in the paper. For an early reflection on writing and revelation see Joseph Blenkinsopp, *Prophecy and Canon: A Contribution to the Study of Jewish Origins* (Notre Dame; University of Notre Dame, 1977). Blenkinsopp's discussion, although not a highly influential one in present day scholarship, was the first to elucidate the essential concepts mentioned here and their relevance for Early Judaism.

[4] See especially Ehud Ben Zvi and Michael H. Floyd (ed.), *Writings and Speech in Ancient Israelite Prophecy* (SBLSymS 10; Atlanta: SBL, 2000); Michael H. Floyd and Robert D. Haak (ed.), *Prophets, Prophecy, and Prophetic Texts in Second Temple Judaism* (LHBOTS 427; New York: T&T Clark, 2006).

[5] Moshe Weinfeld, "The Finding of sepher hatorah," in idem, *From Joshua to Josiah* (Jerusalem: Magnes, 1992), 176–9 (Hebrew). Weinfeld's view is noted in passing by Halbertal (*People of the Book*, 10–11 and n. 18): Josiah, according to Halbertal, may have been an initial sign but not a full manifestation of the religion of the Book.

JBD] attests to a turning point in the relationship between the oral and written traditions."[6] By the end of the seventh century BCE, says van der Toorn, the book was considered the ultimate source of authority. Furthermore, one particular book, i.e., Deuteronomy, was considered already then to be revealed knowledge (Deut 4:44, 29:28). Deuteronomy thus combines two key concepts of the later monotheistic religions which are intensively explored in van der Toorn's book: Writtenness and Revelation. Like Weinfeld, he thus assigns the Josiah narrative an important role in the formation of the new religion of the Book.

Indeed, the Josiah narrative uses the same building blocks that were used to construct a canonical awareness within ancient Israel and outside it in Late Antiquity: the concepts of Prophecy, Law, and the Divine authority of the written word. Moreover, since these concepts certainly were not invented in ancient Israel, but existed already in the cultures of the ancient Near East, where a book culture prospered long before Israelite scribal customs ever existed, it is necessary to examine what extra-biblical scribal practices can teach about the concept of Divine instruction, its writing, and transmission.[7] Taking a serious look at these extra-biblical precedents, we should consider the possibility that Josiah's book was a transition point rather than a revolution. In the words of the medievalist Carolyn Bynum, we may wish "to stress connections and transitions rather than borders, boundaries and breaks."[8]

Reading the Josiah narrative one should constantly be aware of the fact that what he or she reads is a highly pregnant text which fulfilled different functions along its literary life. As is by now widely realized, the context makes the message; one and the same element may have multiple meanings if it appears in different religious and literary settings. Thus, to take up one example, the report on Solomon's horses and chariots (1 Kgs 10:26–29) had originally been written as a praise of Solomon's grandeur; yet at the present it constitutes implicit criticism on Solomon for violating "The Law of The King" (Deut 17:16).[9] Similarly, the book-find by Josiah takes part in two distinctive settings. The

---

[6] van der Toorn, *Scribal Culture*, 221.

[7] I am not the first to claim this, of course. Such a claim had been earlier asserted by others, notably Lowell K. Handy, "The Role of Huldah in Josiah's Cult Reform," *ZAW* 106 (1994): 40–53. Yet my argument differs from that of Handy in significant points (see below).

[8] Carolyn W. Bynum, "Perspectives, Connections & Objects: What's Happening in History Now?" *Daedalus* 138 (2009): 71–86 (80).

[9] See Marc Z. Brettler, "The Structure of 1 Kings 1–11," *JSOT* 49 (1991): 87–97.

Book had initially existed as part of the oracular process in the Judean court, delivering divine approval for the king's intentions to enact a religious reform in the Jerusalem Temple. Later came the legal-canonical setting, in which the book was viewed as part of the legal document that later turned out to be the Torah, Deuteronomy, or the five books of Moses. This is the way Deuteronomistic redactors wanted the book to be understood, and this is how it was actually conceived by traditional and modern scholars alike.[10] I take the opportunity here to present a summary of my previous article about the two views of Josiah's book before continuing to some new trajectories of the same theme with regard to the present title. The discussion here adds some new material I did not have the chance to include in the earlier article. The argument is presented in the following order: (1) The Composition of the Josiah Narrative; (2) the term *tôrāh* —Instruction, Oracle, Law; (3) Books as oracular media; (4) Ancient Near Eastern precedents for the Religion of the Book.

THE COMPOSITION OF THE JOSIAH NARRATIVE

Scholarly opinions still vary between viewing 2 Kgs 22–23 as an essentially pre-deuteronomistic narrative with a Deuteronomistic layer assembled on top of it, to a minimalist view which sees the entire story as Deuteronomistic, except maybe for some short ancient fragments.[11] I suggested to detect the Deuteronomistic presence in 2 Kgs 22–23 primarily in passages which both use characteristic deuteronomistic phraseology and convey an unmistakably deuteronomistic message. These passages are as follows:

22:16–20 Huldah's answer to Josiah.
Huldah has been present also in the pre-Deuteronomistic story, but the actual answer recorded in vv. 16–20 underwent thorough Deuteronomistic rephrasing until very little is left of the original oracle.[12]

---

[10] For a refinement of the view of Josiah's book in the Persian period see most recently Ehud Ben Zvi, "Imagining Josiah's Book and the Implications of Imagining It in Early Persian Yehud," in *Berührungspunkte: Studien zur Sozial- und Religionsgeschichte Israels und seiner Umwelt, Festschrift für Rainer Albertz zu seinem 65. Geburtstag* (AOAT 350; ed. Ingo Kottsieper et al.; Münster: Ugarit Verlag, 2008), 193–212.

[11] See Ben-Dov, "Writing as Oracle and as Law," 229–31, for a more detailed tradition-history of the narrative.

[12] This judgment generally follows Gary N. Knoppers, *Two Nations Under God* (HSM 53; Atlanta: Scholars Press, 1994), 2:131–3. Handy, "The Role of Huldah," supplied a rich and convincing background for the oracle of Huldah in

23:1–3 Covenant
23:15–20 Reform report in Bethel and Samaria[13]
23:21–23 Passover

Other parts of the Josiah narrative are essentially pre-Dtr, i.e., they are based on an antique source or sources whose authors were close in time to Josiah. These authors were free of the Deuteronomistic ideology; in fact this kind of ideology only sprang as a comprehensive historiographical prism some time later, when the influence of the newly-found book increased. One cannot deny that the pre-Deuteronomistic parts were affected (sometimes heavily) by glossators, but the fundamental part of the following passages is early:

22:3–15 Book-Find, report to the king, and inquiry to Huldah[14]

---

ancient Near Eastern literature, but he unnecessarily assigns the entire narrative to an exilic or post-exilic author. Somewhat surprisingly, although Handy takes pains to emphasize the lateness of the Huldah *narrative* (48–49), he downplays the evident deuteronomistic traits preserved in the *oracle*. According to him "The prophecy is a very bland stereotypical couple of phrases which could have been found anywhere in the ancient Near East" (51). Based on v. 20a, Halpern and Vanderhooft view the words of Huldah "as a preexilic document," although they do admit the presence of deuteronomistic reworking in the oracle: Baruch Halpern and David Vanderhooft, "The Editions of Kings in the 7th–6th Centuries B.C.E.," *HUCA* 62 (1991): 179–244 (226–9).

[13] The account of the reform in Bethel and Samaria (vv. 15–20), although not phrased in unequivocal deuteronomistic style, is mostly a later insertion. This conviction is based on the continuity between this passage and the prophetic story from 1 Kgs 12–13. See James A. Montgomery, *A Critical and Exegetical Commentary on the Books of Kings* (ICC; Edinburgh: T&T Clark, 1951) 534–5; Knoppers, *Two Nations Under God*, 2:196–205.

[14] Thomas Römer argued for the lateness of the book-find narrative on the basis of its incongruence with the story of the temple restoration (22:3–7) in which is it embedded (Thomas Römer, "Transformations in Deuteronomistic and Biblical Historiography: On 'Book-finding' and other Literary Strategies," *ZAW* 109 (1997): 1–11 [6]). Römer bases himself on Hans D. Hoffman's contention that the report on temple restoration in 22:3–7 is dependant upon the earlier one in 12:10–16; therefore, says Römer, the fact that the fixed pattern is broken marks the diverging element as an intrusive addition. This argument is not compelling, however. It is in the very nature of biblical type-scenes to change certain elements in each new embellishment of the scene. In fact the

48   *Some Precedents for the Religion of the Book*

22:4–14 Reform report in Judah[15]

Since so many fundamentals of Bible criticism—from deWette's hypothesis to a revisionist view of DtrH as a post-exilic work—depend on the composition of the Book-find narrative, minimalist and maximalist scholars alike in this case risk employing circular reasoning. This problem was justly pointed out by Philip Davies, alert as he always is to methodological flaws:[16]

> ... it takes no genius to see that the identification of Deuteronomy with the Josianic law book is precisely what the author of 2 Kgs 22 intended. The language and ideology of the framework of 2 Kings is Deuteronomistic, and even before Noth's theory of the 'Deuteronomistic History' it could have been realized that any *Deuteronomistic* account of the finding of a law book would present that law book as *Deuteronomy* ... The writer of the law book story wishes to make it clear that in the days of the kings of Judah, the scroll of Deuteronomy, which had been lost temporarily, was recovered and used as the basis for a religious reform, and with a full authority of a Davidic king, no less ... We *know* what the law book of the story was: but we do *not* know if the story of its 'discovery' is true!

According to Davies, the story of the book find is in itself deuteronomistic, and thus cannot be trusted when recounting the history of its own proof text, Deuteronomy. For all we know, Davies would say, 2 Kgs 22 looks like a Deuteronomistic fictional story aimed to credit the book of Deuteronomy with great antiquity. This argument, however, is based on the assumption that a book find could not have had any significance in a pre-deuteronomistic setting, and

---

changes from the type-scene bear most of the meaning of the new narrative. See Robert Alter, *The Art of Biblical Narrative* (New York: Basic Books, 1981), 47–52; Yair Zakovitch, *Through the Looking Glass: Reflection Stories in the Bible* (Tel-Aviv: ha-Kibbutz ha-Meuhad, 1995) (Hebrew).

[15] For the essential authenticity of the Reform report in vv. 4–14 (excluding glosses and insertions) see Christoph Uehlinger, "Was There a Cult Reform under King Josiah? The Case for a Well-Grounded Minimum," in *Good Kings and Bad Kings* (ed. Lester L. Grabbe; LHBOTS 393; New York: T&T Clark, 2005), 279–316; Martin Arneth, "Die antiassyrische Reform Josias von Judah: Überlegungen zur Komposition und Intention 2 Reg 23:4–15," *ZABR* 7 (2001): 189–216.

[16] Philip R. Davies, "Josiah and the Law Book," in Grabbe (ed.), *Good Kings and Bad Kings*, 65–77 (69–70).

thus was only created by Deuteronomistic authors.[17] It is precisely this assumption that I contest. The way out from the vicious circle is to acknowledge that the book find story *did* exist in a pre-Deuteronomistic account of Josiah's reign, but not as the Book of Law. In that original account, the book was conceived as part of the oracular process in the royal court. Davies is right that the story—as it is now—urges the reader to identify the book with Deuteronomy, but this was not necessarily the intention of the *original* story.

The intent of the original story had been to legitimize the intentions of Josiah, who aimed to enact a wide-range cultic reform in Jerusalem. Like many other reformer kings in the ancient world, Josiah had to gain support for his reforming plans, which naturally ran against the interests of this group or another in the establishment.[18] The king presented in support a divine message sent from Heaven. The query to Huldah the prophetess must also be seen on this background: it is a reaffirmation of the Divine instruction by cross-checking it with a different divinatory medium.[19] Such a habit has many parallels in the Mesopotamian divinatory process, both in the Neo-Assyrian context and, earlier, in Mari. I added a Hittite parallel which will be mentioned below.

Interestingly enough, the passages indicated above as pre-Deuteronomistic refer to the book either plainly as *hassēper* or as *sēper hattôrāh* (22:8, 11), while the pronounced Deuteronomistic passages 23:1–3, 21–23, relating to the covenant and the Passover, refer to the book as *sēper habbĕrît* (23:2, 21). This latter term plays on the self-identification of Deuteronomy as a book of the covenant (Deut 28:69), and is accordingly employed in passages which reflect deuteronomic practices: the public reading of the law (2 Kgs 23:1–3, cp. Deut 31) and the celebration of a centralized Passover (2 Kgs 23:21–23, cp. Deut

---

[17] This hidden assumption is made more explicit by Römer ("Transformations," 5–7, 9). The question will be dealt further below.

[18] For a comparison of Josiah with other reforming kings see Handy, "The Role of Huldah" (especially Esarhaddon and Nabunaid), and recently with a wider scope, Nadav Na'aman, "The King Leading Cult Reforms in his Kingdom: Josiah and Other Kings in the Ancient Near East," *ZABR* 12 (2006): 131–68.

[19] This case was masterfully demonstrated by Handy. I add to his argument a parallel from Hittite texts (below), which underscores the use of texts as oracular media already in an ancient period of time. One may therefore doubt the argument by van der Toorn (*Scribal Culture*, 35) that the query to Huldah was performed because the authenticity of the book had been in doubt; the doubt was not greater here than in any other case of rechecking an oracle in the ancient Near East.

16:1–9).[20] The term *sēper habbĕrît* relates to the nomistic aspects of Deuteronomy, while the term *sēper hattôrāh*, I maintain, retains an older prophetic-oracular meaning, which goes back to pre-deuteronomistic concepts.[21]

TORAH

The term *sēper hattôrāh* is usually taken to be a significant marker for identifying Josiah's book with Deuteronomy. However, in 2 Kgs 22 this term is not used in a nomistic connotation, attested for example in Deut 29–31 *passim*. Surprisingly, when a specific law like the Deuteronomic Passah is invoked, the text uses the term *sēper habbĕrît* (23:21), not *hattôrāh*. *Tôrāh* is therefore used in the Josiah narrative in the prophetic-divinatory meaning of "instruction, oracle." I summarize here the fuller argument, to be found with further substantiation in my *JBL* article.[22]

The term *tôrāh* is a keystone of biblical religion, and as such it embodied several divergent meanings in various social settings of ancient Israel. In the Wisdom literature it denoted the meaning of a general, usually secular instruction, which never takes written form. On the other hand, in priestly literature the word *tôrāh* denotes a short instruction which relates to the ritual realm—sacrifices, purity, leprosy, etc. This kind of instruction, always supplied by priests, was committed to writing in a series of short scrolls, and is presently collected into one priestly continuum in the Pentateuch. Side by side with the above connotations, the prophetic literature retained yet another meaning for *tôrāh*, which is closer to the cognate Akkadian term *têrtu(m)*. In Akkadian (especially in Mari and in Neo-Assyrian but also in the Neo-Babylonian inscriptions of Nabunaid) this term means "oracle, decision," as well as "the instruction of the liver by extispicy," and thus remains part and parcel of the semantic field of divination and oracular instruction.

Interestingly, the Akkadian term *têrtum* appears in a prophecy sent from the prophets of Adad in Aleppo to the king of Mari, a typical case of double-

---

[20] For the compliance of 2 Kgs 23:21–23 with the Deuteronomic Passah see Bernard M. Levinson, *Deuteronomy and the Hermeneutics of Legal Innovation* (Oxford: Oxford University, 1998), 95–97.

[21] A distinction between the two terms—*sēper habbĕrît* / *hattôrāh*—was recently employed by van der Toorn, *Scribal Culture*, 160. Yet, while van der Toorn assigns the terms to two consecutive editions of Deuteronomy, both of them post-Josianic, I assign the term *sēper hattôrāh* to an earlier stratum which reflects divinatory-prophetic interests. The evidence adduced below for the meaning of *tôrāh* will account for my preference.

[22] Ben-Dov, "Writing as Oracle," 225–9.

checking the divine message through additional means of divination.[23] Here, the initial divine word came from extispicy (*ina têrētim*), but, as van der Toorn explains, since this ritual was carried out "in the presence of Adad," then the prophets (*āpilū*) standing right there were able to immediately elaborate it and send it in a letter to the king. The use of *têrtum* here sheds some light on the oracular context of the word *tôrāh* in the Josiah episode.

When Isaiah ben Amoz in 2:3 invokes the word pair *tôrāh* // *dābār*, he refers to the pronouncement of the Divine word through the prophet. While this meaning is quite common in prophetic literature for *dābār*, the parallelism makes it clear that *tôrāh* too is used here is a similar sense.[24] The book of Deuteronomy, when referring to itself as *tôrāh*, amalgamates several of the meanings adduced above, on its way to a radical change of the concept of writing and revelation in ancient Israel. Yet, the term *sēper hattôrāh* in the original version of 2 Kgs 22, I maintain, did not relate to the compound, deuteronomic sense of the word, but rather conveyed an older concept about the "Book of Instruction":[25] an oracle in written form which was sent from Heaven to instruct the audience in concrete matters.

In the Josiah narrative, therefore, the term *tôrāh* played different roles in the various literary layers: while originally it had been used in a divinatory-

---

[23] Bertrand Lafont, "Le Roi de Mari et les prophètes du dieu Adad," *RA* 78 (1984): 7–18. This case was discussed by Karel van der Toorn, "From the Oral to the Written: The Case of Old Babylonian Prophecy," in Ben Zvi and Floyd (ed.), *Writings and Speech in Israelite and Ancient Near Eastern Prophecy*, 219–234 (224–5). For an older version see *JNSL* 24 (1998): 55–70. In Mari, the words of prophets were considered a less secure means of communication, and thus required verification by a more "empirical" type of *bārûtu*; see Jack M. Sasson, "The Posting of Letters with Divine Messages," in *Florilegium Marianum II: Recueil d'études à la mémoire de Maurice Birot* (ed. Dominique Charpin and Jean-Marie Durand; Mémoires de NABU 3; Paris: SEPOA, 1994), 299–316 (306–7).

[24] See also Hans Wildberger, *Isaiah 1–12: A Commentary* (trans. Thomas H. Trapp; Continental Commentaries; Minneapolis: Fortress, 1991), 91. This interpretation is slightly different from the one offered by Baruch J. Schwartz, "Torah from Zion: Isaiah's Temple Vision (Isaiah 2:1–4)," in *Sanctity of Time and Space in Tradition and Modernity* (ed. Alberdina Houtman et al.; Leiden: Brill, 1998), 16–17. Schwartz's view that *tôrāh* here means a legal verdict does not fully account for the parallelism with *dābār*, a common technical term for the prophetic word.

[25] Cf. the *NJPS* version in 22:8 "I have found a scroll of the Teaching."

prophetic sense, it later united with other concepts of *tôrāh* under the aegis of the Deuteronomistic redactors (see, e.g., 23:25).

BOOKS AS ORACULAR MEDIA

Some scholars view the book-find of Josiah as a sign for a new tendency in Judahite religion which sought to replace the temple with the book.[26] In recent years Thomas Römer took special interest in exemplifying this new tendency, while identifying it as characteristically Deuteronomistic.[27] In light of the above deliberations, however, I suggest that the book find of Josiah may be interpreted differently. A book find was a perfectly acceptable phenomenon, maybe even a prestigious way for discovering the divine decree, in Judah as in a variety of other ancient cultures in pre-Deuteronomistic times. The best example for such a habit comes from the Hittite account on the days of the king Mursili, preserved in his second plague prayer:[28]

> [The matter of the plague] continued to trouble [me, and I inquired about it] to the god [through an oracle]. [I found] two old tablets: one tablet dealt with [the ritual of the Mala river]. Earlier kings performed the ritual of the Mala river, but because [people have been dying] in Hatti since the days of my father, we never performed [the ritual] of the Mala river.
>
> The second tablet dealt with the town of Kurustamma: how the storm god of Hatti carried the men of Kurustamma to Egyptian territory and how the storm god of Hatti made a treaty between them and the men of Hatti ... the men of Hatti thereby suddenly transgressed the oath of the gods ...
>
> When I found the aforementioned tablet dealing with Egypt, I inquired about it to the god through an oracle ... And it was confirmed by the

---

[26] See for example Weinfeld, "The Finding of *sepher hatorah*"; van der Toorn, *Scribal Culture*, 221–4.

[27] Römer, "Transformations," 9; idem, "Du Temple au Livre: L'idéologie de la centralization dans l'historiographie deutéronomiste," in *Rethinking the Foundations: Historiography in the Ancient World and in the Bible, Essays in Honour of John van Seters* (ed. Thomas Römer and Steven L. McKenzie; BZAW 294; Berlin: de Gruyter, 2000), 207–25.

[28] CTH 378.III; Itamar Singer, *Hittite Prayers* (SBLWAW 11; Atlanta: Society of Biblical Literature, 2002), 58–59; see in greater detail Ben-Dov, "Writing as Oracle," 233–5.

oracle. Because of the plague I also asked the oracle about the ritual of the [Mala] river. And then too it was confirmed that I should appear before the Storm-god of Hatti, my lord. I have [just] confessed [the sin before the storm-god of Hatti]. It is so. We have done [it. But the sin did not] take place in my time. [It took place] in the time of my father ...

In this prayer, the king describes how he turned to the god through an oracle with a specific query about the cause for the plague that devastated the land of Hatti in his times. The answer came in the form two old written tablets found by the king. One of the tablets required the reinstitution of an old ritual which had been abandoned in past years. The king then sought to reenact this ritual, supporting his intention by double-checking the word of the written tablets by a second query to the oracle.[29] This course of events is in many ways similar to the course of events in Josiah's times and could serve as a model for explaining it.

Several points should be emphasized with regard to this extra-biblical source. Earlier attempts to view Josiah's book as an oracular item (notably Handy's article) relied on Assyrian and Babylonian sources, in which divinatory means like astrology and extispicy played a dominant role. In the Hittite case, in contrast, the word of god is conveyed by writing, proving outright that a written oracle must not necessarily be a late, Dtr-oriented element, since it is used in ancient Hatti, hardly a monotheistic Deuteronomistic environment. Furthermore, the king Mursili indicates that he has found "two *old* tablets." The fact that he assigns old age to the books that were found draws strong assonances with the story on Josiah's reform. This is a significant difference from the later, Neo-Assyrian tradition of written prophecy, to be discussed below. Finally, just as Mursili excuses himself by indicating that "the sin did not] take place in my

---

[29] For further information on Hittite oracles see Richard Beal, "Hittite Oracles," in *Magic and Divination in the Ancient World* (ed. Leda Ciraolo and Jonathan Seidel; Leiden: Brill/Styx, 2002), 59–83; Joost Hazenbos, "Der Mensch denkt, Gott lenkt. Betrachtungen zum hethitischen Orakelpersonal," in *Das geistige Erfassen der Welt im Alten Orient: Sprache, Religion, Kultur und Gesellschaft* (ed. Claus Wilcke; Wiesbaden: Harrassowitz, 2007), 95–109. I thank Itamar Singer for his bibliographical help.

time. [It took place] in the time of my father," so Josiah in 2 Kgs 22:13 blames "our fathers" for neglecting to observe the words of the book.[30]

That the Judean royal court made constant use of oracular and divinatory means is suggested by Isa 8:16–20. In this eighth-century piece, the "true" prophet Isaiah seeks to win himself primary place as against a variety of other, exoteric mantic practitioners: "the ghosts and familiar spirits that chirp and moan." In the same chapter, vv. 1 and 16, one encounters the use of a written and authenticated scroll in the process of the verification of a prophecy. This permits us to talk of a *sēper* as a word of god already in the eighth century BCE, a concept which gained further meaning in the days of Josiah.[31]

It is significant that a close parallel to the book-find of Josiah arises from the second millennium BCE Hittite culture rather than from the contemporary activity of prophets and diviners in the Neo-Assyrian court. Josiah's book find can now be more confidently understood on a pre-Deuteronomic background.

Two periods stand out in the history of written prophecy in the Ancient Near East: the prophetic corpus from Mari (ca. eighteenth century BCE) and the Neo-Assyrian prophecies of the seventh century BCE.[32] While both milieus attest to an intensive activity of communication between the king and the god, the Neo-Assyrian corpus lays greater emphasis on written aspects of this

---

[30] The theological question of cross-generational retribution, undoubtedly a burning issue in ancient Israelite historiography, was also highly meaningful in the ancient Hittite literature, as exemplified mainly in the corpus of Hittite prayers. See Itamar Singer, "Sin and Punishment in Hittite Prayers," in *An Experienced Scribe who Neglects Nothing: Ancient Near Eastern Studies in Honor of Jacob Klein* (ed. Yitschak Sefati; Bethesda, Md.: CDL, 2005), 557–67.

[31] Admittedly, as discussed in Ben-Dov, "Writing as Oracle" (236–9, with extensive bibliography), the importance of written documents in Judean prophecy gradually increased, reaching a climax in the late biblical period (Hab 2:2–3, Ezek 2:9–3:2) and beyond (4 Ezra 14:37–47). The late process of textualization does not rule out the existence of early written oracles in Israelite prophecy.

[32] The literature on this aspect of scholarship is immense. On Assyrian prophecies see Simo Parpola, *Assyrian Prophecies* (SAA 9; Helsinki: Helsinki University, 1997). On the topic in general see Martti Nissinen, *Prophets and Prophecy in the Ancient Near East* (SBLWAW 12; Leiden: Brill, 2003); idem, ed., *Prophecy in Its Ancient Near Eastern Context: Mesopotamian, Biblical, and Arabian Perspectives* (SBLSymS 13; Atlanta: SBL, 2000); idem and Matthias Köckert, eds., *Propheten in Mari, Assyrien und Israel* (FRLANT 210; Göttingen: Vandenhoeck & Ruprecht, 2000).

communication.³³ In this later period one finds other aspects which may be useful for illuminating the book find by Josiah. Terms like *šipru*, *šipirtu* connote generally "message, report", but in the Neo-Assyrian period they relate to the written account or "letter" of the king to his god. From the god's side, a term like *šipir mahhê* in the late Assyrian royal inscriptions means "die verschriftliche Form einer göttlichen Mitteilung in Form eines Traums oder eines Orakels."³⁴ However, in all Mesopotamian prophecies from Mari to Assyria the oracle was never given in written form; oracles and other divinatory messages were always transmitted in oral form, while their written version was produced in order to improve the communication rather than as an essential part of the oracular process.

We come then to a fundamental distinction between the Hittite prayer, in which the "book" was the initial form of the word of god about the plague, and the Mesopotamian prophecies which were committed to writing only *post factum*. The pre-Deuteronomistic narrative on Josiah's book-find resembles the Hittite case more than it does the Neo-Assyrian prophecies. However, later Deuteronomistic writers, who acted with advanced concepts of writing, departed from this older concept and gradually related the book that was found with the more familiar concept of a "Book of the Covenant" as designed in the sixth–seventh centuries BCE. Although originating in ancient modes of revelation, the image of the book found renewed strength in the Deuteronomistic edition.

Another distinction which might prove useful for the appreciation of Josiah's book may be culled from the practices of Neo-Assyrian prophecies. Parpola reports that: ³⁵

> The Neo-Assyrian prophecy corpus is extant on two kinds of clay tablets, which differ from each other both in size and in shape .... The horizontal format (*u'iltu*) was used for notes, reports, receipts and memoranda—in short for information primarily meant for immediate use, not for permanent storage. The vertical, multi-column format (*ṭuppu*) was used ... for documents specifically drawn up for archival storage and reference purposes .... We can thus conclude that nos. 5–8

---

³³ The terminology is based on Beate Pongratz-Leisten, *Herrschaftswissen in Mesopotamia* (SAAS 10; Helsinki: Helsinki University, 1999). On prophecy see pp. 47–95; on the written manifestation of prophecy see pp. 202–76, esp. pp. 260–76.

³⁴ Pongratz-Leisten, *Herrschaftswissen*, 261.

³⁵ Parpola, *Assyrian Prophecies*, LIII, and see also the bibliography.

report freshly received oracles, whereas nos. 1–4 are copies made from reports like nos. 5–8.

According to Nissinen, the basic format for a prophetic report was the disposable *u'iltu*.[36] Several such reports were subsequently collected into a standard archival tablet in order to enhance their preservation and circulation. I suggest that a similar distinction might be useful with regard to Josiah's book. While this book first appeared in history as a rather short divine instruction, meant to support the reforming intentions of the king, it was later represented by Deuteronomistic authors as a long and comprehensive book, to be archived and preserved in the temple. The initial document may have contained very small parts of Deuteronomy—possibly only chapters twelve through sixteen and twenty-eight[37]—but the composition gradually accrued to include more text in a longer form. The terminology of Neo-Assyrian prophetic texts may thus throw light on early stages in the growth of Deuteronomy.[38]

The transition from on oral prophetic word to a written format of prophecy, a procedure so well recorded in the prophetic writings from Mari and Assyria, was not so smoothly managed in ancient Israel. As was noted long ago, Jer 8:8–9 preserves an objection to a controversial written *tôrāh*—whether Deuteronomy or a different document unknown

---

[36] Martti Nissinen, "Spoken, Written, Quoted, and Invented: Orality and Writtenness in Ancient Near Eastern Prophecy," in Ben Zvi and Floyd (ed.), *Writings and Speech*, 248; see also Pongratz-Leisten, *Herrschaftswissen*, 272–3. For the process of transforming prophecy from a one-time report to a part of the literary "stream of tradition," see Matthijs J. de Jong, *Isaiah among the Ancient Near Eastern Prophets: A Comparative Study of the Earliest Stages of the Isaiah Tradition and the Neo-Assyrian Prophecies* (VTSup 117; Leiden: Brill, 2007), 395–439. On a similar but not identical process in Mari, see Aaron Schart, "Combining Prophetic Oracles in Mari Letters and Jeremiah 36," *JANES* 23 (1995): 75–93.

[37] I mention chs. 12–16 because they contain most of the laws which could serve as catalysts for the reform: centralization of the cult (ch. 12), intolerance towards worshippers of foreign gods (ch. 13), centralized cult during the festivals (ch. 16), the abolition of Ashera (ch. 16). I include ch. 28 because the curses contained in it gave the scroll the effect of awe, as reported in 2 Kgs 22:13, 16.

[38] van der Toorn (*Scribal Culture*, 144–9) also relied on the habits of ancient scribes when presenting a new hypothesis on the growth of Deuteronomy. He did not mention, however, the two types of prophetic tablets in this regard.

to us—which was propagated by wise men and scribes.³⁹ The two reports in 2 Kgs 22 and Jer 8, when taken together, draw a fuller picture of the acceptance process of written words of god in Israel at the time of the late monarchy.

PRECEDENTS FOR "RELIGION OF THE BOOK"

The notion "religion of the book" is usually invoked to denote a religion in which a book (or collection of books) constitutes the main representative of the word of god, and in which the book is therefore given primary importance. As a result, this kind of religion employs a series of further characteristics, such as the rise to power of agents of writing instead of officiating priests, as well as the development of notions of revelation and the manifestation of the divine in the written word. While biblical religion does not entirely answer to this description, the religion of the rabbinic writings embodies it quite faithfully.⁴⁰ We are now in the position to trace some early forerunners for this type of piety in Ancient Near Eastern and biblical sources, based in part also on the conclusions drawn

---

³⁹ For a survey of recent opinions on these verses see Mark Leuchter, *Josiah's Reform and Jeremiah's Scroll: Historical Calamity and Prophetic Response* (HBM 6; Sheffield: Phoenix, 2006), 129. Quite to the contrary, Leuchter suggests a new reading of Jer 8:8, by which the second half of the verse is *not* Jeremiah's rebuke of the wise but rather a continuation of the wise ones' own words from v. 8a (ibid., 130–2). According to him, the criticism against "the lying pen of scribes" comes from the mouth of Jeremiah's adversaries, who oppose Jeremiah and his association with scribes like Baruch and the Shaphan family. This intriguing new interpretation is, however, problematic from the stylistic aspect. While the actual quotation from the wise ones' words is characterized by the first person plural (as in many popular quotations in biblical prophecy: Ezek 33: 10b, 24b; 37:11b et al.), this formal trait is absent from the rest of the verse. In addition, the word אכן at the beginning of v. 8b marks a strong transition from the words of the people to the prophetic statement (cf. לכן in Ezek 33:25, 37:12).

⁴⁰ Halbertal, *People of the Book*; Michael Fishbane, *The Garments of Torah: Essays in Biblical Hermeneutics* (Bloomington: Indiana University Press, 1989); Robert Goldenberg, "Law and Spirit in Talmudic Religion," in *Jewish Spirituality: From the Bible Through the Middle Ages* (ed. Arthur Green; New York: Crossroad, 1987), 1:232–52.

above about Josiah's book find.[41] The historical development is demonstrated quite well by the transformation of the "book" found by Josiah—from an ominous object to a scroll of the Law.

The ancient kings Assurbanipal and Nabunaid—the former a contemporary of Josiah and the latter subsequent to him—were especially noted in Assyrian and Babylonian literature for their outstanding interest in ancient writings.[42] Assurbanipal invested huge efforts in assembling his celebrated library, to which he collected every possible piece of writing in Assyria and Babylonia.[43] Assurbanipal had a strong interest in the divinatory arts, especially in the "astrological" series *Enūma Anu Enlil*. A case in point is the report SAA 8 19 (= RMA 152, LAS 319). This small tablet begins as a typical astronomical report from the renowned scholar Issar-šumu-ereš, Assurbanipal's chief scribe. After quoting the pertinent celestial omen, however, the scholar changes from the formulaic language of a report to the tone of a letter. Thus we read in Hunger's translation (rev. 1–7): "Let them bring in that polyptich[44] of *Enūma Anu Enlil*

---

[41] For a similar undertaking see Karel van der Toorn, "The Iconic Book: Analogies between the Babylonian Cult of Images and the Veneration of the Torah," in *The Image and the Book: Iconic Cults, Aniconism, and the Rise of Book Religion in Israel and the Ancient Near East* (ed. Karel van der Toorn; CBET 21; Leuven: Peeters, 1997), 229–48. From a different perspective, the canonicity and the role of books in the biblical writings was discussed on the background of Mesopotamian sources in an important article by Victor A. Hurowitz, "'Proto-canonization' of the Torah: A Self-portrait of the Pentateuch in Light of Mesopotamian Writings," in Howard Kreisel (ed.), *Study and Knowledge in Jewish Thought* (The Goren-Goldstein Library of Jewish Thought 4; Beer Sheva: Ben-Gurion University of the Negev, 2006), 31–48.

[42] For Nabunaid see Peter Machinist and Hayim Tadmor, "Heavenly Wisdom," in *The Tablet and the Scroll: Near Eastern Studies in Honor of William W. Hallo* (ed. Mark E. Cohen et al.; Bethesda, Md.: CDL, 1993), 146–51. For Assurbanipal see recently Alasdair Livingstone, "Ashurbanipal—Literate or Not?" *ZA* 97 (2007): 98–118.

[43] See for example: Stephen J. Liebermann, "Canonical and Official Cuneiform Texts: Towards an Understanding of Assurbanipal's Personal Tablet Collection," in *Lingering Over Words: Studies in Ancient Near Eastern Literature in Honor of William L. Moran* (ed. Tzvi Abusch et al.; Atlanta: Scholars Press, 1990), 305–36; Grant Frame and Andrew R. George, "The Royal Libraries of Nineveh: New Evidence for King Ashurbanipal's Tablet Collection," *Iraq* 67 (2005): 265–84.

[44] The original letter in fact reads only *lē'u* (GIŠ.LE.U₅.UM), "writing board." The translation "polyptich" was suggested by Simo Parpola, *Letters from Assyrian Scholars to the Kings Esarhaddon and Assurbanipal, Part II:*

which we wrote, (and) let the king, my lord, have a look. Also, let them give us the Akkadian tablet of the king; the stars, 3 of each, should be drawn therein after (its model)." The royal scribe is asking that the luxury edition of *Enūma Anu Enlil* be sent to him.[45] As noted by Parpola, a polyptich of *Enūma Anu Enlil* of that kind was actually found in archaeological excavations. It is a luxury edition consisting of sixteen ivory boards containing parts of *Enūma Anu Enlil*. The inscription on the cover-board read: "Palace of Sargon, king of the world, king of Assyria: he had the series *Enūma Anu Enlil* inscribed on an ivory writing-board and deposited it in his palace in Dūr Šarrukēn."[46] Note that such copies were made already for Sargon, many years prior to the extravagantly literate Assurbanipal.

In the inscriptions of the last Babylonian king, Nabunaid, the exemplary erudition of the king was demonstrated with recourse to the same astronomical series *Enūma Anu Enlil*. As Machinist and Tadmor demonstrated, this notion is reflected in a passage from the polemical "Verse Account," as well as in a fragment of an inscription reading: "the tablets of the series *Enūma Anu Enlil* the scribes brought before him in a box from Babylon for (him) to peruse. (But) they were not read; no one understood them without his (=Nabonidus) telling them."[47] This divinatory series is depicted here as the prototype for an ancient piece of learning that should be contemplated and copied, with special recourse to the figure of the king. As in the Assurbanipal example, the king holds an unmediated mastery of scholarly knowledge. This body of knowledge is not a

---

Commentary and Appendices (AOAT 5/2; Kevelaer: Butzon & Bercker and Neukirchen-Vluyn: Neukirchener, 1983), 333 on the basis of archeological finds.

[45] For the implications of this report on the administration of the library see Pongratz-Leisten, *Herrschaftswissen*, 297–8. The identity of the second requested document alongside *Enūma Anu Enlil* is debatable: it might be the work called "Astrolabe B" with the title "three stars each," or better the graphic representation of that list on the "circular astrolabe" *CT* 33 11–12 (my thanks to Wayne Horowitz for the information).

[46] Translation follows Parpola, *Letters from Assyrian Scholars*, 333, with further bibliography cited there.

[47] Machinist and Tadmor, "Heavenly Wisdom," 149. The reading and translation by Machinist and Tadmor were accepted also in the recent edition by Hanspeter Schaudig, *Die Inschriften Nabonids von Babylon und Kyros' des Grossen, samt den in ihrem Umfeld enstandenen Tendenzschriften: Textausgabe und Grammatik* (AOAT 256; Münster: Ugarit, 2001).

mere "instruction to the king" but rather a written corpus which requires a significant amount of devotion and practice in order to understand it properly.

The above two examples join other written evidence on the status of authoritative writings. The great corpora of Mesopotamian learning, embodied in the omen series which developed gradually from the late second millennium BCE onwards, are mentioned in the "catalogue of texts and authors" as prototypes of revealed literature.[48] It emerges that these corpora were fertile ground for constant reflection on such conceptions as writing, canonization, inspiration, interpretation, scribal authority, revelation etc.[49] In short: the omen series served as an early laboratory for the development of the religion of the book.

With regard to the Mesopotamian evidence, Parpola took the issue a great deal forward in his following rather bold assertion:[50] "I think it is important to recognize these texts (i.e., scientific-divinatory texts) for what they properly are, religious texts belonging to a large canonized whole comparable to the Holy Writ. It is diagnostic of their character as sacred writings that their origin was attributed to divine revelation..."

On a more modest note, Victor A. Hurowitz has drawn attention to the transmission of *Enūma Anu Enlil* as an example of "proto-canonization."[51] He noted the fact that *Enūma Anu Enlil* is recorded as one of the pieces authored *ša pî Ea* "by the mouth of (the god) Ea."[52] What is more, Hurowitz draws interesting parallels between the transmission of *Enūma Anu Enlil* to humanity—via the famous sage Enmeduranki to the Mesopotamian *ummanū*—and some biblical and post-biblical depictions of how Moses taught the Torah to the Israelites.[53]

While the ancient Mesopotamian reflection on authorship and revelation has been noted before, I draw special attention to the association of these practices with the figure of the king. With regard to the Assurbanipal incident reported

---

[48] Wilfred G. Lambert, "A Catalogue of Texts and Authors," *JCS* 16 (1962): 59–77; van der Toorn, *Scribal Culture*, 42–46, 207–8.

[49] For canonization in the omen series see also Francesca Rochberg-Halton, "Canonicity in Cuneiform Texts," *JCS* 36 (1984): 127–144; eadem, *The Heavenly Writing: Divination, Horoscopy, and Astronomy in Mesopotamian Culture* (Cambridge University, 2004), 210–9. For the emergence of the concept of revelation see van der Toorn, *Scribal Culture*, 207–21.

[50] Simo Parpola, "Mesopotamian Astrology and Astronomy as Domains of the Mesopotamian 'Wisdom,'" in *Die Rolle des Astronomie in den Kulturen Mesopotamiens* (ed. Hannes D. Galter; Graz: Berger, 1993), 56.

[51] Hurowitz, "Proto-Canonization."

[52] Lambert, "A Catalogue of Texts and Authors."

[53] Hurowitz, "Proto-Canonization," 36–38.

above, the fact that the Assyrian king had a luxurious copy of an authoritative text made especially for him and kept in his palace, or sent to him while traveling, conspicuously recalls the Deuteronomic statute commanding the king to make "a copy of this Torah" משנה התורה הזאת (Deut 17:18) and use it for his personal perusal "all the days of his life."

Another important trajectory of the argument outlined above is the significance attributed to the personality of the author of the authoritative text. This factor brings us back to the distinction offered above between the Hittite oracle-book and the prophetic texts from Mesopotamia. While the book found by Mursilli was not imbued to any human figure but rather understood as a direct transmission from some unnamed superhuman source, prophetic oracles are by definition related with the figure of a human mediator or seer.[54] In fact not only prophecy, but also a variety of other textual genres was associated in *The Catalogue of Texts and Authors* (first-millennium-BCE Mesopotamia) with concrete figures as their authors—whether the god Ea or the human figures of famous scribes and scholars from the distant past. Now, it is important that the question of authorship did not arise with regard to Josiah's book; this book was simply accepted as a manifestation of the Divine word. Early sources in the development of the discourse of authority in Israel did not refer to "The torah of Moses" but simply to "the book of Torah" or the like.[55] In 2 Kgs 22–23 the phrase (*sēper*) *tôrat Mōše* was not mentioned throughout the entire narrative until the very late editorial remark in 23:25. The stress on the personality of the mediating figure—a stress so dominant in biblical prophetic literature—should thus be seen as another product of the "New Paradigm" of writtenness and authority developed in the first third of the first milennium BCE.

Conclusion

Reflection on the concepts of writtenness, revelation, and scribal authority began forming in Mesopotamia at the end of the second millennium BCE and reached a peak in the Neo-Assyrian and Neo-Babylonian periods. The high status of the scribal institution and the extent of routine consultation of scholarly texts in

---

[54] Van der Toorn, *Scribal Culture*, 42 and n. 40, where mention of also made of the pseudo-prophetic personality of Kabti-ilāni-Marduk, the author/copyist of the Erra epic.

[55] As a rule, the phrase (*sēper*) *tôrat Mōše* appears in late layers of biblical literature or in late editorial insertions. Thus for example: Josh 8:31–32; 1 Kgs 2:3; Mal 3:22; Neh 8:1; Dan 9:11, 13; 2 Chr 23:18.

Mesopotamia came more or less simultaneously with the acculturation of writing and of scholarly habits in ancient Israel. It is not surprising, therefore, to find some lines of similarity between the two cultures. This is not to say in a *Babel und Bibel* type of argument that whatever scholarly concepts one finds in Judah were all imported from the intellectually advanced imperial culture from Mesopotamia. In contrast, one sees how the Judean culture entertained some "indigenous" concepts on the authority of writing even before the stamp of the imperial ideas achieved full prominence. The Josiah narrative is an important case in point here, because the origins of that narrative are rooted before the great advent of writing and revelation in Mesopotamia in the late Neo-Assyrian and Neo-Babylonian periods.

The evidence collected here would suggest that the conceptions of *Torah* in both biblical and post-biblical religion may find some precedents in non-Israelite sources of prophetic and divinatory literature. Judaic religion during the monarchy was not a religion of the book. Under the Davidic dynasty, the Judahite state was a monarchy based on a divinely-supported royal family, which in turn relied on a divinatory-prophetic establishment. This ancient divinatory milieu gave rise to some early connections between writing and revelation even before the creation of a full-fledged reflection on writtenness. Later on, when this kind of reflection did come to exist in Judah, and as Jewish literati became acquainted with the Mesopotamian scholarly establishment, the older stories were refashioned to fit this new agenda. The story on the book find of Josiah came into existence as part of the early tendency, while it was still tightly close to the divinatory process pursued in the royal court. With the strengthening of the Deuteronomistic ideology, this story became the hinge on which to suspend a reformulated conception of the book.

*THE WEBERIAN CONSTRUCT OF PROPHECY
AND WOMANIST AND FEMINIST
RECUPERATIVE CRITICISM*

Steve Cook

INTRODUCTION

In its history, biblical scholarship has been very attentive to the nature of prophets in the Hebrew Bible. Surveying the perspectives used to understand prophets in history and the biblical text, one notices almost as many "types" of prophets as there are interpreters. Prophets are theologians, social critics, intercessors, future tellers, priests, and intermediaries of divine information, among others. As good as biblical scholarship has been in bringing to light multiple ways by which to understand the idea of "prophet," it has often not proceeded with clear articulations about the significance of its work, or, simply put, what interests its constructions of "prophet" serve. Granted, those who study Hebrew prophets have conducted their scholarship with unspoken assumptions and objectives. Protestant scholarship in Europe and the United States, for example, sometimes exalts the categories of "prophet" and "prophecy," as well as the Hebrew Bible's "writing prophets," at the expense of the categories of "law" or Torah—often carried along by the worst Christian prejudices.[1] More positively, work that attends to the dynamics of ancient Near Eastern prophecy for elucidating biblical prophecy and/or historical Israelite prophecy has the potential to promote greater awareness of similarities between cultures and

---

[1] For some discussion of prejudices in Christian scholarship that relates to the consideration of prophets, see the introduction and chapter one of Johanna W. H. van Wijk-Bos, *Making Wise the Simple: The Torah in Christian Faith and Practice* (Grand Rapids, Mich.: Eerdmans, 2005).

people often thought to be mutually exclusive, if not adversarial. While study of ancient Near Eastern and biblical and/or Israelite prophecy rarely considers this payoff, this scholarship could bear fruit for interreligious dialogue.

The scholars who have spoken most clearly about their intentions in the context of the study of prophecy are womanists and feminists. Feminists and womanists highlight that the category of "prophet" presented in the biblical text includes women (starting with those named as such in the Bible), excavate women's contributions to biblical prophetic texts (especially of "writing prophets"), critique prophetic language that perpetuates harmful social relations (Hosea, Jeremiah, and Ezekiel), and contribute to understanding the language, theology, history, and biblical representations of women prophets and prophecy in general. With their work, these scholars often advocate for the full inclusion of people in society and expose and challenge societal attitudes that harm and dehumanize. The first part of this essay intends to demonstrate an overlap between one type of "prophet" prevalent in scholarship and the aims and hermeneutics of one strand of feminist and womanist attention to prophets. Specifically, it wants to demonstrate how and where womanist and feminist critics who employ a hermeneutic of recuperation reinforce notions of what a prophet is and does as understood by Max Weber. That Weber's construction of prophecy in some respects dominates womanist and feminist recuperative scholarship on prophets merits attention.[2] The overlap speaks loudly to the interestedness of scholarship (not a bad thing) and the potential, positive political gains that it can have. The second half of this essay will further clarify some of the ways that embracing Weber-like ideas about "prophet" advances the interests of womanist and feminist recuperative scholars and explore ramifications that could go overlooked.

---

[2] This essay does not argue that all scholars who think about prophets in ways that have affinities with Weber draw upon him consciously or explicitly. Chronology alone does not allow such an argument. This essay uses Weber more as a convenient point of reference with which to group certain ideas about and expectations of prophets.

THE WEBERIAN CONSTRUCT OF PROPHECY AND FEMINIST RECUPERATIVE CRITICISM

By the most simple of readings of Weber's seminal chapter "The Prophet" in his *Sociology of Religion*, a prophet performs the role by virtue of charisma, preaches, and advances the renewal or establishment of a religion. The following quote from Weber encapsulates many of his thoughts:

> We shall understand "prophet" to mean a purely individual bearer of charisma, who by virtue of his mission proclaims a religious doctrine or divine commandment. No radical distinction will be drawn between a "renewer of religion" who preaches an older revelation, actual or supposititious, and a "founder of religion" who claims to bring totally new deliverances. The two types merge into one another.[3]

This quote and Weber's other writing also include a negative definition of prophet. A prophet is *not* established in the role by virtue of institutional standing, lineage, tradition, or the like; a prophet is *not* a ritual functionary; a prophet is *not* a "priest." Furthermore, Weber's writing on prophets considers them extremely important. If "prophet" is best exemplified by Zoroaster, Jesus, Muhammad, Buddha, and prophets of the Hebrew Bible, "prophet" is an exceptionally significant designation and those included in the designation partake in its significance.[4] It deserves mention that two of the most influential biblical scholars of the last one hundred plus years, Julius Wellhausen and William F. Albright, anticipate and echo aspects of Weber's ideas about a prophet. Speaking on prophets in Israel's history, Albright wrote: "The prophet was thus a charismatic spiritual leader, directly commissioned by Yahweh to warn the people of the perils of sin and to preach reform and revival of true religion and morality."[5] While he does not highlight the feature of charisma, Wellhausen understood prophets as essential to the formation of Israelite religion before its decline at the hands of the "Mosaic theocracy."[6] By noticing

---

[3] Max Weber, *Sociology of Religion* (4th English ed.; Boston: Beacon, 1963), 46.

[4] Ibid. Also, Weber could have included Ellen G. White (1827–1915) in his list of prophets.

[5] W. F. Albright, *From Stone Age to Christianity: Monotheism and the Historical Process* (2d ed.; Garden City, N.Y.: Doubleday, 1957), 303.

[6] Two quotes from Wellhausen's *Prolegomena* are relevant here. "Thus the

how scholars of divergent perspectives on the development the Hebrew Bible and Israelite religion share similar ideas when it comes to prophets, we can better recognize the pervasiveness of thoughts like those of Weber.[7] It also merits noting that Weber's writing about prophets reflects and reinforces classic Protestant ideals about religious leadership. Protestant preachers are called to their roles, and they advance the Christian faith by proclaiming the Word. And like biblical scholars who hold radically different stances on certain topics but share some sort of common ground around the idea of "prophet," Protestant ministers of vastly different ideological and political orientations can see something of themselves in Weber's concept of prophecy.

Weber's construction of prophecy has much that is widely appealing. By virtue of the mechanism by which one becomes a prophet (charisma) and by virtue of their importance (they stand at the very heart of a religion's formation and continuance), anyone has the potential to create and sustain a social force (religion) deemed positive by many. Put another way, the Weberian paradigm of prophecy promotes the idea that anyone can participate not just in religion but also in religious leadership. Additionally, by virtue of the significance of the category of "prophet," anyone can participate in a role of great esteem.

Ideas about the role of "prophet" as universally accessible and of great social import are recurrently operative in womanist and feminist recuperative work on female prophets, especially those in the Hebrew Bible.[8] In the context of nineteenth-century women's appeal to the biblical text for authorization of callings to preach and speak in public arenas, African Americans like Jarena Lee and Maria Stewart made direct reference to the tradition of women prophets in the Hebrew Bible. Lee, the first woman officially recognized to preach in the African Methodist Episcopal Church, prefaced her autobiography that recounts

---

whole historical movement now under our consideration [the centralization of worship], so far as it was effective and thereby has come to our knowledge, is in its origin and essence prophetic, even if latterly it may have been aided by priestly influences." Julius Wellhausen, *Prolegomena to the History of Israel* (1885; trans. J. Sutherland Black and Allan Menzies; repr. Atlanta: Scholars Press, 1994), 48. "The great pathologist of Judaism is quite right: in the Mosaic theocracy the cultus became a pedagogic instrument of discipline. It is estranged from the heart... It no longer has its roots in childlike impulse, it is a dead work..." Wellhausen, *Prolegomena*, 425.

[7] That Weber does not distinguish between a "renewer" and a "founder" of religion does assist in bringing Wellhausen and Albright together on their Weber-like thinking about prophets.

[8] For a discussion of womanist and feminist recuperative hermeneutics, see The Bible and Culture Collective, "Feminist and Womanist Criticism," in *The Postmodern Bible* (New Haven: Yale University Press, 1995), 245–47.

her life in ministry with Joel 2:28 (MT 3:1) italicizing the word "daughters."[9] Maria Stewart drew upon Deborah to argue for the legitimacy of her public role as an abolitionist.[10] Neither Lee nor Stewart thought that they required the authorization of a hierarchical community to preach or orate. Rather, they took their warrant from biblical witness and divine intention. Their use of the biblical text also drew upon the recognized authoritative position that the Bible had in the religious and public life of the United States. The nineteenth-century project headed by Elizabeth Cady Stanton, *The Woman's Bible*, also sought to capitalize on the authority of the Bible in the United States and its inclusion of women prophets.

> Seeing that the Lord has endowed "the daughters of men" also with the gift of speech, and they may have messages from Him to deliver to "the sons of God," it would be wise for the prophets of our day to admit them into their Conferences, Synods and General Assemblies, and give them opportunities for speech.[11]

While neither Lee, Walker, nor Stanton were "heirs" to Weber, just as Wellhausen was not, all of them operated with expectations of "prophet" that he helped to imprint further in people's minds. Furthermore, working with these expectations served Lee's, Walker's, and Stanton's important political goals of advancing women's status in the life of the United States.

In the discourse of contemporary feminist and womanist scholarship, the retrieval of biblical women prophets also proceeds with the specific intention of advancing women's status. In her recent work *Daughters of Miriam: Women Prophets in Ancient Israel*, Wilda C. Gafney calls attention to the fact that:

> More than three thousand years after the prophet Miriam led the Israelites dancing and drumming across the Sea of Reeds, some Jewish and Christian communities still restrict the role

---

[9] Jarena Lee, *Religious Experience and Journal of Mrs. Jarena Lee* (Philadelphia, 1846), 3. For another reference to Joel 2:28 (MT 3:1), see page 63.

[10] For discussion of Maria Stewart's appeal to Deborah, see Wilda C. Gafney, *Daughters of Miriam: Women Prophets in Ancient Israel* (Minneapolis: Fortress, 2008), 8, 170.

[11] Elizabeth Cady Stanton, *The Woman's Bible* (New York: European Pub. Co., 1895–1898; repr., Boston: Northeastern University Press, 1993), 114.

of women in proclamation, leadership, and presence in the pulpit on what they call biblical and traditional grounds.[12]

Like those before her, Gafney notices an incongruity between the biblical record of woman prophets in the Hebrew Bible and the inclusion of women in Jewish and Christian religious communities. Lisa Wilson Davison, writing on women in the Bible and preaching, states: "No matter what has been done in the more recent past to exclude women from positions of religious authority, this [Huldah's] story presents an irrefutable counter-witness."[13] For both Gafney and Davison, women in the Bible served as prophets; therefore, women today should be allowed to participate in religious communities with connections to the biblical text. Furthermore, the frameworks for thinking about what a prophet does bear much in common with Weberian prophecy. Modern-day analogues to the Hebrew Bible's prophets, most importantly, contribute to a religious community's understanding of its faith through the activity of preaching.[14] Granted, Gafney's extensive treatment of women prophets in the Hebrew Bible does not equate the activity of biblical prophets only with preaching. Given her introductory comments (quoted above), however, her work presents itself, at one level, as most interested in the value of reclaiming women prophets for women as modern-day preachers.[15]

In her work on women in religious life of ancient Israel as viewed through the biblical text, Phyllis Bird proceeds from the perspective that prophets occupy

---

[12] Gafney, *Daughters of Miriam*, 1. On another note, while this essay uses the terms "womanist" and "feminist," it does not presume that an African American woman necessarily self-identifies as a womanist scholar. For Gafney's self-consideration, see eadem, "A Black Feminist Approach to Biblical Studies," *Encounter* 64, no. 4 (Autumn 2006): 381–403, especially 397.

[13] Lisa Wilson Davison, *Preaching the Women of the Bible* (St. Louis, Mo.: Chalice, 2006), 70.

[14] While not included in the brief, earlier comments about Weber, his thoughts about distinguishing prophets from philosophers is significant: "What primarily separates such figures [philosophers] from the prophets is their lack of vital emotional preaching which is distinctive of prophecy." Weber, *Sociology of Religion*, 53.

[15] In the conclusion of *Daughters of Miriam*, Gafney lists fifteen activities associated with biblical, women prophets. In some regards, the word "prophet" becomes a way to recognize and expand the realms in which women act with authority—authority that derives from esteem for the idea of a "prophet." While there are fifteen items, the last on the list, "Proclaiming the word of YHWH," brings one back full-circle to the introduction. Gafney, *Daughters of Miriam*, 152.

an especially important social position. In her 1974 essay "Images of Women in the Old Testament," Bird recognizes the presence of women prophets in the biblical text and notes their significance.

> In addition to the primary roles of wife and mother, women appear in the historical writings in a number of other, more specialized roles, occupations and professions .... Foremost among these is the prophetess, of which the Old Testament canon knows only three by name: Deborah (Judg 4:4-16), in the premonarchic period; Huldah (2 Kgs 22:14-20), in the late monarchic period (seventh century BCE); and Noadiah (Neh 6:14), in the post-exilic period (fifth century BCE).[16]

The consideration of the role of the prophet as "foremost" deserves attention as it suggests that the position of prophet stands over and above all other roles, occupations, and professions, including that of monarch. In step with Weber, the category of "prophet" carries tremendous weight for Bird. Writing on women in the Israelite religion, Bird demonstrates even more affinities with Weber's ideas. More specifically, Bird works from the perspective that prophets and priests occupy their positions due to different sources of legitimation.[17]

> The most important and best-documented religious office occupied by women in ancient Israel, that of prophet, stands in ambiguous relationship to the cultus. Whatever the role of the

---

[16] Phyllis A. Bird, "Images of Women in the Old Testament," in *Missing Persons and Mistaken Identities: Women and Gender in Ancient Israel* (OBT; Minneapolis: Fortress, 1997), 41; repr. from *Religion and Sexism: Images of Women in the Jewish and Christian Traditions* (ed. Rosemary R. Ruether; New York: Simon & Schuster, 1974).

[17] A relevant quote by Weber: "For our purposes here, the personal call is the decisive element distinguishing the prophet from the priest." Weber, *Sociology of Religion*, 46. For a discussion that treats the usefulness of Weber's thoughts on charisma for understanding biblical prophecy, see: R. E. Clements, "Max Weber, Charisma, and Biblical Prophecy," in *Prophecy and Prophets* (ed. Yehoshua Gitay; Atlanta: Scholars Press, 1997), 89–108; for important, "early" discussions on priests vis-à-vis prophets, see: Peter L. Berger, "Charisma and Religious Innovation: The Social Location of Israelite Prophecy," *ASR* 28 (1963): 940–50; James G. Williams, "The Social Location of Israelite Prophecy," *JAAR* 37 (1969): 153–65.

prophet within the cultus, it was clearly not a priestly office. Since recruitment was by divine designation (charismatic gift) and not dependent upon family or status, it was the one religious office with broad power that was not mediated or directly controlled by the cultic or civil hierarchy and the one religious office open to women.[18]

Weber provided an important articulation of prophet that reflected orientations of previous scholarship and supported later discussions, even if it is only one way to think about prophets among many. Most significantly, he raised the role of prophet to one of great importance (in serving to articulate religious doctrine) accessible to anyone (on the basis of charisma). The Weberian paradigm of prophet often finds expression within womanist and feminist scholarship. To identify women as prophets in the biblical text with affinities to the Weberian construct of prophecy serves as a useful tool to argue for women's greater inclusion in modern religious communities and, if it grants the biblical text a place of authority, in society as a whole.

Issues for Consideration

The work of womanist and feminist scholars who retrieve women prophets from the pages of the Hebrew Bible makes a vital contribution to academic biblical studies. For generations of (male) scholars, prophets were men. In his classic work on the subject, Abraham Heschel titled the first chapter: "What Manner of Man is the Prophet?"[19] Pleasant surprises do dot the landscape of the scholarly past. As Gafney notes, Walther Eichrodt demonstrated a high regard for Deborah.[20] Ivan Engnell, in distinction from scholars like Wellhausen, did not explain away the attribution of the prophetic title to the woman in Isa 8:3. He calls her a "professional prophetess."[21] Those who explore and draw upon

---

[18] Phyllis A. Bird, "The Place of Women in the Israelite Cultus," 98.

[19] Abraham Joshua Heschel, *The Prophets* (New York: Harper & Row, 1962; repr., New York: Perennial, 2001). In so far as this book has been widely read and utilized in theological education, one should ask how this book has hindered the recognition of women prophets in the Hebrew Bible.

[20] Gafney, *Daughters of Miriam*, 7.

[21] Ivan Engnell, *A Rigid Scrutiny: Critical Essays on the Old Testament* (trans. John T. Willis; Nashville, Tenn.: Vanderbilt University Press, 1969), 141. By way of contrast, Julius Wellhausen wrote: "Isaiah was so completely a prophet that even his wife was called the prophetess after him." Wellhausen,

women as prophets in the Hebrew Bible help maintain all scholars' attention to prophecy as a role not limited to men. Furthermore, within contexts that value the Bible as a source of authority, womanist and feminist scholarship has made substantial inroads for advancing opportunities for women's leadership—even as there is still work to be done.

In part, the real-world gains that can be and have been made by womanist and feminist recuperative scholars comes from advancing "prophet" as a role that is freely open, especially significant, and analogous to modern professions, especially preachers. If recuperative readers were to promote the participation of women in religious leadership by drawing upon prophets in ancient Near Eastern contexts—who as a "profession" were often secondary to extispicy experts for providing monarchs with divine information—recuperative hermeneutics might not have the same impact.[22] Feminist and womanist criticism that attends to women prophets in the Hebrew Bible in tune with Weber-like expectations of "prophet," therefore, raises the ante on what it means to speak about women as prophets. Additionally, considering prophets in ways consistent with Weber appeals to an understanding of "prophet" shared by many who have and still do oppose advancing women's access to religious and social leadership.

In thinking about the costs of painting prophets in ways that resemble Weber's prophets, we should consider the prejudices that Weber's "prophets are not equal to priests" dynamic can harbor and promote. In the history of Protestant, theological interpretation of texts like Jer 7, for example, prophets denounce temple activities as hollow ritual.[23] With such readings, interpreters often permit their audiences to differentiate themselves with contempt from

---

Prolegomena, 484.

[22] For discussion of prophets vis-à-vis extispicy experts and the relevance for studying biblical prophets, see: Jack M. Sasson, "About 'Mari and the Bible,'" *RA* 92 (1998): 118–19.

[23] For example: "Jeremiah, in his teaching, hinders their ['a group of temple frequenters, apparently quite numerous, who have taken over the catchword promulgated by the priests and who like to make full use of the temple as the welcome asylum in these dangerous times'] cause. Let the priests be satisfied with the external performance of certain ceremonies with the intention of getting once again the people into the hollow of their hands! As far as the prophet was concerned, there lay in this behavior not only incomparable hypocrisy and self-delusion, but a defiance of God himself, which must lead to the most severe judgments." Walther Eichrodt, "Right Interpretation of the Old Testament: A Study of Jeremiah 7:1-15," *ThTo* 7, no. 1 (April 1950): 18–19.

modern Jewish and Christian traditions perceived of as devoid of the "true religiosity" exemplified by "the prophets."[24] In short, the Weberian paradigm of a prophet participates in and often contributes to Protestant attitudes that wrongly disparage other religious traditions. Even though womanist and feminist criticism retrieves women prophets of the Hebrew Bible for positive social gains, it could unintentionally promote denigration of other religious traditions.

To speak of women prophets in the Hebrew Bible in ways consistent with Weber can also do a disservice to the interest of promoting women in society in general. Attention to women prophets in the Hebrew Bible is often accompanied by advancing "prophet" as an especially noble, divinely appointed position. As such, it could focus attention away from advancing women in other social positions and professions. If a prophet-preacher, for example, is so great, why should anyone aspire to anything else? In my experience of teaching at seminaries, I have noticed that students have a great enthusiasm for women prophets in the Hebrew Bible. In many ways, the topic reconfirms and supports people, especially women, in their preparation for ministry. While this is certainly a good thing, I sometimes worry that the exaltation of prophets fosters an estimation of students' future lives as ministers that can devalue by extension all other professions. If such devaluation does occur, future ministers risk not recognizing the important contributions that their parishioners make in the world.

The appeal to the biblical text and its representations of women prophets for legitimating women's calls to participation in religious life can also unintentionally create a criterion for access that does not benefit others who unjustly experience exclusion. By its nature, recuperative hermeneutics interested in women prophets with social or political ends appeals to biblical authority in connection with expectations of what prophets are and do. As a member of the Episcopal Church of the United States of America and as one who follows the activities of Christian religious communities in general, I am sympathetic to lesbian, gay, bisexual, and transgender persons who are denied the ability to follow calls to ministry. Amidst the controversies, I regularly ask myself: "Does the (and my) study of women prophets help these people?" If recuperative hermeneutics reinforces the biblical text as a source of legitimation, I cannot offer a confident, "Yes." One could, I suppose, investigate the biblical text for examples of LGBT persons engaged in prophecy. However, I am not

---

[24] For discussion of Christian "teaching of contempt" of Judaism, see: van Wijk-Bos, *Making Wise the Simple*, xvii; idem, "The Writing on the Water: The Ineffable Name of God," in *Jews, Christians, and the Theology of the Hebrew Scriptures* (eds. Alice Ogden Bellis and Joel S. Kaminsky; SBLSymS 8; Atlanta: SBL, 2000), 50.

certain that such reconstructions would find wide acceptance as plausible, even if there were possible starting points, nor am I certain that I would want to reinforce the biblical text as authoritative in this way because of the negative witness that can be made of it.[25]

CONCLUSION

When Max Weber discusses prophets and prophecy, he invokes the names of Jesus, Zoroaster, Muhammad, and others. As a result, Weber reinforces prophets as especially important in the eyes of many of his readers. Furthermore, he grants prophecy a pivotal role in religion and attributes their authority to charisma. Biblical scholars, including womanists and feminists, have had similar high esteem for and ideas about the prophets of the Hebrew Bible. Readers who employ a hermeneutic of recuperation have often demonstrated affinities with the Weberian paradigm for prophecy to advance the interests of women in modern religious communities and society at large. While there are other constructions of prophecy available for framing discussions of biblical women, there is much to be gained by thinking about women prophets with expectations consistent with those of Weber. In so far as they often implicitly or explicitly embrace a Weberian paradigm of prophet, womanist and feminist recuperative hermeneuts remind us that named and unnamed interests are at work in academic pursuits. And, by recognizing this, we have a better sense of the choices people make as readers as well as the impact that reading choices can have. In the end, I hope that this modest contribution profitably affirms attention that has been paid to women prophets of the Hebrew Bible and encourages further work on prophecy that continues to promote greater respect for all people.

---

[25] For thoughts related to ancient Near Eastern prophecy, see Martti Nissinen, *Homoeroticism in the Biblical World: A Historical Perspective* (trans. Kirsi Stjerna; Minneapolis: Fortress, 1998), 28–36.

1 SAMUEL 1–8
The Prophet as Agent Provocateur

Serge Frolov

Prophecy is an important, one might even say pivotal, phenomenon in the Hebrew Bible; suffice it to say that properly prophetic books (the Latter Prophets of the Jewish tradition) constitute almost 25% of its total volume. Yet, with the Bible read consecutively, the concept and the associated terminology take more than a little while to emerge. It is possible to argue that sustained communication with God characterizes Noah, Abraham, Jacob, Moses, and Joshua as prophets and that the last two characters are especially qualified for the title, given that they not only receive messages from the deity, but also pass them on to an awe-stricken audience. At the same time, the term נביא is very rare in the Hexateuch. It is used only once of Abraham (Gen 20:7), three times of Moses (directly in Deut 34:10 and indirectly in Num 12:6–8 and Deut 18:18), once of Miriam (Exod 15:20), once of Aaron (who is rather unexpectedly referred to in Exod 7:1 as נביא of the divine Moses), and never of Noah, Jacob, or Joshua. In addition, Num 11:28–29 applies the *Hitpael* form of the verb נבא "to prophesy," often translated "to prophesy ecstatically," to the behavior of spirit-stricken Eldad and Medad. Prophecy-related commandments appear only in the Deuteronomic collection (13:2–6, 18:15–22). The trend does not change in Judges, where Deborah and an unnamed emissary of God are each referred to once as a prophet (respectively, 4:4 and 6:8).

It is only in the book of Samuel and in association with its title character that the root נבא goes into sustained use (eventually to be employed more than four hundred times in the Hebrew Bible) and certain related terms begin to show up, such as ראה "seer" (1 Sam 9:9) and חזון "vision" (1 Sam 3:1).[1] Two major stages in the literary unfolding of the biblical concept of prophecy can be consequently singled out: first, Deut 18 with its concise "prophetic statute" and second, the opening chapters of 1 Samuel where the first biblical character emerges who not only walks and talks like a prophet but also is consistently characterized as such. This paper compares the concepts implicitly operative in the above-mentioned texts and argues that there is a substantial tension between these concepts, one that can be plausibly and profitably resolved in both synchronic and diachronic terms.

Samuel's first prophetic experience is recounted by 1 Sam 3. This well-known narrative, where YHWH speaks to Samuel at night while the latter lodges in the inner sanctum of the temple, where the ark is also housed, is unique in at least two respects. First, the message that Samuel receives from the deity (vv. 11–14) is entirely redundant; it does not go even a small step beyond what the audience and Samuel's mentor, Eli, already know from 2:27–36: that Eli's priestly house is doomed to destruction because of the blasphemies of his sons. Of course, for Samuel himself it is definitely news, but that does not matter because he is not asked to do anything, not even to make the revelation public. Several exegetes have tried to resolve this apparent incongruence in diachronic terms, but such solutions tend to overlook the second enigmatic

---

[1] Mark Leuchter argues that by referring to Samuel's birthplace as Ramathaim–zophim and one of his ancestors as Zuph, 1 Sam 1:1 in fact uses a term for a distinctive prophetic guild, צופים "Watchers" (*Josiah's Reform and Jeremiah's Scroll: Historical Calamity and Prophetic Response* [HBM 6; Sheffield: Sheffield Phoenix, 2006], 18–32). This interpretation is highly speculative. Although Leuchter is correct in pointing out that some late ancient and medieval Jewish sources interpret צופים as "disciples of prophets" or "seers" (*Reform* 23–24), it does not follow that biblical traditions actually know such a group. The reference to "the land of Zuph" in 1 Sam 9:5 strongly suggests that this is a clan name (it would border on the bizarre for a region to be named after a prophetic guild), and otherwise the term never occurs in the narratives featuring Samuel or, for that matter, any other biblical prophet. Demonstrable occurrences of צופה or צופים are limited to prophetic books, but these rare occurrences are either highly obscure and therefore open to multiple alternative construals (Hos 9:8) or much more plausibly interpretable as references to generic "sentinels" (Jer 6:17; Ezek 3:17; 33:2, 6–7; note the mentions of the shofar, a sentinel's instrument, in Jer 6:17 and Ezek 33:6). Leuchter's claim that the term also twice occurs in Psalms (*Reform* 27–29) is erroneous: in Ps 19:11, צופים is a plural of צוף "nectar" (Abraham Even-Shoshan, *A New Concordance of the Bible* [Jerusalem: Kiryat Sefer, 1988], 982), and in Ps 37:32 צופה is clearly a verbal form ("the evildoer stalks the righteous").

feature of the story.² At the outset, the theophany it recounts is strictly auditory: the deity repeatedly calls Samuel by name, and the boy repeatedly runs to Eli, thinking that the master is calling him (vv. 4–8a). Only on the third try does Eli realize that his apprentice is being addressed by God and suggest an appropriate response (v. 8b–9). In the next verse, the format of the theophany dramatically changes: by "coming and standing erect," YHWH apparently adds a visual component to it (v. 10a). Remarkably, this happens before Samuel has a chance to show that he knows who is speaking to him (v. 10b); the change in the deity's behavior seems to be prompted by Eli's, rather than Samuel's, realization what is going on. This suggests that by neglecting to "come and stand erect" from the very beginning God was making sure that Eli knew that Samuel was experiencing a theophany.³ Its otherwise redundant content served the same purpose: by providing Eli with what amounted to a confirmation of the dire, and therefore unforgettable, message that he had received previously (2:27–36) and that Samuel could not be privy to (or properly understand, for that matter) the boy proved beyond reasonable doubt that he had indeed had a conversation with God.

It appears therefore that the main, if not the only, objective of Samuel's first prophetic experience was to lay the foundation of his prophetic reputation. And indeed, the narrator almost immediately confirms that as Samuel was growing up, the deity "let none of his words fall to the ground" so that he "became accredited as a prophet of YHWH" on the national level (1 Sam 3:19–20). In other words, up to a certain point Samuel's entire prophetic activity was largely, if not exclusively, about beefing up his oracular resume. In this respect, Samuel's emergence fulfills the divine promise quoted by Moses in Deut 18:18: "I will raise them up a prophet from among their brethren… and will put my words into his mouth; and he shall speak to them all that I shall command him."

---

² E.g., Otto Eissfeldt, *Die Komposition der Samuelisbücher* (Leipzig: Hinrichs, 1931), 4–6; Richard Press, "Der Prophet Samuel: Eine traditionsgeschichtliche Untersuchung," *ZAW* 56 (1938): 177–225; Timo Veijola, *Die ewige Dynastie: David und die Entstehung seiner Dynastie nach der deuteronomistischen Darstellung* (AASF B193; Helsinki: Suomalainen Tiedeakatemia, 1975), 35–43.

³ The syntactic layout of the narrative points in the same direction by reporting Eli's realization and YHWH's response to it in close succession (vv. 8–10) and detaching them from the deity's two initial addresses to Samuel (vv. 4–6) by means of a narrator's digression in v. 7. See Serge Frolov, *The Turn of the Cycle: 1 Samuel 1–8 in Synchronic and Diachronic Perspectives* (BZAW 342; Berlin: de Gruyter, 2004), 110–13.

However, the consequences of this fulfillment, and indeed its very purposes, do not appear to be the ones that the Deuteronomic author had in mind.

In 1 Sam 4:1a, Samuel's word goes out to "all Israel." The narrator does not specify the content of the address, but what follows leaves little doubt as far as its overall thrust is concerned. With Israel going to war with the Philistines in the next sentence, it is difficult to deny that Samuel's message must have called upon the people to confront their foreign oppressors for the first time in several generations (discounting Samson's pointless escapades, there is no mention of Israel challenging the Philistines since Judg 13:1 reports the establishment of their overlordship). Given Samuel's well-established reputation as the deity's reliable mouthpiece, the people interpret his call as YHWH's promise that the campaign will be a success and grab the rare opportunity to set themselves free. However, they are in for a bitter disappointment: two successive battles are lost, and 34,000 Israelite warriors are killed (4:2, 10). Even the ark's presence on the battlefield (vv. 3–6) fails to ensure divine intervention; YHWH does not lift a finger even to prevent the sacred object from ending up in the enemy's hands (4:11) and ultimately in the temple of the enemy's deity (5:2). Heeding Samuel's instructions lands Israel and its palladium in a deadly trap.

Almost all existing commentaries and studies avoid this rather disturbing conclusion by drawing a thick line after the first half of 1 Sam 4:1—a scholarly tradition most prominently expressed in Leonhard Rost's concept of 1 Sam 4–6 (plus 2 Sam 6 and minus 1 Sam 4:1a) as an originally self-contained "ark history."[4] However, apart from the preconceived notion of divine deception as a theological impossibility (a notion that ignores other, more explicit instances of this modus operandi in the Hebrew Bible),[5] there is nothing to indicate a major discontinuity close to the beginning of 1 Sam 4. The sequence of *waw*-consecutive imperfect clauses that form the master sequence of the biblical narrative stretches without significant interruptions from 3:15b all the way through 4:4. As far as the storyline is concerned, 1 Sam 2 adequately explains why the deity would set Israel up for a military defeat: angry at Eli's sons, Hophni and Phinehas, for their misappropriation of sacrificial meat (vv. 12-17),

---

[4] Leonhard Rost, *Die Überlieferung von der Thronnachfolge Davids* (BWANT 3/6; Stuttgart: W. Kohlhammer, 1926), 4–47. See also Antony F. Campbell, *The Ark Narrative (1 Sam 4–6; 2 Sam 6): A Form-Critical and Traditio-Historical Study* (SBLDS 16; Missoula: Scholars Press, 1975).

[5] See James L. Crenshaw, *Prophetic Conflict: Its Effect upon Israelite Religion* (BZAW 124; Berlin: Walter de Gruyter, 1971) 77–90; J. J. M. Roberts, "Does God Lie? Divine Deceit as a Theological Problem in Israelite Prophetic Literature," in *Congress Volume Jerusalem 1986* (VTSup 40; ed. John A. Emerton; Leiden: Brill, 1988), 211–20 (repr. in idem, *The Bible and the Ancient Near East: Collected Essays* [Winona Lake, Ind.: Eisenbrauns, 2002], 123–31).

it announces that both of them will die on the same day (v. 34), and this is precisely what happens as a result of the campaign apparently launched at Samuel's instigation (4:11). Conversely, with a literary boundary drawn down the middle of 4:1, a self-standing narrative would begin with a *waw*-consecutive imperfect other than ויהי (something that never happens elsewhere in the Hebrew Bible), and there would be no way to determine the nature of Samuel's address to all Israel (which would render the reference to this address meaningless) and to explain God's reluctance to help the people on the battlefield. With these considerations in mind, it appears likely that in 1 Sam 3 YHWH carefully establishes Samuel's prophetic credentials in order to use him in the next chapter as an *agent provocateur*.

A similar pattern can be traced at a much later stage of Samuel's career, in 1 Sam 8. When the people ask Samuel to give them a king (vv. 4–6), the deity immediately and unambiguously characterizes the move as another kind of apostasy: "They have rejected me, that I should not reign over them, according to all the deeds which they have done since I brought them up out of Egypt, and to this day, in that they have forsaken me, and served other gods" (vv. 7–8). However, this ominous response is intended strictly for Samuel—and, to an even greater extent, for the narrative's audience. The prophet is instructed to forewarn the people by summarizing the usual practices of monarchs while apparently withholding from the listeners the institution's most pernicious aspect, its essentially blasphemous nature (v. 9). The reason for this glaring omission is obvious: God wants to punish Israel for requesting a king by letting it have one (vv. 7, 9) and therefore avoids scaring the people into withdrawal of their request by adding alienation from the divine to the list of kingship's expected costs that takes up much of the chapter (vv. 11-18).[6] Admittedly, in this case, Samuel's role is passive: he is asked to mislead the people by omission rather than by bald deception. Moreover, there are indications that Samuel, perhaps mindful of the disastrous consequences of his previous assignment, may be trying this time to sabotage the mission. He tells the people "*all* the words of YHWH" (v. 10), tops the mandated review of the monarchic ruler's rights by the statement that once the monarchy is in place God will not heed any complaints about its being too burdensome (v. 18), and dismisses the petitioners without

---

[6] This modus operandi is detectable elsewhere in the Hebrew Bible. In Judg 2:1–3, YHWH decides to leave the Canaanites in place because the Israelites are willing to coexist with them (1:27–36) and despite foreseeing dire consequences of such coexistence. In Ezek 16, the prophet threatens female Jerusalem that she will be punished with too much of what she liked to have, that is, sex with male neighbors (see especially vv. 36–39).

appointing a king (v. 22). This, however, does nothing to change the fundamental nature of what transpires in the chapter: the deity commissions the prophet to cause the people to bring a disaster upon themselves. In other words, he is cast again in the role of an *agent provocateur*.

One noteworthy aspect of this role is its congruence with the prophet's job description in Deut 18:15–22. The piece apparently sees him or her as a conduit for God's day-to-day instructions: "I… will put my words in his mouth; and he shall speak to them all that I shall command him" (v. 18). In full accordance with this promise, the deity uses Samuel to convey its specific commands: to go to war with the Philistines in 1 Sam 4 and to appoint a king (after approving his privileges) in 1 Sam 8. The two chapters thus can be seen as real-life tests (or as consecutive stages of a single test) of the Deuteronomic model of prophecy. Conducted in the situations where the deity does not appear to have Israel's best interests in mind, the tests reveal at least two sinister aspects of this model.

First, it may land the people in a Catch-22 situation. In Deut 18:19, Moses quotes God as stipulating: "Whoever will not hearken to my words which he [sc. the prophet] shall speak in my name, I will require it of him." When the intent of the deity's words is malevolent, as it apparently is in 1 Sam 4 and 8, under this provision the people are required, in a twist that Kafka would appreciate, to shoot themselves in the foot. Even more paradoxically, in such a situation the above-mentioned provision of the Deuteronomic "prophetic statute" clashes with the concept of reward and punishment, laid out at considerable length in Deut 28. If blindly obeying the prophet is a commandment (and the Deuteronomic formulation suggests that it is), the observance of this requirement should be rewarded with a blessing, but in 1 Sam 4 and 8 the people who do what Samuel tells them to do (or what he is commanded to tell them to do) find themselves under a curse.

Second, Deuteronomy's instructions on identification of true and false prophets are grossly misleading in the case of divine deception. According to Deut 18:22, "when a prophet speaks in the name of YHWH, if the thing follow not, nor come to pass, that is the thing which YHWH has not spoken, but the prophet has spoken it presumptuously; you should not be afraid of him." From this perspective, the outcome of Samuel's call to arms in 1 Sam 4 (which clearly presupposed a divine promise of victory, even if no such promise was given explicitly) rendered him a presumptuous prophet whose punishment in Deut 18:20 is death. The same is true of his appointing a king and keeping mum about the monarchy being another kind of idolatry—as he was apparently commissioned to do by the deity. Yet, in both cases, Samuel serves as God's faithful mouthpiece—too faithful, in fact, in 1 Sam 8, where he seems to disclose to the people the revelations that YHWH meant only for his ears. Deuteronomy thus potentially exposes an innocent, loyal individual to the stigma of a false oracle and perhaps even to capital punishment (if Deut 18:20 is understood as an instruction to put such an oracle to death rather than a promise that the deity would take care of this).

In addition to exposing the problems inherent in the Deuteronomic concept of the prophet as a conduit for day-to-day divine instructions, 1 Sam 1–8 may be offering an alternative to this concept. Arguably, the crowning achievement of Samuel's career is the national repentance that he engineers in 1 Sam 7 and the concomitant military victory that puts an end to the long period of Philistine oppression. Significantly, in this case he acts without any specific prompting and prodding from the deity—a circumstance emphasized above all by the fact that this happens while the most tangible symbol of God's presence, the ark, stays outside Israel proper, in the Gibeonite town of Kirjath-jearim (1 Sam 6:21–7:2).[7] Rather than acting at the deity's behest, Samuel takes initiative in calling upon fellow Israelites to renounce foreign gods (7:3–4) and thereby, in a certain sense, causes, if not forces, YHWH to act against Israel's oppressors (vv. 9–10). In other words, by spontaneously reminding the people of their covenantal obligations, the first of which is to worship YHWH alone (Exod 20:3), the prophet scores a major success that looks especially striking when contrasted with the bleak consequences of his missions in chs. 4 and 8.

The first eight chapters of 1 Samuel thus stand, as far as the notion of prophecy is concerned, in no small tension to Deut 18. This conclusion is valid regardless of the intent, or lack thereof, behind the intertextual relationship outlined above; conceptual patterns demonstrably detectable in a text are there *ipso facto*.[8] It does not follow, however, that a plausible, if inevitably hypothetical, and intellectually rewarding reconstruction of the authorial or redactional design that generated the text would not contribute to its meaning. Among several possible lines of investigation, two appear promising in this respect. One would view the stance of 1 Sam 1–8 on prophecy as an extension and refinement of the Deuteronomic thought. The setting of both chs. 4 and 8 is that of disrupted relationship between YHWH and Israel, in the former case due to the abuses of the Shiloan priests (1 Sam 2:12–17), not to mention foreign worship (which is renounced only in ch. 7), in the latter due to the people's request for a king (8:7–8).[9] In terms of Deut 28, Israel deserves punishment in

---

[7] For Kirjath-jearim as a Gibeonite locale, see Josh 9:17.

[8] In essence, validity of an interpretation hinges not on correct reconstruction of what the text was supposed to mean, but rather on whether the proposed construal can sway other readers.

[9] Further complicating the matter is the fact that this request seems to be made in full accordance with Deuteronomic guidelines (compare Deut 17:14–15

both cases, and it does not matter whether the penalty comes as a result of following the prophet's guidance or in response to ignoring it. In this synchronic perspective, 1 Sam 1–8 builds upon Deut 18:15–22 to make a stark, rhetorically powerful addition to the threats of Deut 28:15–68: failure to observe the commandments results in not only natural phenomena, human body, social networks, political structures, and personal relationships, but also the communication with the divine ceasing to function the way they were intended to. From a source of guidance, prophecy turns into a source of confusion, because there is no way to ascertain the prophet's credentials and the intent of the instructions communicated through him or her. Under such conditions, anything that Israel does in response to a prophet's ad hoc advice is much more likely to aggravate the situation than to improve it. The only way out of the mess is to fall back on the timeless requirements of the Torah, and the best an individual prophet can do to help the people is to bring these requirements to their attention.

An even more intriguing possibility is that 1 Sam 1–8 is polemically directed against the Deuteronomic and Deuteronomistic concept of prophecy. The chapters' stance on the phenomenon is nowhere to be found in the subsequent parts of Samuel, where the book's title character again serves as a conduit for God's ad hoc instructions, this time without identifiably negative consequences (one example is his, and the deity's, successful orchestration of Saul's enthronement in chs. 9–10).[10] The same is true of Samuel's successors Gad (1 Sam 22:5) and Nathan (2 Sam 7, 12), as well as of the prophets featured in Kings, such as Ahijah, Elijah, Elisha, and Isaiah.[11] First Samuel 1–8

and 1 Sam 8:5). For a more detailed discussion of the issue, see Frolov, *Turn* 152–60, 176–7, 185–9.

[10] See Frolov, "The Semiotics of Covert Action in 1 Samuel 9–10," *JSOT* 31 (2007): 429–50.

[11] The only exception is 1 Kgs 22:1–38, a piece that bears substantial resemblance to 1 Sam 2–4: YHWH wants King Ahab dead and through four hundred prophets incites him to launch a campaign against Aram, in which the king is ultimately killed, despite the precautions that he takes. The plot is complicated by several twists, including the appearance of a vaguely proto-Satanic supernatural figure who volunteers, at YHWH's request, to "be a lying spirit in the mouth of all prophets" (v. 22) and the exposure of the deity's true intentions by the prophet Micaiah (whose revelation lands him in jail; vv. 15–28). The text may be another post- and anti-Deuteronomistic interpolation: note that Ahab's violent demise in vv. 35–37 is incompatible with the formula "Ahab slept with his fathers" in v. 40 that is consistently used elsewhere of natural death and that the purported realization in v. 38 of Elijah's prophecy in 1 Kgs 21:19 clashes with its apparent cancellation in 21:28–29.

consequently presents itself from this diachronic viewpoint as an anti-Deuteronomic and anti-Deuteronomistic addition to the largely Deuteronomistic substrate of the Former Prophets. Pointing in the same direction are the stances the unit takes on the monarchy, the priesthood, the cult, and the ark; as I have argued elsewhere, these stances can be interpreted as heavily anti-Deuteronomic and anti-Deuteronomistic.[12]

Significantly, the clash between the notions of prophecy operative in Deut 18 and 1 Sam 1–8 may be indicative of a crucial step in the historical evolvement of the Israelite, and later Jewish, concept of the phenomenon. Genetically, this concept is rooted in Israel's ancient Near Eastern milieu, where the prophet was mostly seen as a mouthpiece for the deity's day-to-day instructions (as it is strongly suggested, for example, by the Mari documents).[13] However, ultimately Jewish tradition came to reject any direct communication from God as a source of authority—as shown most graphically and most forcefully by the famous "oven of Akhnai" story in the Talmud, where the sages ignore explicit divine intervention in their debate, citing the statement of Deut 30:12 that, "the Torah is not in heaven."[14] Situated between these two extremes of the historical continuum, the tension between Deut 18 and 1 Sam 1–8 may signify the point where reminding the people of the covenant's enduring terms came to be seen as a more efficient way to ensure their well-being than transmitting to them God's ad hoc advice. This is the point where consulting the Torah became more important than consulting God, and the prophet ... well, the prophet began to morph into a rabbi.[15]

---

[12] Frolov, *Turn*, 152–78.

[13] *ANET* 623–26, 629–32.

[14] *b. B. Meṣ'ia* 59a–b.

[15] A related transformation takes place in 1 Kings 22: by eavesdropping on the divine council and bringing back crucial information that they deity would prefer to withhold, the prophet Micaiah acts like a mystic. In the Jewish tradition, all legitimate mystics of the post-biblical times are identified as rabbis and many prominent rabbis are identified as mystics. Although the date of the rabbis' emergence as a distinctive group cannot be established with any degree of certainty, it is possible that already in Neo-Babylonian and early Persian times certain classes of community leaders in the diaspora performed similar functions. In the famous chain of tradition that opens *Pirke Aboth*, prophets are immediately followed by "men of the Great Assembly" who are implicitly marked as first rabbis by a quotation of their sayings (*m. Abot* 1:1).

DANIEL
Sage, Seer . . . and Prophet?

Lester L. Grabbe

It may seem an act of great folly—or great hubris—to raise seriously the question of whether Daniel is a prophet.[1] Haven't we known since the nineteenth century that prophetic literature differed in an essential way from apocalyptic literature, and were not prophets the bedrock of Israel's ethical and moral religion, in contrast to the decadent, late, rather superstitious foretellers of the future like Daniel? Consider the following summary statement by no less than Georg Fohrer:

> More important than the professional prophets—indeed, second only to Moses in importance for the history of Yahwism—is the small group comprising the great individual prophets, including Amos and Hosea, Isaiah and Micah, Zephaniah and Jeremiah, Ezekiel and in part Deutero-Isaiah. They did not exercise their prophetical ministry as members of a profession but on the basis of a special call that snatched them from their original profession. In them Israelite prophecy reached its summit; and although they are lumped with other forms under the common heading of "prophecy," there is more to distinguish them from than to identify them with these forms. They came forward among their

---

[1] In other contexts, I have raised questions about apocalyptic, such as my article ("Prophetic and Apocalyptic: Time for New Definitions—and New Thinking") and the "Introduction" in Lester L. Grabbe and Robert D. Haak, eds., *Knowing the End from the Beginning: The Prophetic, the Apocalyptic, and their Relationships* (JSPSup 46; London: T&T Clark, 2003), 2–43, 107–33, not to everyone's satisfaction (see the response by John J. Collins in the same volume, "Prophecy, Apocalypse and Eschatology: Reflections on the Proposals of Lester Grabbe," p. 44–52).

people not as members of a guild or of a class, not as representatives of a tribe or of a clan, not as functionaries of a sanctuary or of the king, but as conscious representatives and messengers of their God.[2]

If large numbers of the Twelve do not make it, what hope does Daniel have?

There are several points to establish at the beginning of any discussion: first, there is the difference between prophetic literature and the persona of a prophet. That is, we tend to use different methods to research the one as opposed to the other. There is also the danger of using arguments for one investigation that properly belong to the other. Another point is that to establish any common ground, we have to deal intially with the writings as they exist in their final form. Later on in the discussion, we might bring in traditio-historical insights or theories, but that is not where we begin.

AMOS AND DANIEL

The place to start is with the question of literature, beginning with a comparison. No book is more quintessentially prophetic than Amos, so we shall make some comparisons between Daniel and Amos. Many would immediately see a great contrast, and there is no doubt that Amos and Daniel differ in a great many ways. But then you could say that about Amos and Ezekiel or Amos and Nahum.

We should be careful not to confuse temporal factors and influence with essential components of parallel writings. A number of Amos passages have no specific parallel elsewhere in prophetic literature (e.g., "cows of Bashan" [4:1–3], criticism of festivals [5:21]). Two crime novels may differ greatly in characters, setting, and plot, but there will still be parallel structures that can be compared. The prophetic books differ from one another in language, imagery, and specific references but still have parallel structures. The same applies to Amos and Daniel.

Amos 1–2 contains oracles against various nations. I am not aware of a precise parallel to the oracles against the nations in apocalyptic literature. Rather than criticism of individual nations, what we find is a review of and prophetic statements against a succession of historical empires and periods (e.g., the dark

---

[2] Quote from Georg Fohrer, *History of Israelite Religion* (trans. D. E. Green; Nashville: Abingdon; London: SPCK, 1972) 237 (ET of *Geschichte der israelitischen Religion* [Berlin: de Gruyter, 1968]); cf. also his statements in his *Introduction to the Old Testament* (Nashville: Abingdon, 1968) 345–6.

waters of *2 Baruch* 53–76). The book of Daniel (2, 7, 8, and 11) clearly sees the succession of world empires and their activities negatively. Under a symbol (a statue, various beasts, and regional kings) it prophesies the end of the Babylonian, "Median," Persian, and Greek empires—all within the writer's horizon of concern. The mode of communication is somewhat different, but the general concept and—especially—the end result are very much parallel.

Amos 3–6 contains a lengthy critique of the kingdom of Israel, with a detailed catalogue of sins and a sustained rant against the people in general and against various social groups in particular. Here we can find much in common with apocalyptic literature which frequently contains paranaetic passages, condemning the wicked and encouraging the righteous. These passages are usually couched in individual rather than ethnic or national terms, but threat, admonition, and general exhortation to do the right and avoid the wrong is common to much religious literature. The national disaster outlined in Amos has closest parallels in some of the other prophets, but this could be explained by the particular circumstances in which the book was written.

In Amos 7–9 is a series of visions. First a vision is described, then its significance is explained; however, there is a sort of progression. In the first vision (7:1–3), a plague of locusts seems to be a fairly literal threat, but YHWH relents. In the second vision (7:4–6), the threat of a fire is also withdrawn. The third vision (7:7–9) is more symbolic: the vision of a plumb line signifies the destruction of the high places and holy places of Israel.[3] The fourth vision is also symbolic: Amos sees YHWH standing by the altar and commanding to strike the capitals of the temple. This appears to represent God's seeking out and punishing all the sinners. The important thing, though, is that we can compare the visions in the book of Daniel and also other apocalypses and related writings.

But I hear my reader saying, "Yes, Amos may have some visions, but many other prophetic books do not." My reader would be correct in this observation, but then many prophetic books do not have oracles against the nations. Of course, there are significant differences between Daniel and Amos, but considering the variations between prophetic books and the differences between various apocalyptic writings, simply pointing out differences is not sufficient. Naturally, pointing out similarities without recognizing differences can be

---

[3] Between the third and fourth visions is an inset about Amos's interaction with Amaziah the priest of Bethel (7:10–17). This appears to be anchored to the vision context by catchwords ("Jeroboam" [7:9, 10], "Isaac" [7:9, 16], "plumb line"/"measuring line" [7:7–8: אנך; 7:17: חבל]).

equally hazardous. But at least the issue deserves to be debated, whereas many see it as already settled.

When you start to read Amos as a prophetic book, one of the first things that strikes you is the statement at 3:7: "For the Lord YHWH will do nothing except that he reveals his purpose to his servants the prophets." Could any statement be truer of the sage *Daniel* to whom God has granted a veritable panorama of future history? Of course, it is conventional to ascribe this passage to an editor rather than to Amos, but it is part of the book as we have it. The prophetic book of Amos says that God does exactly what he does in the book of Daniel. Amos says that God will reveal the future before carrying out his planned actions; in Daniel God reveals the future before carrying out his planned actions.

JEREMIAH AND DANIEL

Now let us turn to the persona of the prophet. There is not a lot of information in Amos about the prophet, so it would be helpful to turn to another prophet, Jeremiah, about whose life the book of Jeremiah gives a great deal of information. Notice the similarities:

Jeremiah	Daniel
Called by God (1).	Daniel and friends chosen (1).
Associated with temple and royal court.	Associated with king and court.
Receives messages/revelations from God.	Receives messages/revelations from God.
Opposed/persecuted by priests/nobility.	Opposed/persecuted by priests/officials.
Supported by powerful individuals (38).	Supported by king (2, 4, 6).
Given oracles against various nations (46-51).	Given visions of fall of empires (2, 7, 8).
Jeremiah's 70-year prophecy (25, 29).	Jeremiah's 70 weeks of years prophecy (9).
Symbolic vision/action with interpretation (13, 18, 24, 32, 35).	Symbolic vision with interpretation (2, 5, 7, 8, 9).

The fact is that Daniel *looks* like a prophet, as much as Jeremiah. As he putters around the Persian court, God communicates with him, sometimes via visions sent to him, sometimes via visions sent to someone else who calls on Daniel for an explanation, and sometimes a heavenly lackey brings the word and its interpretation (Dan 9, 10–12). Note that heavenly speech makes up part of the revelation; the book does not consist entirely of visions. Jeremiah is beaten (Jer 20:2), threatened with death (26:8–9), forced to go into hiding from the wrath of the king (36:5), thrown into a well or cistern (38:6–13), and accused of deserting to the Babylonians (37:11–16). But the lives of Daniel and his friends are also threatened on a number of occasions: Nebuchadnezzar threatens to execute all the wisemen of the court (Dan 2), and he has the three friends thrown into the fiery furnace (3); Darius has Daniel put in the lion's den—if reluctantly (6). Deliverance comes in each case, sometimes by more miraculous means than others, but God's providence is assumed in each set of writings.

It seems hardly surprising, then, when Daniel is referred to as a "prophet"—*nābî'*—in the Qumran scrolls (4QFlor frag. 1, II, 3, 24, 5:3: "[a]s is written in the book of Daniel, the prophet [הנביא]") and as a προφήτης in the New Testament (Mark 13:14 variant reading // Matt 24:15).

INSPIRED SCRIBES?

"But," someone will say to me, "Jeremiah was a real individual whereas Daniel was a fictitious figure." This may or may not be true. I happen to think that Jeremiah was a real figure who also did a number of things ascribed to him in the book, but the late lamented Robert Carroll was much more skeptical.[4] As for Daniel, there may have been a Jewish mantic figure in the Persian or at least the Babylonian court on whom the book of Daniel is based. This reconstruction is much less secure, but it is a possibility. The point we have to realize and accept is that there is a distance between the story and historical reality in the prophetic books as well as in the apocalyptic literature. Apocalypses are often assigned to an ancient patriarch and are therefore patently an invention of a later writer, but this may also be the case with prophetic writings.

This raises another issue: the prophetic books were not necessarily written

---

[4] Among Robert Carroll's writings, the two following contain much of his perspective on the book: *From Chaos to Covenant: Uses of Prophecy in the Book of Jeremiah* (London: SCM, 1981); *Jeremiah: A Commentary* (OTL; London: SCM, 1986).

by prophets, any more than the various books of Enoch were written by an antediluvian patriarch. In some cases we may indeed have words or messages from prophetic figures preserved in prophetic writings, though where and to what extent is often still debated. Yet we must keep in mind that the contents of a prophetic book may come from a variety of sources, not just prophets. Just because we have a book in the name of Isaiah we cannot assume all the words are from Isaiah of Jerusalem in the eighth century—which is a standard assumption of scholarship, anyway. But—very important—neither can we assume that all the words are from a prophet of any sort. The books were ultimately assembled by scribes, and scribes may have composed some or even many passages. This means that we cannot make an automatic equation between prophetic book and prophetic utterances of a prophet. A prophetic book may be as fictional as an apocalyptic one, as far as the claims made about the source of prophecies within it.

Yet there is a further consideration. Although some of the contents of a prophetic book may not be from the prophet named at the top of the page, those who wrote might well have done so in a state of ecstasy or be describing a genuine vision. Similarly, the fact that an apocalyptic book has a fictional setting and a fictional main character does not mean that everything about it is created by a scribe in his study. Just as poets may see inspiration behind the verses they write or prophets might undergo ecstatic experiences or see actual visions, so the composers of apocalyptic writings might themselves be the recipients of visions or auditions or revelations that they perceive as divine. This is a difficult area because in most cases we have no external information about how the book was composed. But analogies from other periods in Jewish history, from hints in mystical literature, and from anthropological studies suggest that those who wrote apocalyptic works assumed in all seriousness that their work was inspired and ultimately originating with the deity.

Thus, there are a number of reasons to question the sharp distinction often made between the prophetic and the apocalyptic spheres. Notice the following points:

- Both prophecy and apocalyptic present themselves as delivering a divine message to human recipients.
- Both have the function of addressing the contemporary audience with regard to their current situation and offering hope or advice or perspective.
- Both contain significant paranetic material, warning, advising, and admonishing the reader not only for the present but also for the future.

- Both presuppose a mythical worldview in which the unseen but very real heavenly world determines what will happen on earth and in the affairs of humans.
- Both look forward to an ideal age in which earth (and heaven, in some cases) will be transformed and the righteous will live in peace and happiness.
- Both prophetic and apocalyptic writings might be the product of a community, but equally they might be produced by a single individual.
- Both have a large element of pseudepigraphic material.

The purpose of this comparison is not to suggest that one cannot distinguish between Amos and *1 Enoch*; the purpose is rather to draw attention to the problematic nature of some past arguments and conclusions.

Proposed Solution

There are, no doubt, various ways to approach this dilemma. If we stick to the horizon of ancient Jewish literature, we do indeed have a problem, which is to find that biblical scholarship has often dealt with the issue in an unsatisfactory way—frequently privileging the canonical writings over other products of the community. But if we are willing to cast our net wider, we find some interesting comparisons. Studies in anthropology indicate that prophecy is not the isolated phenomenon that some biblical scholars want to fence off and protect from contamination. Not only in the ancient Near East but in many cultures around the world, we find individuals who look something like Israelite prophets and who engage in something like Israelite prophecy. But when we attempt to classify this activity in its cultural context, we often find some relation to divination, just as Israelite prophets had some relation to priestly divination. Indeed, most prophecy can be classified as a form of spirit divination.[5] There are

---

[5] See Evan M. Zuesse, "Divination," in *The Encyclopedia of Religion* (New York: Macmillan, 1987) 4:375–82. Zuesse gives a typology of divination which includes "possession divination" as one of three main categories. This category is further divided into several different subdivisions, including one which includes prophecy and another which includes spirit mediumship. He states: "Full diviniatory possession of human beings may be of several theoretical forms: prophetic inspiration, shamanistic ecstasy, mystical illuminations and visions, and mediumistic or oracular trance. They differ according to the degree of ego awareness and lucity, awareness of the ordinary world, and the theoretical

also different modes of divination, and the mechanical type is only one. Divination by control of spirits is another.

Thus, I would classify prophecy as a form of divination. This is a matter of academic judgment and convenience and not meant to be a way of dismissing the importance of prophecy nor is it meant to be an *a priori* determination of the source of the prophecies in question. But once we start the classifying process, we can then ask what else might fall under divination. That is a discussion for another context, but a further question is about how the category of prophecy might be delineated. I would make apocalyptic a subdivision of prophecy. In other words, we do not necessarily have to decide whether Daniel or another apocalyptic writing is a form of prophecy: by my categorization Daniel is a special form of prophecy. The resemblances between prophetic and apocalyptic literature noted above occur because we are not dealing with two separate categories but with a single category that can be subdivided.

I appreciate that this has been a brief discussion of a complex subject. But if my reasoning has merit, the issue may be more simply dealt with than has been assumed. At the very least, my suggestion recognizes something that we have all felt—that generations of Bible readers have felt—that Daniel is in some sense also among the prophets. It also raises annoying questions about conventional scholarly wisdom which, to my mind, is always a good thing.

---

recipient of the divinatory message. The prophets of the Bible seem to retain a lucid sense of themselves and the world..." (p. 377) The last statement might well be disputed by some, since it is not necessarily certain what the prophet's state of mind was when receiving the revelation, though the message had to be lucid when it was delivered.

CULT OF PERSONALITY
The Eclipse of Pre-Exilic Judahite Cultic Structures in the Book of Jeremiah

Mark Leuchter

The prophet Jeremiah—whether viewed as an historical figure or a literary icon—remains among the most enigmatic personalities in the Hebrew Bible. The book bearing his name creates his prophetic personality in antonymic terms in almost every chapter: he hails from Anathoth (Jer 1:1), then calls for the destruction of his kinfolk there (Jer 11:21–23) only to finally provide a message of hope and redemption to them shortly before the fall of Jerusalem (Jer 32:6–15). He protests the centrality of the temple (Jer 7:3–15) one moment while championing the Deuteronomic reform in the next (Jer 22:15–16). He revels as a prophet in the divine word (Jer 15:16) while lamenting his prophetic responsibility (20:14–18), castigating the office of the prophet (Jer 23:13–14) and complaining that the divine word he carries burns as a fire (20:9). And while closely associated with a variety of scribes throughout the book, Jeremiah's words preserve a harsh critique of scribal initiatives (Jer 8:8–9).[1] The book of

---

[1] I have elsewhere suggested that the anti-scribal tone of this oracle did not originate with Jeremiah but, rather, with adversaries that are quoted in this passage (*Josiah's Reform and Jeremiah's Scroll: Historical Calamity and Prophetic Response* [HBM 6; Sheffield: Sheffield Phoenix, 2006], 129–32). Nevertheless, the oracle's current literary context indeed creates a degree of ambiguity regarding with whom this sentiment originates, and many scholars make strong arguments for its contribution to a prophetic critique of written traditions in the late seventh through mid-sixth centuries BCE. See William M. Schniedewind, *How The Bible Became a Book: The Textualization of Ancient Israel* (New York: Cambridge University, 2004), 115–6; Baruch Halpern, "Why

Jeremiah may present us with more details about his life than that of any other prophet, but the abundance of details provide an abundance of contradictions that make it difficult to place the prophet within discernible social or religious parameters.

This, however, is precisely the point of the book, or at least the goal of its primary contributors. For if the majority of material from the book of Jeremiah reflects upon the twilight years of Judah and the early conditions of the exilic period, the presentation of the prophet as repeatedly cast adrift in social and religious terms creates a symbol appropriate to the times, when the older national institutions had failed and uncertainty loomed on every horizon.[2] As Frank Moore Cross famously argued, "classical" prophecy was born in the context of the national cult at the dawn of the monarchy,[3] and thus the debilitation suffered by that cult under Babylon would invariably have affected the potency of the prophetic office. And yet—as the examples of Ezekiel and Deutero-Isaiah demonstrate—it is clear that prophecy flourished without a strong national cult as its basis. The roots of this survival of prophecy in the face of overwhelming destruction may be traced in no small part to the Jeremiah tradition. Facing the devastating circumstances of exile (impending or experienced), the authors of the book of Jeremiah created a model for survival by placing the prophetic personality above and beyond the tattered cult that in large part spawned it. We shall consider three major themes in the book of Jeremiah that lay the foundations for this strategy, all of which are representative of a recurring motif within the book that tackles the challenges of the exile with the same aggression as the Babylonian forces that perpetrated it.

THE LEVITICAL CULT

Most commentators recognize the depths of Jeremiah's connection to his Levite heritage. The very beginning of the book boldly declares that what is to follow should be credited to a prophet who comes from the Mushite Levites of

---

Manasseh is Blamed for the Babylonian Exile: The Evolution of a Biblical Tradition," *VT* 48 (1998): 505.

[2] Mark Leuchter, *The Polemics of Exile in Jeremiah 26–45* (New York: Cambridge University, 2008), 145.

[3] Frank Moore Cross, *Canaanite Myth and Hebrew Epic* (Cambridge: Harvard University, 1973), 223. By "national" cult I mean the official cult of the monarchic period applied broadly throughout territories governed by the royal officers and firmly connected to the religious interests of the royal court.

Anathoth,⁴ and the inaugural vision reports in the prophet's call narrative are steeped in ritual symbols that reveal his own background as a Levite and his familiarity with the paraphernalia of the Levitical cult.⁵ Similarly, the structure of the call narrative echoes the figures of Moses and Samuel,⁶ who are elsewhere invoked as Levite standards against which the prophet should be measured (Jer 15:1). The connection between Jeremiah and these archetypal Levites informs his appearance in Jer 34, where an author presents his protest of Zedekiah's covenant ceremony as that of a Levite dutifully proclaiming *tôrāh* as mandated in Deut 31:9–12.⁷ In all of these cases, the reliance upon Levite typologies acts as a legitimizing force to undergird the rhetoric of the surrounding literature, but it is important to note that just as the text affirms Jeremiah's heritage as a Levite it also explodes the preconceptions regarding what that means in broader social/historical context. Jeremiah's Levite identity is founded on the prophet's lineage but is ultimately divorced from it in a variety of passages. The first and most blatant example is in the prophet's call for punishment against his own kin, the men of Anathoth (Jer 11:21–23):

> Therefore thus says YHWH concerning the men of Anathoth, that seek your life, saying: 'Do not prophesy in the name of YHWH, lest you die by our hand'; Therefore thus says YHWH of hosts: Behold, I will punish them; the young men shall die by the sword, their sons and their daughters shall die by famine; And there shall be no remnant of them; for I will bring evil upon the men of Anathoth in the year of their visitation.

Part of the reason for this harsh call for punishment against his kin at Anathoth may be connected to their rejection of Jeremiah's prophetic role and his advocacy of Deuteronomic principles; the tone and scope of the prophet's words are consonant with the Deuteronomic legislation against sedition (Deut

---

⁴ For the connection of the priests of Anatoth to the Mushite line, see Cross, *Canaanite Myth*, 205–15.

⁵ Marvin A. Sweeney, "Review of Martti Nissinen and C. L. Seow and Robert K. Ritner, *Prophets and Prophecy in the Ancient Near East*," *Review of Biblical Literature* (2005) (www.bookreviews.org).

⁶ Leuchter, *Josiah's Reform and Jeremiah's Scroll*, 76–78.

⁷ The timing of this event coincides with the scheduled septennial reading of the Deuteronomic Torah (assuming that the dating of the episode to 587 BCE is accepted). Reinforcing this is the introduction to the prophet's invective with the מקץ שבע שנים formula also found in Deut 31:10 in relation to the Levites' reading of the *torah*.

13:7–12).[8] But notable also is the specific imagery employed in the oracle, which closely matches that of the Song of Moses and its vision of violent punishment (Deut 32:25–26, 35–36, 41–42). Before its redaction into Deuteronomy, the Song of Moses functioned as a traditional liturgy cultivated by Levites marginalized from the central religious establishment in Jerusalem.[9] Here, however, the old poem is turned against its trustees, the threats it once voiced now lodged against its originators. A similar strategy involving the poem is worked into other oracles currently located in Jer 2–6 in an implicit manner,[10] but its role here is far more dramatic. If the poem had been part of the Levitical cult for generations, the turning of its threats of destruction against the important family of Levites in Anathoth is more than a matter of drawing from a familiar pool of lexemes for rhetorical impact. Rather, it signals the end of cultic authority that such a family could claim based solely on matters of lineage, and it is *lineage* which formed the crux of the Levite cultic infrastructure.[11] The Levite cult fostered for generations—one that boasted the Song of Moses as part of its repertoire[12]—was to be "cut off," for the Song of Moses was now part of the Deuteronomic stream of tradition (advocated in a particular rhetorical-compositional stratum in Jeremiah though later challenged; see below), one that leveled lineage hierarchies and atomistic ancestral traditions.[13]

---

[8] Leuchter, *Josiah's Reform and Jeremiah's Scroll*, 100–101.

[9] On the liturgical origins and character of the Song of Moses, see Matthew Thiessen, "The Form and Function of the Song of Moses (Deut 32:1–43)," *JBL* 123 (2004): 407–10, 418–9. See also Mark Leuchter, "Why is the Song of Moses in the Book of Deuteronomy?" *VT* 57 (2007): 314.

[10] William L. Holladay identifies a variety of places in the Jeremianic oracles where the language of the old poem appears to left a notable impression ("Elusive Deuteronomists, Jeremiah and Proto-Deuteronomy," *CBQ* 66 [2004]: 59, 63–64).

[11] Examples of lineage bases for Levite sacral authority may be found in Judg 18:30; 1 Sam 2:11–26; 8:1–4. For the centrality of lineage to the traditional Levite cult, see Stephen L. Cook, *The Social Roots of Biblical Yahwism* (Studies in Biblical Literature; Atlanta: Society of Biblical Literature, 2004), 231–66 (esp. 259ff.).

[12] Leuchter, "Song of Moses," 314.

[13] The literature demonstrating the affinities between Jeremiah and Deuteronomy is well known, exhaustive and need not be rehearsed here. But it is clear that these affinities are complex and it is not sufficient to simply assume a Deuteronomistic redaction of an originally independent oracular corpus as a profound degree of Deuteronomic language and ideology permeates the poetic oracles as much as the parenetic passages and narratives. See the brief but useful discussion of Richard E. Friedman, "The Deuteronomistic School," in *Fortunate*

It is debatable as to whether or not the oracle in Jer 11:21–23 advocates a genuine deathblow to be inflicted upon the men of Anathoth; that the prophet later returns to Anathoth and redeems his ancestral territory (Jer 32:6–15) suggests that this was not the intention of the oracle. Rather, the severity of the oracle was to suggest that the cultic authority of the Mushite Levites in Anathoth could no longer function in competition with the prevailing Deuteronomic ideology of the time.[14] Deuteronomy obviously recognizes Levite heritage as a determinative factor in cultic matters,[15] but Deuteronomic policy restricted Levite participation in the cult to praxes connected and subordinate to the central administration in Jerusalem (Deut 18:6–8). Outside of this paradigm, "Levite" cultic identity could no longer matter, regardless of long-standing kinship and lineage roles. It is for this reason that the icons and personnel of the traditional Levitical cult in the prophet's call narrative are abstracted from their original and independent functions and made mere vehicles for the prophetic message

---

the Eyes that See: Essays in Honor of David Noel Freedman in Celebration of his Seventieth Birthday (ed. Astrid B. Beck et al; Grand Rapids: Eerdmans, 1995), 78–79, though Friedman's conclusions regarding the relatively uniform consistency between the "Deuteronomistic" authors in Jeremiah, Kings, and Deuteronomy requires additional consideration. The presentation and use of language and ideology in Jeremiah diverges from its Deuteronomic basis in important ways, as will be discussed below.

[14] William M. McKane's model of the Jeremianic material as a "rolling corpus" is a useful point of departure in understanding the relationship between its disparate layers of composition (*A Critical and Exegetical Commentary on the Book of Jeremiah* [ICC; London: T&T Clark, 1986], l–lxxxiii), though his view that the primary accumulation of material represents a centuries-long process is open to question. There is good reason to see significant turns or opinion in the Jeremianic corpus within a more limited period of time and representing varied strata of composition from a more limited circle of authorship in response to the political turbulence of the late seventh through mid-sixth centuries BCE (Leuchter, *Polemics of Exile*, passim). In relation to the current passage under discussion, we may detect a pro-Deuteronomic position from an early period in the formation of the corpus related to the prophet's Josianic-era career (see Marvin A. Sweeney, *King Josiah of Judah: The Lost Messiah of Israel* [New York: Oxford University, 2001], 208–33, though Sweeney does not discuss Jer 11 in this regard) that is later developed into a more nuanced qualification of Deuteronomy; see the ensuing discussion herein.

[15] The repeated qualification of priests as "Levitical" (הכהנים הלויים) makes this conclusion nearly inescapable in virtually every chapter in the book.

that was to override pre-Deuteronomic sacerdotal ideologies.[16] This concept is reinforced by the oracle in Jer 16:1–2, which sees the prohibition on the paramount place of Levite lineage applied to the prophet himself: "The word of YHWH came also to me, saying: You shall not take for yourself a wife, neither shall you have sons or daughters in this place." Some scholars have noted similarities between this oracle and the oracles of Jeremiah's eighth century predecessor Hosea, a prophet who also possessed Levite lineage and who used the issue of marriage and family to symbolize the state of the covenant between YHWH and Israel.[17] Marriage and family were obviously fair game for the formation of prophetic metaphors, but Jer 16:1–2 differs insofar as there is no metaphor to speak of in this verse or the unit in which it appears (Jer 16:1–4). These verses use the concept of Jeremiah's lack of progeny as a symbol of impending doom and, in a sense, may constitute some reprieve for the prophet who will not be forced to mourn for his children the way other families will have to mourn for their own. The potency of the oracle, however, is felt in the fact that the denial of progeny is to a Levite. This symbolizes more than just the impending doom facing the nation; it symbolizes the debilitation of the Levitical cult as handed down within the lineage. A running theme throughout various strata of Biblical narrative emphasizes the importance of Levite heritage as a prerequisite for priestly authority, for better or for worse (Judg 18:30; 1 Sam 2:11–36; 8:1–4).[18] For Jeremiah to be prohibited from following that norm is a powerful statement against its ongoing applicability, and it is no coincidence that similar threats accompany the prophet's criticism of adversaries who may have also possessed priestly heritage.[19]

But perhaps the greatest challenge to the Levitical cult in Jeremiah is the "New Covenant" oracle in Jer 31:31–34. Volumes have been written on the purpose and importance of this oracle in the development of covenant theology in the Hebrew Bible and beyond,[20] but an oft-overlooked dimension of this

---

[16] Sweeney, "Review"; Leuchter, *Josiah's Reform and Jeremiah's Scroll*, 76–78.

[17] Cook, *Social Roots*, 74 and references cited there.

[18] See further Cook's discussion in *Social Roots*, 259–66.

[19] Jack R. Lundbom, *Jeremiah 21–36* (AB; New York: Doubleday, 2004), 363.

[20] See among others H. D. Potter, "The New Covenant in Jeremiah 31:31 – 34," *VT* 33 (1983): 349–50; William L. Holladay, *Jeremiah 2* (Hermeneia; Philadelphia: Fortress, 1989), 198; James Swetnam, "Why Was Jeremiah's New Covenant New?" in *Studies in Prophecy* (ed. G. W. Anderson et al.; VTSup 26; Leiden: Brill, 1974), 111–5; Lundbom, *Jeremiah 21–36*, 467–9; Moshe Weinfeld, "Jeremiah and the Spiritual Metamorphosis of Israel," *ZAW* 88

oracle is the degree to which it purports to empower the laity in terms of sacral knowledge. The oracle falls into a Deuteronomic category of thought with regard to the impulse for populist religious enculturation,[21] but at least as important as what it says about populism is what it leaves out regarding elite traditions of instruction:

> But this is the covenant that I will make with the house of Israel after those days, says YHWH, I will put My instruction in their inward parts, and on their heart will I write it; and I will be their God, and they shall be My people; and they shall teach no more every man his neighbor, and every man his brother, saying: Know YHWH; for they shall all know Me, from the least of them unto the greatest of them, says YHWH ... (Jer 31:33–34)

Nowhere in this passage is there a traditional place for a Levite to instruct the laity. Every individual is charged with knowing *tôrāh* on a personal level without intervening input from an outside authority. This is not necessarily an argument for social egalitarianism, for the oracle acknowledges that social hierarchies will persevere (v. 34). Nevertheless, all levels of society will benefit from equal access to the *tôrāh*. This stands in great contrast to traditions such as the one preserved in Deut 33:8–11 where divine instruction is entrusted to Levi.[22] The passage also contrasts with the earlier presupposition of Jer 2:8, where the priestly caste is identified as the "handlers of the torah,"[23] and Jer

---

(1976): 29–32; Helga Weippert, "Das Wort vom neuen Bund in Jeremia xxxi 31 –34," *VT* 29 (1979): 336–51.

[21] This populist bias regarding education in Deuteronomy is discussed by David M. Carr, *Writing on the Tablet of the Heart: Origins of Scripture and Literature* (New York: Oxford University, 2005), 136–7, though it is likely that this was a theoretical construct rather than an ideology meant to be implemented in a pseudo-democratic manner. For a discussion regarding the political-philosophical implications of this bias, see most recently Joshua A. Berman, *Created Equal: How the Bible Broke with Ancient Political Thought* (New York: Oxford University, 2008), 51–80.

[22] Though the dating of Deut 33 is widely debated, most scholars recognize that it preserves old fragments, among which Deut 33:8–11 may be counted. For the pre-Deuteronomic antiquity of these verses, see Bernard M. Levinson, *Deuteronomy and the Hermeneutics of Legal Innovation* (New York: Oxford University, 1997), 111.

[23] William L. Holladay, *Jeremiah 1* (Hermeneia; Philadelphia: Fortress, 1986), 88–89.

31:33–34 may possibly be read as a corrective to the problems addressed in the earlier oracle.

That the "New Covenant" oracle has been redacted into the larger unit of Jer 30–31 is also significant in placing limits on the Levitical cult, as the original purpose of these chapters was to address Levites in the former northern kingdom to adopt the Deuteronomic policies of the Josianic court and serve as mediators of Jerusalemite policy to outlying regions.[24] Working a passage that eliminates the traditional pedagogical role of Levites into a complex of material once meant to support their authority constitutes a powerful hermeneutical statement; it affirms the covenantal blessings enshrined in the earlier oracle in the same breath as it negates its original meaning.[25] Levites may contribute a role in supporting a particular *tôrāh* theology, but not because they are to sustain independent traditions of teaching legitimized by lineage and ancestral precedent. Rather, like Jeremiah, individual Levites must put aside their kin-based cultic allegiances and contribute to a larger theological enterprise.

THE ROYAL AND FAMILY CULT

The attitude toward kingship in the book of Jeremiah, as is well known, is overwhelmingly negative. Almost every reference to kingship identifies it as abusive, corrupt, misguided, inept, or any combination thereof. The exceptions to this pattern, therefore, demand closer attention. There are only two kings to receive a degree of sympathy or support within the Jeremianic corpus, namely, Josiah and Jehoiachin; the support shown for the memory of Josiah is often

---

[24] Mark Leuchter, "'The Levite in your Gates': The Deuteronomic Redefinition of Levitical Authority," *JBL* 126 (2007): 429–32.

[25] A similar literary flourish may be found in 1 Kgs 6:11–13, a passage that legitimizes the earlier material recounting the construction of the Temple, but only according to Deuteronomistic principles (see Leuchter, "Song of Moses," 308). This evidences the close connection between the methods deployed by the redactor of Kings and the redactor behind Jer 31:31–34, though the appeal made in Kings to the landed gentry of Judah in a few important passages contrasts with Jeremiah's critique of the hinterland culture of the late seventh century (see below). Thus while redactors of Kings and the book of Jeremiah may have benefitted from a shared sort of scribal training (see Lundbom, *Jeremiah 1–20*, 92), the minor but notable differences between them suggest different hands at work in these respective corpora (*pace* the implications of Friedman, "The Deuteronomistic School," 79–80). I address this issue in more detail in a forthcoming study on the rhetorical and sociolinguistic significance of the source citations in the book of Kings.

ascribed to his association with the Deuteronomic reform and thus compliance with Deuteronomic law (Jer 22:15–16), but this does not explain the relative sympathy visited upon Jehoiachin. There is no indication in any of the biblical texts relating to Jehoiachin that this king supported Deuteronomic ideology or engaged in cultic/administrative activity akin to that in Deuteronomy during the few months that he sat on the throne before his deportation to Babylon in 597 BCE.[26] It is likely that accompanying Jehoiachin into exile were many members of the Shaphanide scribal family and other members of the Deuteronomistic movement;[27] this may signal that king's implicit sympathies with the ideology that informed Josiah's reign. However, the book of Jeremiah does not emphasize Jehoiachin's allegiances in this regard. What the book does emphasize is the king's complete separation from the ongoing royal cult in Jerusalem now helmed by Zedekiah, and Jer 24:1, 5 is especially clear on this matter:

> YHWH showed me, and behold two baskets of figs set before *the temple of the YHWH*; after that Nebuchadrezzar king of Babylon had carried away captive Jeconiah the son of Jehoiakim, king of Judah, and the princes of Judah, with the craftsmen and smiths, from Jerusalem, and had brought them to Babylon...Thus says YHWH, the God of Israel: Like these good figs, so will I regard the captives of Judah, whom I have sent *out of this place* (מן־המקום הזה) into the land of the Chaldeans, for good.

The oracle sets the cultic מקום terminology in apposition to the Jerusalem Temple,[28] and specifies that it is good that Jehoiachin and his retinue have been sent away from this sacred place. What saves Jehoiachin from condemnation, then, is the very thing that stands out so uniquely regarding Josiah's reign—both kings appear distant from the traditional appurtenances of the royal cult in Jerusalem preserved and advanced for so long by the Davidic family.[29] In the

---

[26] Indeed, the evaluation of Jehoiachin in Kings (2 Kgs 24:9) is formulaically negative akin to the evaluation of all the post-Josianic kings.

[27] Norbert Lohfink, "Die Gattung der 'Historischen Kurzgeschichte' in den letzten Jahren von Juda und in der Zeit des Babylonischen Exils," *ZAW* 90 (1978): 333–42.

[28] On this term's application to the Jerusalem Temple in the Deuteronomistic idiom, see Levinson, *Deuteronomy*, 35–36, 50–52; this is presupposed also in Jer 7:3 (see below).

[29] This presupposes that the stipulations of Deut 17:14–20 emerged during Josiah's reign and that the report of his adherence to the Deuteronomic law (2 Kgs 23:25) has these stipulations in mind; regardless of the questionable

case of Josiah, this is (ostensibly) due to the composite influence of the landed gentry, rural Levites and the sympathetic Jerusalemite priests during the early years of the king's reign, leading to the limits on royal cultic agency encoded within Deuteronomy.[30] In the case of Jehoiachin, it is the physical separation from Jerusalem and, therefore, his *de facto* inability to indulge in the traditional role of the Davidic king as the chief executive of national religion. But for both kings, the separation from the cult preserved by the Davidic family signals a larger trend within the book of Jeremiah and its assault on (what it considers to be) invalid religious tradition, namely, the dissolution of cultic praxes preserved on the family level.[31] Like the book of Kings, the book of Jeremiah conceives of the Davidic kings as representatives of entire communities;[32] the deportation of

---

historicity of 2 Kgs 22–23, Jer 22:15–16 appears to know and agree with it. Both Bernard M. Levinson and Gary N. Knoppers have raised important questions regarding notable inconsistencies between the Deuteronomic legislation and the presentation of Josiah as chief executive of the cult in 2 Kgs 22–23 (Levinson: "The Reconceptualization of Kingship in Deuteronomy and the Deuteronomistic History's Transformation of Torah," *VT* 51 [2001], 511–34; Knoppers: "Rethinking the Relationship between Deuteronomy and the Deuteronomistic History: The Case of Kings," *CBQ* 63 [2001]: 393–415). Nevertheless, 2 Kgs 22–23 does not overtly present Josiah in a priestly capacity in terms of generating law or engaging in sacral jurisprudence, but relates that the king rallied his resources to support the law, and implicitly in conjunction with the sacral caste (the "priests" and "prophets" in 2 Kgs 23:2) in conformity with Deut 17:18–20; 18:15,18.

[30] For a study of the variety of social forces involved in the "Deuteronomistic" movement backing Josiah's reign, see Patricia Dutcher-Walls, "The Social Location of the Deuteronomists: A Sociological Study of Factional Politics in Late Pre-Exilic Judah," *JSOT* 52 (1991), 77–94.

[31] I adopt here the terminology of "family" religion/cult as opposed to "popular" religion/cult or even "household" religion/cult, as the former is an umbrella term extending over several categories irrespective of families, and the latter is too narrow a term for the present discussion as it relates to individual homes and not clan networks sharing common ancestral religious traditions. For a thorough discussion of family religion in ancient Israel and further qualifications of these terms, see Saul M. Olyan, "Family Religion in Israel and the Wider Levant of the First Millennium BCE," in *Household and Family Religion in Antiquity* (ed. John Bodel and Saul M. Olyan; Oxford: Blackwell Publishing, 2008), 113–126.

[32] The strongest evidence of this is in the repeated claim that the kings of the north "caused Israel to sin" by following in the footsteps of Jeroboam. See Paul

597 BCE created two Judahite communities, one of which is roundly condemned (the homeland group ruled by Zedekiah) while the other is redeemed (the *gôlāh* group surrounding Jehoiachin). Oracles within the book of Jeremiah repeatedly identify the deficiencies inherent to family-based religious practices and imperatives initiated or sustained by the homeland group. The exiles of 597 may have shared in this qualification before their deportation, but it is extended to those who stay fixed in Jerusalem and its satellite communities. A prominent example is found in Jer 7:16–20:

> Therefore do not pray for this people, neither lift up cry nor prayer for them, neither make intercession to Me; for I will not hear you. Do you not see what they do in the cities of Judah and in the streets of Jerusalem? The children gather wood, and the fathers kindle the fire, and the women knead the dough, to make cakes to the Queen of Heaven, and to pour out drink-offerings unto other gods, that they may provoke Me. Do they provoke Me? says YHWH; do they not provoke themselves, to their own shame? Therefore thus says the lord YHWH: Behold, My anger and My fury shall be poured out upon this place, upon man, and upon beast, and upon the trees of the field, and upon the fruit of the land; and it shall burn, and shall not be quenched.

This passage accurately reflects the traditional cult of the domicile preserving a dedication to religious ideas that Deuteronomy had earlier attempted to displace (Deut 6:5–9), especially with regard to devotion to "the Queen of Heaven."[33] Yet Deuteronomy nowhere speaks of "the Queen of Heaven"; allusion is made of the illegality of devotion to Asherah, but no details

---

S. Ash, "Jeroboam I and the Deuteronomistic Historian's Ideology of the Founder," *CBQ* 60 (1998): 16–24.

[33] Carr notes, for example, how the emphasis on constant enculturation under Deuteronomic standards was to replace older religious ideas that used the paradigm of family structures (*Tablet of the Heart*, 129–30, 134–5), and this would have included the traditional family-based cults in the domicile and beyond. See Carol L. Meyers, *Househoulds and Holiness: The Religious Culture of Israelite Women* (Minneapolis: Fortress, 2005) 27–56. Susan A. Ackerman also discusses the family-rooted devotion to the "Queen of Heaven" ("At Home with the Goddess," in *Symbiosis, Symbolism, and the Power of the Past* [ed. William G. Dever and Seymour Gitin; Winona Lake, Ind.: Eisenbrauns, 2003], 461–465).

are provided in Deuteronomy regarding the nature of this devotion.[34] Though Jer 7:16–20 does not identify Asherah as the object of devotion, it provides the type of details that Deuteronomy leaves out. Furthermore, it reveals the marginal place of Deuteronomic thought among wide swaths of the population, specifying that the cult to the Queen of Heaven was found in every household. This may be hyperbolic with regard to every" household, but it indicates the popularity of these praxes.

Many scholars attempt to identify the Queen of Heaven with a particular Judahite goddess based on the details contained in Jer 7:16–20 and its "companion" text, Jer 44:15–19.[35] However, the ambiguity regarding the identity of the Queen of Heaven is a deliberate rhetorical strategy, allowing for all variations on the dedication to the numinous female concept (Asherah, Astarte, Tanit, etc.) to fall under the same category of illegitimacy. The critique is thereby applied to all kinship groups preserving their own traditions and variations of the numinous female principle in association with the veneration of the ancestral deity.[36] As a result, the family-based cult is elevated to the level of

---

[34] Deut 7:5 and 12:3 speak of אשריהם ("their *asherim*"); this is suggestive of cult objects related to Asherah worship (see also Deut 16:21) but there lacks in these passages an overt censure of Asherah herself. This, however, may be a deliberate rhetorical strategy in Deuteronomy, which elsewhere engages in "exegetical silence" (to use a term by Levinson, *Deuteronomy*, 126) where older norms are to be eradicated from the discourse altogether. Once we dig beneath the text's rhetorical stratum, the reference to אשריהם should be understood as the outlawing of the cult of Asherah. For a detailed discussion of the biblical references to the Asherah symbol in relation to the goddess, see Mark S. Smith, *The Early History of God: Yahweh and the Other Deities in Ancient Israel* (2d ed.; Grand Rapids: Eerdmans, 2002) 108–18.

[35] Notably, this later text is the climax to the extended criticism of homeland community and the cultic structures intimately bound to ancestral territories; the purpose of this criticism was to eliminate such presuppositions from the ideological vocabulary of the exilic audience. See Leuchter, *Polemics of Exile*, 131–5. For attempts to identify the Queen of Heaven in these verses, see Smith, *The Early History of God*, 127, 182, 197; Ackerman, "At Home with the Goddess," 461–3; Jill Middlemas, *The Troubles of Templeless Judah* (Oxford: Oxford University, 2005), 85–90.

[36] The antiquity of such traditions may be seen in the old layers of Gen 38, which originated as an apology for the hinterland-clan origins of the Davidic line over against the elite urban royal circle in Jerusalem. The tale establishes Tamar as the savior-figure who restores life and fertility to the line of Judah which had otherwise begun to wither; that both David and Absalom name their daughters "Tamar" (2 Sam 13; 2 Sam 14:27) points to an early myth regarding

competing national theology rather than remaining a matter of private religious expression, replaying in a sense the "showdown" between Yahwism and Baalism conducted by Elijah in 1 Kgs 18. Indeed, when the book of Jeremiah criticizes the Judahite public, it is a charge of Baalism that is most often leveled; the book expands the parameters of the charge of Baalism to include any practice or concept that conflict with what the authors (Jeremiah or those who wrote in his name) adapt from Deuteronomy.[37] Possible areas of conflict include, for example, political alliances, improper veneration of written or oral traditions, the preservation of outdated iconography, and misguided ritual practices—all of these things become "Baal" in the Jeremianic corpus, and thus intolerable.[38]

The family cult in all of its manifestations thereby becomes a target of this critique, whether in the hinterland village or in the palace (and temple) in Jerusalem.[39] The ongoing adherence to traditions rooted in the Davidic/Zion

---

this character as the sacred matron of the Davidic line connected to the old hinterland culture, a culture cut off from royal politics with the rise of Solomon. For Tamar as a numinous figure, see Yoel I. Arbeitman, "Tamar's Name: Or Is It? (Gen 38)," *ZAW* 112 (2000): 341–55; Michael C. Astour, "Tamar the Hierodule: An Essay in the Method of Vestigial Motifs," *JBL* 85 (1966), 185–196. Geographical references and allusions to certain hinterland religious festivals (Jeffrey C. Geoghegan "Israelite Sheepshearing and David's Rise to Power," *Bib* 87 [2006]: 55–63) suggest an origin to the tale sometime before the urbanization policy of Hezekiah (ca. 705–701 BCE) after which many of the locales and religious practices would not have been sustained due to the damage wrought by Sennacherib's campaign of 701.

[37] See especially the discussion by Baruch Halpern, "Brisker Pipes than Poetry: The Development of Monotheism in Ancient Israel," in *Judaic Perspectives on Ancient Israel* (ed. Jacob Neusner et al; Minneapolis: Fortress, 1987), 98–102.

[38] Leuchter, *Josiah's Reform and Jeremiah's Scroll*, 75, 90–91, 100, 139–40.

[39] Jer 7:11 identifies the temple as a מארת פרצים, a "den of thieves," but the wordplay on the Davidic clan ancestor פרץ recognizes the genetic association of the royal family with this structure, a staple of the relationship between royalty and temples in the ancient near east. Victor A. Hurowitz discusses this in detail with respect to Mesopotamian temple construction in *I Have Built You an Exalted House: Temple Building in the Bible in Light of Mesopotamian and Northwest Semitic Writings* (JSOTSup 115; Sheffield: JSOT, 1992), 271–7. See

mythos represents on the royal level the same dysfunction the prophet delineates in Jer 7:16–20 (however stereotyped) within the private domicile. This is especially the case with Jehoiakim and Zedekiah, both of whom retreat into ignoble sacral recesses granted them through the inheritance of the royal office and tolerated due to their antiquity.[40] Jehoiakim reclaims Solomonic norms for himself (including the violent dispatching of dissenting voices, or the threat of such action)[41] and Zedekiah's attempt to secure a peaceful oracle from Jeremiah reveals his delusions regarding the role of the prophetic word as subordinate to the royal covenant.[42] Both of these kings thereby exploit the legacy of the Davidic-Solomonic institutions preserved by the royal family, but the influence of these institutions resonated beyond Jerusalem throughout the hinterland. Regional shrines and family-based religious structures emulated the royal cult and its sanctuaries;[43] a loose symbiosis thus obtained between the state cult and that of the individual domicile or network of domiciles, with families of all types taking their cues from the mores and praxes of the royal line.[44]

It is for this reason that Jer 8:1–3 identifies all typologies aligned with the royal cult as an illegitimate family who will suffer collectively for turning away from the prophet's call to piety:

---

also the presuppositions of Amaziah's castigation in Amos 7:13, where Beth El is identified as a "royal house."

[40] One prominent example of this is Zedekiah's דרור declaration in Jer 34:8–9, which is roundly condemned by the author of the chapter (Mark Leuchter, "The Manumission Laws in Leviticus and Deuteronomy: The Jeremiah Connection," *JBL* 127 [2008]: 640–6).

[41] Leuchter, Josiah's Reform and Jeremiah's Scroll, 174.

[42] This is found in the drama of Jer 37–38, where Zedekiah uses psychological warfare against Jeremiah to secure his desired oracle (A. R. Pete Diamond, "Portraying Prophecy: Of Doubts, Variants, and Analogies in the Narrative Representatives of Jeremiah's Oracles—Reconstructing the Hermeneutics of Prophecy," *JSOT* 57 [1993]: 104–6). The redactors of the book of Jeremiah considered this delusional attempt to subordinate the prophetic word so significant a problem that the tale was told and retold in the doublet found in Jer 21//37. On the creation and function of this doublet, see William M. McKane, "The Construction of Jeremiah Chapter 21," *VT* 32 (1982): 59–73.

[43] Olyan, "Family Religion," 116–7.

[44] This was reinforced, no doubt, by the patrimonial nature of Judahite statecraft beginning in the tenth century BCE and persisting down to the Neo-Babylonian period. See Lawrence E. Stager, "The Patrimonial Kingdom of Solomon," in Dever and Gitin (ed.), *Symbiosis, Symbolism and the Power of the Past*, 63–73.

At that time, says YHWH, they shall bring out the bones of the kings of Judah, and the bones of its princes, and the bones of the priests, and the bones of the prophets, and the bones of the inhabitants of Jerusalem, but of their graves; and they shall spread them before the sun, and the moon, and all the host of heaven, whom they have loved, and whom they have served, and after whom they have walked, and whom they have sought, and whom they have worshipped; they shall not be gathered, nor be buried, they shall be for dung upon the face of the earth. And death shall be chosen rather than life by all the residue that remain of this evil family, that remain in all the places from where I have driven them, says YHWH of hosts.

This oracle is an appropriate finale to a rhetorical unit including a critique of family-based religious practices.[45] It specifies that those who engage in these practices will receive the harshest of all punishments, namely, having their bones removed from their ancestral tombs and thus from their assured place in *Sheol*. Engaging in the family cult results in being cut-off from the family in the afterlife, with no way to commune with living descendants during festivals set aside for the veneration of ancestors. All of this only heightens the significance of the benign attitude shown to Jehoiachin and the deportees of 597, who were separated from these festivals through the conditions of exile and who faced the prospect of death without interment in the ancestral tombs.

The paradox is obvious: those who indulge in traditional family-based praxes will be cursed to have their remains strewn out in the open, but those who are removed from family-based cultic institutions—by choice or otherwise—receive blessing despite sharing the same basic fate of separation from the family tomb. The implication is that the family cult and afterlife scenarios may possess potency (why otherwise would the threat of Jer 8:1–3 be lodged?) and one may sustain them and adhere to them, but they are alien to proper Israelite religious experience and identity. In essence, to maintain the family cult is to opt out of Israelite religion. Though the book of Jeremiah treats seriously the threat of non-burial in a variety of places,[46] bigger issues are addressed in light of a

---

[45] W. Boyd Barrick considers this oracle against the historical background of Josiah's reform and suggests that it preserves memories of temporally proximate events that would resonate in public memory (*The Kings and the Cemeteries: Toward a New Understanding of Josiah's Reform* [VTSup 88; Leiden: Brill, 2002], 164).

[46] This is especially the case in Jer 26 and 36, which frame a major unit of discourse within the book; see Kathleen M. O'Connor, "'Do Not Trim a Word': The Contribution of Chapter 26 to the Book of Jeremiah," *CBQ* 51 (1989): 625–

developing theology of the sixth century BCE. For example, Jer 24:5–7 develops the same line of though as Deut 5:2–3, where the matter of the ancestral covenant is no longer at the center of religious thought and with it, the family cult: Jehoiachin and Zedekiah, both of the same family, obviously do not share in the same covenantal fate. Here, then, the parenetic material in Jer 24 is rightfully "Deuteronomistic" in general theological outlook, as a legitimate collective ideology and standard of communal identity is proposed as a replacement for older models.[47] But there is a significant break between the rhetoric of Jeremiah and the contents of Deuteronomy with regard to cultic matters that present difficulties in identifying Jer 24 and other prose passages in the book as simply a subset of Deuteronomic discourse, as demonstrated below.

THE DEUTERONOMIC CULT

In a way, the (traditional) Levitical and royal/family cults are expected targets within the book of Jeremiah, as the Deuteronomic ideology informing Jeremiah itself redefines Levitical and royal/family tradition. What is surprising is that despite this, the Deuteronomic cult is itself subjected to a significant critique. Deuteronomy, of course, is relatively unconcerned with the cult when compared with the P and non-P traditions in the Pentateuch dealing with the particulars of ritual, priesthood, and sacrifice. But whatever cultic concerns Deuteronomy does emphasize are significantly dismantled (and periodically redefined) within the Jeremianic corpus. The outstanding example of this is to be found in the Temple Sermon (Jer 7:[1–2]3–15), where the prophet brazenly calls out the pretentions of the temple establishment that must have obtained by the late pre-exilic period among the pious of Jerusalem. It is often assumed that this Temple Sermon is part of a Jeremianic complaint against the very idea of a temple in the religion of Judah, but this is not the case. In the debate with Hananiah (see below), tacit support of the temple infrastructure is voiced (Jer 28:6). Moreover, it would have been self-defeating to completely invalidate the legitimacy of the temple with the central importance of Deut 12 to the account of Josiah's reform (and

---

7; J. Andrew Dearman "My Servants the Scribes: Composition and Context in Jeremiah 36" *JBL* 109 (1990): 409. On interment in Israelite thought, see Saul M. Olyan, "Some Neglected Aspects of Israelite Interment Ideology," *JBL* 124 (2005): 601–16.

[47] Levinson discusses Deuteronomy's replacement of these antecedent traditions (*Deuteronomy*, 144–51).

one that Jeremiah is presented as supporting),[48] as this would have compromised the viability of Deuteronomic discourse in general as the basis for the other oracles in the book.

Recognizing this, the author of the Temple Sermon adopts a more subtle and ultimately more effective rhetorical strategy. The temple is not invalidated, but the cult identifying it as the substance of YHWH's covenant itself is dismantled. The Temple Sermon retains the concept of the temple as a sacred place, but redefines the very idea of what constitutes a sacred place; it is no longer a locale governed by sacrifice or the sacrificial calendar, as these receive no mention whatsoever in the Sermon. The notion of a מקום as a dwelling-place remains (Jer 7:3), but not as the locus of a divine hypostasis. Instead, it appears as a symbolic home for the people (ואשכנה אתכם—"and I will cause you to dwell"). The conditions under which the temple may retain this role are primarily a social and ethical matter, as evident in Jer 7:5–6: "But if you thoroughly amend your ways and doings; if you thoroughly execute justice between a man and his neighbor; if you do not oppress the stranger, the fatherless, and the widow, and do not shed innocent blood in this place[49] or go after other gods to your detriment...."

The temple is still connected, then, to the central principles of Deuteronomy, and like the repeated refrain found in that book, it is the cornerstone of ongoing life in the land. But unlike Deut 12, where the temple *cult* anchors surrounding hinterland life, the Temple Sermon suggests that the temple in Jerusalem fills this role as a symbolic locus of social and ethical values. The delivery of the Temple Sermon exemplifies this, as its proclamation within the temple precincts redefines the purpose of the sacred space in question, and the sermon is addressed to a broad audience warned not to trust in delusional ritual formulae (Jer 7:4, 8). Indeed, the temple is ultimately revealed to be equivalent—not superior—to any other structure or local, as the term מקום which was once reserved for the temple is now applied to the entire land (Jer 7:7).[50]

---

[48] Ergo the early stratum of the oracles in Jer 30–31 discussed above, which appear to support the aims of the Josianic reform and that king's designs on the northern population(s). See Sweeney, *King Josiah*, 232–233.

[49] Thus far in the Sermon the מקום is expectedly the Temple, though the semantic range of this term is expanded in the following verse in an emphatic manner; see the ensuing discussion.

[50] This, too, follows a decidedly Deuteronomic impulse, as Deuteronomy presents the king not as hierarchically superior in any way but, rather, as

But the critique of the Deuteronomic "cult" does not end with the redefinition of the practical and symbolic purposes of the temple. The book of Jeremiah presents consistent challenges to the temple faculty in sharp distinction from the conditions that obtained during the reign of Josiah.[51] Though Deuteronomy specifies a place for a single Mosaic prophet during the Josianic period (Deut 18:15–18), several passages in both Kings and Jeremiah suggest that several prophets worked under the aegis of the central establishment and engaged populations in the outlying regions as advocates of Deuteronomic policy and ideology.[52] Jeremiah himself appears to have had such a role in relation to his own kinship group and in relation to the northern populations more generally, and other figures within the book of Jeremiah possess characteristics that suggest that they once held a similar role.[53] Yet the authors of the book of Jeremiah are almost entirely unforgiving or unsupportive of these other prophetic figures, none of whom advocate the worship of deities other than YHWH or who suggest ritual traditions that counter the Deuteronomic tradition.[54] The example of Hananiah (Jer 28) stands out most dramatically in this regard. Hananiah is obviously revealed to be inaccurate in his reading of history and in his predictive abilities, and this is generally regarded as a prime example of Deut 18:21–22 in action.[55] However—the vicissitudes of history aside—there is nothing particularly anti- or non-Deuteronomic about Hananiah's

---

symbolic of all Israelites in his prescribed submission to the law (Deut 17:15, 18–20). See Berman, *Created Equal*, 60–61.

[51] I assume here, with many scholars, that Deuteronomy is primarily a Josianic-era composition.

[52] Leuchter, "The 'Prophets' and the 'Levites,'" 36–44.

[53] Ibid.

[54] Compare this to the presentation of "enemy" prophets in Deut 13:2–6. This passage is cast as the anti-type to the legitimate prophetic typology in Deut 18:15–22 by virtue of the inclusio formed by these two passages; see Jack R. Lundbom, "The Inclusio and Other Framing Devices in Deuteronomy 1–28," *VT* 46 (1996): 309–312.

[55] The relationship between this episode and Deut 18:21–22, however, is very complex, and it is difficult to determine whether or not Jer 28 spawned the Deuteronomic passage or vice versa. For a full discussion of this literary inter-relationship, see Carolyn J. Sharp, *Prophecy and Ideology in Jeremiah: Struggles for Authority in the Deutero-Jeremianic Prose* (New York: T&T Clark, 2003), 152–153. One indication that Deut 18:21–22 may well have been added to the rest of the chapter at a subsequent stage (and thus perhaps in response to Jer 28) is that the lexemes of Deut 18:20 (ומת הנביא ההוא) reverse those initiated in Deut 13:6 (... יומת הנביא ההוא) thus closing the *inclusio* initiated in the latter (Lundbom, "The Inclusio," 309–12).

words, and viewing him as a non-Deuteronomic prophet is therefore problematic. The book's opposition to Hananiah and the other prophets in Jer 27–29 is similar to its opposition to what it considers misconceptions regarding the temple: these prophets are too tightly connected to Deuteronomic understandings of the central sanctuary's cult as the lifeblood of the covenant. This is not to be confused with allegiance to the royal court; Hananiah does speak of the return of Jehoiachin from exile, but more important for him is the independence of the temple and its cult from foreign influence, an important concept encoded within Deuteronomy.[56] Hananiah's rhetorical choices in Jer 28:2–4 reveal his interests in this regard:

> Thus says YHWH of hosts, the God of Israel, saying: I have broken the yoke of the king of Babylon (על מלך בבל) Within two full years will I bring back into this place (המקום הזה) all the vessels of the house of YHWH, that Nebuchadnezzar king of Babylon took away from this place (המקום הזה), and carried them to Babylon; and I will bring back to this place (המקום הזה) Jeconiah the son of Jehoiakim, king of Judah, with all the captives of Judah, that went to Babylon, says YHWH; For I will break the yoke of the king of Babylon (על מלך בבל)

The dominant role of Babylon (על מלך בבל) is kept at the margins of Hananiah's discourse, while the temple (המקום הזה) remains the central category, with cult icons and royal figures both subordinated to it.[57] Hananiah is no "court prophet" on the royal payroll but instead supports the Deuteronomic concept of the independent cultic establishment as the basis for the national character. By contrast, the מקום terminology used in opposition to Babylon by Hananiah is

---

[56] Richard H. Lowery identifies this anti-imperialist theme in Deuteronomy; see his *The Reforming Kings: Cults and Society in First Temple Judah* (JSOTSup 120; Sheffield: JSOT, 1991), 151–5. Lowery ascribes the ideology enshrined in the passages he examines to the Hezekian period, though it is just as likely that it derives from a Josianic context as a response to residual impulses for allegiance to Assyria.

[57] Leslie C. Allen notes the structural features of this unit (*Jeremiah: A Commentary* [OTL; Louisville: Westminster John Knox, 2008], 316), though the marginal placement of בבל על מלך is not addressed. Within the context of the larger book of Jeremiah, however, the structure pulls double-duty; Hananiah keeps Babylon's power at the margins, but the reader—knowing the events of 587—invariably recognizes that the force of Hananiah's hopeful oracle is doomed to unfold in an unfortunate manner within the context of Babylon's dominance.

taken up by Jeremiah and applied to Babylon itself in various oracles, and the book further highlights other locales where binding prophecy is declared, applied, or preserved.[58] Jeremiah himself is the prophetic agent in some of these cases; in others, the agents of prophecy are Jeremiah's scribal supporters (e.g., Jer 51:59–64). But the essential message of the book regarding prophecy is that while it is to be guided by Deuteronomic principles, it is not an intrinsic part of the Deuteronomic "cult." Since the book of Deuteronomy is itself presented as a prophetic utterance from Moses, the implication is that Deuteronomy may propose a cultic macrostructure but, in the end, must transcend it along with the prophets licensed to preserve and contribute to its stream of tradition.[59]

CONCLUSION

The book of Jeremiah creates a discourse that diminishes the cult of exterior objects, rituals, and social structures[60] and promotes an alternative cult—that of the prophetic personality, where this literary *persona* forms the authoritative basis for norms of devotion above and beyond older standards and praxes. The figure of Jeremiah stands in isolation from and in opposition to all previous categories of religious practice and experience, even as he draws from these categories in offering the oracles that take them to task. This must be seen in distinction from other major prophets such as Isaiah and Ezekiel, both of whom offer harsh criticism of national religious institutions but who base their oracles upon the unwavering legitimacy of particular ancient traditions (the Zion tradition for Isaiah; the Zadokite tradition for Ezekiel). By contrast, Jeremiah's rhetoric dismantles all dominant cultic and theological traditions from the pre-exilic period, orchestrating the remnants of these thought structures into an ideology and foundation for belief in which the sanctity of older institutions are affirmed as the basis for discourse and yet persistently challenged. This would be especially potent during the period of the Babylonian exile, when the exilic audience was divested of any cultic bastions—royal, Levitical, Deuteronomic, or family-based—from which a sense of order and security could be derived. As a result, the personality of Jeremiah emerging from the book bearing his name becomes a theological, social, historical, and didactic symbol to which exiled

---

[58] Mark Leuchter, "The Temple Sermon and the term מקום in the Jeremianic Corpus," *JSOT* 30 (2005): 107–109.

[59] Here, Sharp's observations about the reciprocal literary/hermeneutical relationship between Jeremiah and Deuteronomy are of paramount significance, as the former provides bases for evaluating or re-evaluating the purpose, scope, and applicability of the latter (*Prophecy and Ideology*, 152–3).

[60] So also Halpern, "Brisker Pipes," 101–2.

Judahites could look as a model of faith and behavior during times of uncertainty.[61]

The impact of Jeremiah was clearly felt in the Persian period, with the prophet and his oracles making appearances in both Ezra-Nehemiah and Chronicles in order to advance the rhetorical aims of those works.[62] But the cult of personality emerging in the book of Jeremiah informs the rhetorical topography of other works from the exilic and post-exilic periods. The most prominent example of this is the eventual creation of the Pentateuch as the Torah of Moses, with its diverse contents all falling under the category of Mosaic teaching and Moses himself outshining all other typologies alluded to within (and beyond!) the work (Deut 34:10–12).[63] The evolution of Israelite religion into Judaism was invariably aided by the cult of personality, as older traditions once fused to distinct lineages and socio-political factions were subsumed within these personality types. They, in turn, established a sacred history which superseded the role and memory of social types and institutions no longer suited for the complexities of a largely Diasporatic Jewish world. As a result, texts like Jeremiah and the Pentateuch ensured the submergence of once-atomistic traditions of religious thought and practice into a larger ideological matrix that could transcend international borders and ensure that dispersed communities could persevere as a unified religious community.

---

[61] This is facilitated by the subsuming of the material in Jer 26–45 within the "words of Jeremiah" *inclusio* in Jer 1:1/51:64, thus hermeneutically providing a major unit of exilic discourse with a Jeremianic pedigree; Leuchter, *Polemics of Exile*, 146–7.

[62] Ezra 1:1; 2 Chr 35:25; 36:22–23. On Jeremiah's symbolic role in Chronicles and Ezra–Nehemiah, see Leuchter, "The 'Prophets' and the 'Levites,'" 34–36. The connections between Jer 34 and Neh 5 are discussed by Simeon Chavel, "'Let My People Go!': Emancipation, Revelation and Scribal Activity in Jeremiah 34:8–11," *JSOT* 76 (1997): 93–95, and Ezra 9:11/Jer 2:7;16:18 and Ezra 9:12/Jer 29:6–7.

[63] Konrad Schmid, "The Late Persian Formation of the Torah: Observations on Deuteronomy 34," in *Judah and Judeans in the Fourth Century B.C.E.* (ed. Oded Lipschits, Gary N. Knoppers and Rainer Albertz; Winona Lake, Ind.: Eisenbrauns, 2007), 244–7. One might also see this feature at work in the midrashic ascription of the entirety of various Biblical books to specific authors, e.g., Samuel, Joshua, David, etc. (*Baba Bathra* 14b–15a).

ZEPHANIAH
How This Book Became Prophecy

Christoph Levin

WRITTEN PROPHECY CAME INTO BEING BY "FORTSCHREIBUNG"

The book of Zephaniah, and the first part of it (Zeph 1:1–2:3) in particular, forms a good example of the possibility that a prophetic tradition did not start with the preaching of an individual prophet in a particular historical setting, but that prophecy came into being only in course of the literary growth of a writing, which—moreover—was at first non-prophetic.

Though no more than fifty-three masoretic verses in length, the book reads as an extremely heterogeneous composition. Prophetic speech and divine speech change frequently, and with no obvious reason. There is also a sudden change of addressees, and the themes of the book vary greatly—"a rather remarkable package for so brief a book."[1]

Usually the literary nature of the book is explained as being a collection of short prophetic sayings, composed by the pupils of the prophet or by later editors. The text is seen as built on individual units, comparable to collections like the book of Proverbs or a law-book like the Covenant Code. In collections of proverbs or of law, each short literary unit has its own independent origin. According to this view unity is lacking because the literary entities stem from different situations and from different times addressed by the prophet. If the collection shows a meaningful order (which may be lacking), this is put down to secondary arrangement. However, this model does not fit in explaining the

---

[1] David L. Petersen, *The Prophetic Literature: An Introduction* (Louisville: Westminster John Knox, 2002), 205.

composition of most prophetic books, because the single sayings are closely interwoven.

Recent exegetical research on the book of Zephaniah still holds to a process of three steps: (1) collecting and (2) editing/composing and (3) commenting/ annotating. This is true of the studies of Guy Langohr,[2] the comprehensive investigation of Hubert Irsigler,[3] the literary-historical and form-critical outline of the book by Klaus Seybold,[4] and the thorough study by Ehud Ben Zvi, who concludes: "There is a compositional level, several units that reflect pre-compositional material, and a few additions that are likely to be post-compositional."[5] In this way Seybold, taking up the investigations of Langohr and Irsigler, counts fourteen to fifteen pre-compositional prophetic sayings within the book.[6] For Lothar Perlitt it is a matter of course that "at the beginning of the tradition that was collected under the name of Zephaniah there were sayings of YHWH that this man had received and put into words."[7]

On the other hand, in the book of Zephaniah (as in most prophetic books), many of the individual literary entities are closely linked with each other.

---

[2] Guy Langohr, "Le livre de Sophonie et la critique d'autenticité," *ETL* 52 (1976): 1–27; idem, "Rédaction et composition du livre de Sophonie," *Museon* 89 (1976): 51–73.

[3] Hubert Irsigler, *Gottesgericht und Jahwetag: Die Komposition Zef 1,1– 2,3, untersucht auf der Grundlage der Literarkritik des Zefanjabuches* (Arbeiten zu Text und Sprache im Alten Testament 3; St. Ottilien: EOS, 1977).

[4] Klaus Seybold, *Satirische Prophetie: Studien zum Buch Zefanja* (SBS 120; Stuttgart: Katholisches Bibelwerk, 1985).

[5] Ehud Ben Zvi, *A Historical-Critical Study of the Book of Zephaniah* (BZAW 198; Berlin: de Gruyter, 1991), 347. Marvin A. Sweeney, *Zephaniah: A Commentary* (Hermeneia; Minneapolis: Fortress, 2003), 2, holds the same view, underlining "that the present form of the book is the product of extensive exilic or postexilic redaction, which added a great deal of material concerned with worldwide eschatological punishment and salvation in an effort to transform the book from one concerned only with the fate of Jerusalem and Judah in the days of king Josiah to one concerned with the fate of the entire world in the Second Temple period and beyond." See also the most recent investigation by Jakob Wöhrle, *Die frühen Sammlungen des Zwölfprophetenbuches: Entstehung und Komposition* (BZAW 360; Berlin: de Gruyter, 2006): (1) Pre–Deuteronomistic stock dating from the seventh century; (2) Deuteronomistic Edition; (3) late additions.

[6] *Satirische Prophetie*, 83. See also his translation of "the poems of Zephaniah," 109–12.

[7] Lothar Perlitt, *Die Propheten Nahum, Habakuk, Zephanja* (ATD 25/1; Göttingen: Vandenhoeck & Ruprecht, 2004), 97.

Sayings frequently react to their literary context in one way or another. There are in fact only a few sayings which can be read as independent units. This observation might be explained in two ways: the one is that the editors reshaped the sayings that came into their hands to put them into their present context; the other is that most of the sayings grew out of the written stock of the book step by step and were written *ad hoc* in regard to their literary context. The first possibility would mean nothing less than that the editors altered the word of God as transmitted by the prophet. This is highly improbable, because in this case the editors would have spoiled the real basis of their work. In fact, form-criticism differentiates between transmitted sayings secondarily framed for their context, and sayings written for their context. The latter are much more frequent. In prophetic books it is even the rule. Walther Zimmerli aptly called this phenomenon *Fortschreibung*, that is "a process of successive development of a kernel element, which has been developed further in new additions at a somewhat later time."[8] Zimmerli gained his insights from the book of Ezekiel. However, it is the same as William McKane and Robert Carroll observed in the book of Jeremiah as the "rolling corpus" or "snowball" effect.[9]

If most of the sayings are editorial in this way, we have to look for a nucleus from which the *Fortschreibungen* could have advanced. Most scholars concur that the origin of the book of Zephaniah is to be found in ch. 1, and that chs. 2–3 did not belong to the initial stock. With high probability the oracles to the nations in 2:4–14 and 3:6, 8 as well as the salvation oracles in 3:9–20 are late additions.[10] The same may be true of the sayings against the wicked town in 2:15–3:5, 7, which are interwoven with the oracles against the nations. From this follows a caesura between 2:3 and 2:4.[11] This does not exclude the possibility that 1:1–2:3 contains additions which may be as late as 2:4–3:20 or even later. Additionally, this does not exclude the possibility of literary and/or thematic layers which cover the entire book.

---

[8] See Walther Zimmerli, *Ezekiel: A Commentary on the Book of the Prophet Ezekiel*, Vol. 1 (trans. Ronald E. Clements; Hermeneia; Philadelphia: Fortress, 1979), 69.

[9] William McKane, *A Critical and Exegetical Commentary on Jeremiah*, I–II (ICC; Edinburgh: T&T Clark, 1986 and 1996); Robert P. Carroll, *Jeremiah: A Commentary* (OTL; London: SCM, 1986).

[10] Perlitt, *Nahum, Habakuk, Zephanja*, 132: "I share the insight of Schwally's of 1890, that chapter 3 as a whole 'had its setting in post-exilic times.'" Cf. Friedrich Schwally, "Das Buch Sefanjâ, eine historisch-kritische Untersuchung," *ZAW* 10 (1890): 165–240 (238).

[11] See especially Irsigler, *Gottesgericht und Jahwetag*.

Seven Main Layers in Zeph 1:1–2:3

The literary critical analysis of Zeph 1:1–2:3 uncovers seven main written layers which are marked in the following translation by indentation. There are also many intertextual quotations and allusions which are indicated by *italics*, their origin given in parentheses.[12]

(1) A liturgy for the celebration of the theophany on the Day of YHWH-festival (cf. Hab 2:20; Zech 2:17; Ps 97:2–5; 47:6)
    (2) is interpreted according to Amos 5:18a, bb, 20b as a prophetic threat
        (3) and later used to explain the catastrophe of Jerusalem as predicted (and caused) by YHWH himself: The punishment came because the people and especially the courtiers practised the sin of Manasseh: They behaved as before Josiah's reform.
            (4) They did not serve YHWH alone, and did not expect to be punished by him.
                (5) In the near future the Day of YHWH shall come again in form of a divine judgment on all beings. A cosmic catastrophe like the flood shall be repeated.
                    (6) Other than by the flood in primeval times, no one shall escape,
                        (7) especially not the wicked traders and people like those. But the pious shall survive.
                            (8) Some more additions.

1.1 The word of YHWH that was unto Zephaniah son of Cushi son of Gedaliah son of Amariah son of Hezekiah, *in the days of Josiah son of Amon, king of Judah.* (Jer 1:2)
    2 I will surely sweep away everything *from upon the face of the ground* (Gen 6:7; 7:4), utterance of YHWH. *3* I will sweep away human and animal; I will sweep away the bird of the heavens, and the fish of the sea.
        'I will overthrow'[13] the wicked.

---

[12] The translation follows Sweeney, *Zephaniah*, with a few alterations.
[13] Thus according to the usual emendation וְהִכְשַׁלְתִּי. Having no support by the ancient versions, this reading remains, however, quite unsure. Cf. the discussion by Ben Zvi, *Historical-Critical Study*, 59–60, and by Sweeney, *Zephaniah*, 64.

And I will cut off (v. 4) humanity *from upon the face of the ground, utterance of YHWH.* (v. 2)

4 And I will stretch out my hand against (Jer 51:25; Ezek 6:14; 14:9, 13; 25:13; 35:3) Judah and against all the inhabitants of Jerusalem, *and I will cut off from* (Jer 51:25; Ezek 6:14; 14:9, 13; 25:13; 35:3) this place (cf. Jer 19:3 a.o.) the remnant of *Baal* (cf. 2 Kgs 23:4-5; Jer 19:5 a.o.)

and the name of the *idolatrous priests* (2 Kgs 23:5) [MT + with the priests];

5 and those who prostrate themselves *upon the rooftops to the host of heaven* (Jer 19:13);

and those who prostrate themselves (v. 5a) [who swear] to YHWH and swear by '*Milcom*';[14] (2 Kgs 23:13)

6 and those who turn aside from after YHWH, and who do not seek YHWH and do not inquire of him.

7 Silence! from before my Lord YHWH!

For *the Day of YHWH is near*; (v. 14)

For YHWH has prepared a sacrifice, he has sanctified his invitees.

8 And it shall come to pass on the day of YHWH's *sacrifice* (v. 7), and I shall punish the officers and the sons of the king,

and all who are dressed in foreign attire. *9 And I shall punish* (v. 8) those who leap over the threshold in that day,

who fill the house of their lord with violence and deceit.

10 And it shall come to pass on that day, utterance of YHWH, sound of a cry from the Fish Gate and wailing from the Second Quarter, and a loud crash from the hills.

11 Wail, O inhabitants of the Mortar!

Because all the people of Canaan are destroyed, and all who weigh out silver are cut off.

12 And it shall come to pass at that time, I will search out Jerusalem with lamps, *and I shall punish* (v. 8) the people, those who linger over their wine dregs, who say in their heart, YHWH does no good, and he does no evil. *13* And their wealth *shall become booty* (cf. 2 Kgs 21:14), and their houses desolation,

---

[14] Vocalize בְּמִלְכֹּם instead of בְּמַלְכָּם "by their king."

> *and they shall build houses, but they shall not dwell in them, and they shall plant vineyards, but they shall not drink their wine.* (Amos 5:11)

14 The great Day of YHWH is near! Near and coming very fast.
> The sound of the *Day of YHWH* (v. 14a) is bitter, a warrior cries out there.

15 That day is a day of wrath, a day of distress and stress, a day of destruction and devastation, *a day of darkness and gloom,* (Amos 5:18bβ, 20b)
a day of clouds and thick darkness, *16* a day of trumpet blast and cry
> against the fortified cities and against the high towers.
>> *17* And I shall afflict humankind, and they shall walk like the blind,
>>> because they have sinned against YHWH;
>> and their blood shall be spilled out like dust, and their guts like dung,
>>> *18* Neither their silver nor their gold shall be able to save them on the day of *the wrath of YHWH,* (v. 15)

And by the fire of his jealousy, all the earth shall be consumed because destruction, indeed, sudden devastation, he will make of all the inhabitants of the earth.

> *2:1* Assemble yourselves and gather, O worthless nation,[15] *2* before bearing a statute, like chaff a day has passed,[16]
>> *before there comes upon you* the angry *wrath of YHWH,* (v. 2bβ)
> before there comes upon you *the day of the wrath of YHWH.* (v. 3)
> *3* Seek YHWH, all you humble of the land who have done his law. Seek righteousness; seek humility; perhaps you will be hidden *in the day of the wrath of YHWH.* (1:18)

---

[15] Julius Wellhausen, *Die kleinen Propheten* (4th ed.; Berlin: de Gruyter, 1963), 152, comments on 2:1: "The wording is not transmitted in a trustworthy state; in any case it cannot to be understood."

[16] The reading of v. 2a is difficult, see Sweeney, *Zephaniah,* 110.

THE BOOK'S SUPERSCRIPTION (ZEPH 1:1)

The superscription of the book is obviously editorial. This makes it doubtful whether the information the editors gave may rely on real memory. The definition of prophecy as "word of YHWH" represents a theological concept that was developed in late exilic times only.[17] With high probability the dating to the time of King Josiah is secondary, for it is identical with one of the dates given—additionally—to the book of Jeremiah (Jer 1:2aβ).[18] We therefore cannot exclude that the dating of Zephaniah's prophecy is an editorial conclusion which grew out of the comparison with the edited form of the book of Jeremiah. Nevertheless the similarities of the book of Zephaniah to the book of Ezekiel and to the Book of the Twelve are even more obvious.

The prophet's person is only mentioned in the superscription. Elsewhere in the Old Testament the name Zephaniah can be found twice, both among the people around Jeremiah. The second priest according to 2 Kgs 25:18 is called Zephaniah, as well as the priest Zephaniah son of Maaseiah according to Jer 21:1; 29:25, 29; 37:3. The prophet's father Cushi shares his name with Ebed-melech, the man who saved Jeremiah from the cistern, for whom it is used as gentilicium (Jer 38:7, 10, 12; 39:16). According to Jer 36:14, a man called Jehudi son of Nethaniah son of Shelemiah son of Cushi read Baruch's scroll to King Jehoiakim. The name of Zephaniah's grandfather Gedaliah son of Amariah recalls the name of Gedaliah son of Ahikam Jer 39:14, and the name of Gedaliah son of Pashhur Jer 38:1. Surprisingly enough the chain of forefathers is pursued back four steps to a man called Hezekiah. It is not improbable that this person is to be identified by the reader with the king of that name. In this case the prophet's genealogy forms a kind of bridge between the two alleged reforms of King Hezekiah on the one hand and of King Josiah on the other. The chain of

---

[17] See Christoph Levin, "The 'Word of Yhwh': A Theological Concept in the Book of Jeremiah," in *Prophets, Prophecy, and Prophetic Texts in Second Temple Judaism* (ed. Michael H. Floyd and Robert D. Haak; LHBOTS 427; New York: T&T Clark, 2006), 42–62.

[18] See Christoph Levin, "Noch einmal: Die Anfänge des Propheten Jeremia," *VT* 31 (1981): 428–40 (430–1); repr. in idem, *Fortschreibungen: Gesammelte Studien zum Alten Testament* (BZAW 316; Berlin: de Gruyter, 2003), 217–26 (218–9). The idea that Jeremiah prepared for King Josiah's reform seemed reasonable in later times. However it causes problems in regard to the coherence of the prophet's message. Moreover, after his early preaching he must have fallen for decades into a "prophetic hibernation."

ancestors also prevents identifying the prophet with the Cushites, which are threatened in 2:12.

It is a matter of course that in the Old Testament the mentioning of names does not guarantee historicity.[19] All observations make it highly probable that the superscription of the book of Zephaniah is composed by inner-biblical combination. We may therefore conclude that the book was first transmitted as an anonymous and undated writing. We better read it as a pseudepigraphon. "The book does not claim to be the work of its author; ... The individuality of the author is simply ignored."[20] In any case we are bound by methodological reasons to get the historical coordinates from the content of the book only, not from external evidence—the superscription being always external to some degree.

THE PRESENT BOOK'S MOTTO (ZEPH 1:2–3)

After the superscription the book starts with kind of a motto: "I will surely sweep away everything (כֹּל) from upon the face of the ground, utterance of YHWH."[21] It is common that the Hebrew expression מֵעַל פְּנֵי הָאֲדָמָה "from the face of the ground" is to be understood as an allusion to the story of the flood in its Yahwistic version (see Gen 6:7; 7:4).[22] Though relating to the future, this is no prophecy, but an exegetical hint at the flood story of the book of Genesis. It reads as a repetition of YHWH's prologue to the flood (Gen 6:5–8). Repeated for the future, the memory of primeval times becomes an eschatological vision. This is emphasized by the details: it is "everything" (כֹּל), that should be swept away. In late postexilic times the expectation that the flood of primeval days

---

[19] Otherwise the book of Chronicles would be historically more reliable than the book of Kings, and the book of Numbers would be one of the best sources for the early history of Israel—which is obviously not the case.

[20] Ben Zvi, *Historical-Critical Study*, 347.

[21] A motto of this kind was also applied to the book of Amos; see Amos 1:2. It is secondary as well, anticipating Amos 3:4, 8.

[22] This is all the more true as the use of אֲדָמָה "ground" in the sense of אֶרֶץ "earth" is peculiar to the language of the Yahwistic editor, cf. Christoph Levin, *Der Jahwist* (FRLANT 157; Göttingen: Vandenhoeck & Ruprecht, 1993), 399–400. Instances such as Exod 32:12; 33:16; Num 12:3; Deut 6:15; 7:6; 14:2; 2 Sam 14:7; 1 Kgs 13:34; Isa 23:17; Jer 25:26; 28:16; Ezek 38:20; Amos 9:8; Zeph 1:2–3 depend on the Yahwist. Seybold, *Satirische Prophetie*, 23, seeks to save the saying for the prophet: "It is Zephaniah's own soil ... on which the harvest begins." This is an obvious mistake.

shall come again at the end of history was wide spread.²³ The motto turns the book of Zephaniah into an eschatological writing.

The reference to Genesis 6–8 becomes even clearer in the second line of the saying: "I will sweep away human and animal; I will sweep away the bird of the heavens, and the fish of the sea." The expression אָדָם וּבְהֵמָה "human and animal" is a reminder of the fate all beings suffered from the flood (Gen 6:7; 7:23). "Bird" and "fish" which are explicitly mentioned are those who could escape the former flood. In the cosmic catastrophe to come no one shall be saved. The devastation shall be comprehensive. The same idea is added also in Hos 4:3 for to give the book of Hosea an eschatological focus: "Therefore, the land mourns and all who dwell in it languish [including the beasts of the field and the bird of the heavens {and even the fish of the sea are swept away}]."²⁴

The saying was later expanded by v. 3b, as is to be seen from the resumptive repetition מֵעַל פְּנֵי הָאֲדָמָה נְאֻם־יְהוָה "from upon the face of the ground, utterance of YHWH." The verb וְהִכְרַתִּי "and I will cut off" is probably taken from v. 4. The reason for the expansion may have been to limit the punishment to humankind only—i.e., to correct the threat of vv. 2–3aα—because only humankind is able to be guilty. If God punishes the beast, he would be unjust. Again the tradition of the flood is altered, this time the opposite way as before. In v. 3aα the beasts have been explicitly included into the catastrophe, in v. 3b they are saved from punishment. The emphasis on humankind is also to be found in v. 17aα, b.

Verse 3aβ forms a still later expansion, missing in some part of the Greek textual tradition. "The phrase והמכשלות את־הרשעים is commonly considered a gloss."²⁵ Now the final judgment is restricted to the impious: "I will overthrow [txt. em.] the wicked." The same idea is to be found in v. 6 and v. 17aβ. In contrast the pious shall get the chance to escape punishment, see 2:3.

---

²³ Cf. Hermann Gunkel, *Creation and Chaos in the Primeval Era and the Eschaton: A Religio-historical Study of Genesis 1 and Revelation 12* (1895; trans. K. William Whitney, Jr.; The Biblical Resource Series; Grand Rapids: Eerdmans, 2006).

²⁴ Cf. Jörg Jeremias, *Der Prophet Hosea* (ATD 24/1; Göttingen: Vandenhoeck & Ruprecht, 1983), 62–63 (with reference also to Amos 8:8; 9:5); Gale A. Yee, *Composition and Tradition in the Book of Hosea* (SBLDS 102; Atlanta: Scholars Press, 1987), 142–4. Hos 4:3b may be copied from Zeph 1:3aα.

²⁵ Ben Zvi, *Historical-Critical Study*, 58. For the reading see above note 13.

The Sin of Manasseh (Zeph 1:4-6)

The next unit, 1:4–6 is related to the superscription of the book. This again supports that vv. 2–3 is a later insertion. The sin described in these verses mirrors the situation just before the cultic reform of King Josiah as it is told in 2 Kings 23. Moreover, the matter of the polemics is similar to the sermon, which the editors of the book of Jeremiah inserted into the symbolic action with the broken flask in Jer 19.[26] A closer look however shows that the language of the prophetic threat is that of the book of Ezekiel. The two phrases: וְנָטִיתִי יָדִי עַל "and I will stretch out my hand against ..." (Ezek 6:14; 14:9, 13; 16:27; 25:7, 13; 35:3) and וְהִכְרַתִּי מִן "and I will cut off from ..." (Ezek 14:8, 13, 17; 21:8, 9; 25:7, 13; 29:8; 35:7) are frequent in this book. Since the phrases occur in Zephaniah only once, it is obvious that the book of Zephaniah borrowed from the book of Ezekiel, and not vice versa.[27] According to Ezek 1:1–2, the prophet's preaching began in 593, i.e., sixteen years after Josiah's death in 609, and twenty-nine years after his alleged reform in 622.

Some of the details mentioned in vv. 4–5 are quoted from or at least alluded to Jer 19 and 2 Kgs 23.[28] This is true for "the remnant of Baal" (שְׁאָר הַבַּעַל), i.e. the worshippers of the deity who remained after Josiah had destroyed its cult (v. 4bα, cf. 2 Kgs 23:4–5; Jer 19:5). This is true as well of the cult of the host of heavens celebrated on the roofs (v. 5a) which is elsewhere told of in Jer 19:13 exclusively.[29] The emphasis on "this place" (הַמָּקוֹם הַזֶּה) also reminds on Jer 19 (vv. 3–7, 12). It is significant that King Manasseh was accused for the cult of Baal as well as of the host of heavens (2 Kgs 21:3). For the theologians at the second temple who conceived the reform of Josiah as the return to the exclusive worship of YHWH, the sin of Manasseh counted for the main reason why YHWH nevertheless let Jerusalem to be conquered by Nebuchadnezzar (2 Kgs 21:11-12; 23:26; 24:3; Jer 15:4). Zephaniah 1:4–5 maintains that the people of Jerusalem continued sinning like Manasseh contrary to Josiah's reform. The related texts should not be read as announcement of coming punishment; they are intended to show YHWH's justice in history.

---

[26] This editorial insertion was first observed by Friedrich Giesebrecht, *Das Buch Jeremia* (HK III 2,1; Göttingen: Vandenhoeck & Ruprecht, 1894), 108–11. Cf. Carroll, *Jeremiah*, 386.

[27] The saying starts with a perfect consecutive וְנָטִיתִי. This is because of the quotation.

[28] Cf. Levin, "Anfänge des Propheten Jeremia," 224–6.

[29] The only further parallel Jer 32:29 is quoting Jer 19:13. 2 Kgs 23:12 tells of altars on the roof without mentioning the deity to whom the cult was addressed.

Later the catalogue of idolatrous details was enlarged in v. 4bβ. The false priests (הַכְּמָרִים) are added from 2 Kgs 23:5. It is their name (שֵׁם), i.e., the memory of them, which shall be destroyed—because they themselves have already been deposed by Josiah. In the Hebrew textual tradition the rare noun[30] was later explained by הַכֹּהֲנִים "priests." In v. 5b those who worship YHWH as well as the Milcom (txt. em.)—taken from 2 Kgs 23:13—have been added to those who worship the host of heavens. The supplement is easily recognized by the repeated catchword וְאֶת־הַמִּשְׁתַּחֲוִים "and those who prostrate themselves"[31] from v. 5a.

In v. 6, which belongs to the latest textual layer, the people practising idolatry are identified with the apostates who do not seek for YHWH, i.e., the members of the Jewish community who do not participate in the temple cult of Jerusalem and not strictly follow the will of God. The different origin of this verse is to be seen from the fact that divine speech changes into speech about YHWH.[32] The verse mirrors the conflicts the pious fought with the un-pious in late Persian and Hellenistic times under the threat of the coming final judgment. The terminology is that of late piety, see for בִּקֵּשׁ אֶת־יהוה "to seek YHWH" Isa 51:1; Zeph 2:3; Ps 105:3–4 par. 1 Chr 16:10; Prov 28:5, for דָּרַשׁ אֶת־יהוה "to inquire of YHWH" Ps 9:11; 34:11; 105:4 par. 1 Chr 16:11; Ezra 6:21; 1 Chr 22:19; 28:9; 2 Chr 12:14; 14:3, 6; 15:12, 13; 16:12; 20:3; 22:9; 26:5. This addition cannot be earlier than the late Persian era.

THE PROCLAMATION OF THE THEOPHANY (ZEPH 1:7)

In v. 7 we come again upon a sudden change of style:

הַס מִפְּנֵי אֲדֹנָי יְהוִה...
כִּי־הֵכִין יְהוָה זֶבַח הִקְדִּישׁ קְרֻאָיו

Silence! from before my Lord YHWH! ...
For YHWH has prepared a sacrifice; he has sanctified his invitees.

The saying is a liturgical exclamation, with no reference to the threat and the listening of sins in the preceding verses. The double כִּי probably marks an

---

[30] The noun כֹּמֶר is only to be found in 2 Kgs 23:5; Hos 10:5; Zeph 1:4.

[31] This was enlarged and interpreted still later by הַנִּשְׁבָּעִים "who swear," which is anticipated from v. 4bβ. Septuagint avoids the doublet by deleting הַמִּשְׁתַּחֲוִים. The Greek reading is doubtless secondary.

[32] Cf. Bernhard Duhm, *Anmerkungen zu den zwölf Propheten* (Gießen: Töpelmann, 1911), 56.

expansion: The first כִּי phrase כִּי קָרוֹב יוֹם יְהוָה "for the Day of YHWH is near" anticipates v. 14 in order to underline that it is the Day of YHWH that claims for cultic silence.[33] "The call for silence on the one hand and the announcement of the Day of YHWH on the other stem from quite different traditions and are combined this one time only."[34]

The unexpanded form of the saying follows a fixed formula, as can be seen from two close parallels:

הַס כָּל־בָּשָׂר מִפְּנֵי יְהוָה
כִּי נֵעוֹר מִמְּעוֹן קָדְשׁוֹ

Silence, all flesh, from before YHWH;
for he has roused himself from his holy dwelling (Zech 2:17).

And

וַיהוָה בְּהֵיכַל קָדְשׁוֹ
הַס מִפָּנָיו כָּל־הָאָרֶץ

YHWH is in his holy temple;
silence from before him, all the earth! (Hab 2:20).

"The cry הס expresses the normative attitude of human beings before the appearance of YHWH."[35] "No doubt the cultic exclamation ... has its *Sitz* in the cultic service and signals the climax of the worship that is the theophany of the almighty."[36] Surprisingly the two other examples are addressed to "all flesh" / "all the earth" which in reality cannot have been participants in worship. This is in accordance with the fact that in Zech 2:17 and Hab 2:20 the temple is described from outside as "his holy dwelling" / "his holy temple," which would not have been done in the course of the celebration. Therefore Zeph 1:7 seems to be nearest to the original shape of the formula.

The theophany was celebrated by the worshippers with sacrifices, and the invited (cf. Gen 31:54; 1 Sam 9:22; 16:3) had to be consecrated in advance (cf. 1 Sam 9:13; 16:5). The only irregularity in Zeph 1:7 is that YHWH himself is the one who prepares the sacrifices and sanctifies the participants. This is used elsewhere metaphorically to illustrate YHWH's threat against foreign nations (cf. Isa 34:5; Jer 46:10; Ezek 39:17).

Zephaniah 1:7 has often been explained as directed against the Judeans. However the cultic proclamation is obviously no prophetic saying. It is not the prophet's task to call for cultic silence. Exegetes concluded that the prophet

---

[33] See Seybold, *Satirische Prophetie*, 14; Perlitt, *Nahum, Habakuk, Zephanja*, 107.

[34] Perlitt, *Nahum, Habakuk, Zephanja*, 107.

[35] Ben Zvi, *Historical-Critical Study*, 80.

[36] Seybold, *Satirische Prophetie*, 24.

imitated and possibly parodied the cultic exclamation. It is supposed that Zephaniah quoted the liturgy in an ironic manner for to couch his prediction of YHWH's punishment.[37] However the saying is not transmitted within the prophet's preaching, but as part of a (prophetic) book. The irony—if there is any—goes back not to the prophet but to the editors.

WHY THE CATASTROPHE HAS/SHALL COME (ZEPH 1:8–13)

Scholars usually follow the traditional idea about prophetic preaching, and see the verses 1:8–13 as being original at least in part. "People and conditions accused here are so precisely defined that this must have been said by the prophet himself."[38] "If anywhere in the book the prophet himself is speaking, it is in the details of vv. 8–9, 10–11."[39] But this conclusion is circular. It is only based on the content. "The main question is not whether Zephaniah said these words or not, but whether they are secondary additions to an existent text of Zephaniah ..., or compositional devices used to attach a certain unit to an existent text."[40] It is fairly certain from the literary form and the syntax, that all of these verses have been inserted between v. 7 and vv. 14–16.

This can be seen from the connecting formulas וְהָיָה בְּיוֹם זֶבַח יְהוָה "and it shall come to pass on the day of YHWH's sacrifice" (v. 8), בַּיּוֹם הַהוּא "in that day" (v. 9a), וְהָיָה בַיּוֹם הַהוּא נְאֻם־יְהוָה "and it shall come to pass on that day, utterance of YHWH" (v. 10) and וְהָיָה בָּעֵת הַהִיא "and it shall come to pass at that time" (v. 12), which are editorial by nature. It is common to remove these formulas as secondary additions for to get the supposed original shape of the sayings.[41] But this is arbitrary.[42]

---

[37] Cf. Irsigler, *Gottesgericht und Jahwetag*, 284–5; Seybold, *Satirische Prophetie*, 24.

[38] Perlitt, *Nahum, Habakuk, Zephanja*, 108. Because of this view of the text Perlitt, 107, considers 7 to be a later insertion. See already Karl Marti, *Das Dodekapropheton* (KHC 13; Tübingen: Mohr Siebeck, 1904), 363. This is turning the text's growing process upside down.

[39] Perlitt, *Nahum, Habakuk, Zephanja*, 110.

[40] Ben Zvi, *Historical-Critical Study*, 89.

[41] Thus the apparatus in *BHS* by Karl Elliger; Marti, *Dodekapropheton*, 363–4; Duhm, *Anmerkungen*, 56–57; Seybold, *Satirische Prophetie*, 14–15, and many others. Cf. Ben Zvi, *Historical-Critical Study*, 88 with n. 192.

Verse 8 has grown out of v. 7. This is to be seen from the connecting catchword זֶבַח "sacrifice." The verse already presupposes the announcement of the Day of YHWH that was later added in v. 7bα. The cultic exclamation is now focused so as to become a threat against the Judean courtiers. YHWH announces that he will punish them (וּפָקַדְתִּי, v. 8aβ). The reason is to be found in v. 9b, which must have followed immediately: the courtiers have filled their lord's house (בֵּית אֲדֹנֵיהֶם) with violence and deceit. The saying gives the impression to have been proclaimed when the kingdom in Judah still existed. But this is not necessarily so. We should not exclude the possibility that the saying wants to explain why YHWH did not avert the dynasty of the Davidides to break off: not the king (Josiah) himself but his entourage committed the deeds YHWH was not ready to forgive anymore.

Later this saying was split off by vv. 8b–9a. This can be seen from the repetition of וְעַל "and against" and וּפָקַדְתִּי עַל "and I shall punish against" in combination with the connecting formula בַּיּוֹם הַהוּא "in that day." The sin of the courtly upper class is specified: they clothe themselves in foreign (gentile) garments and use superstitious practices.

The first expansion of vv. 8a, 9b is to be found in vv. 12–13a. Again the supplement is marked by the connecting formula וְהָיָה בָּעֵת הַהִיא "and it shall come to pass at that time" in combination with the repetition וּפָקַדְתִּי עַל "and I shall punish against." Again the threat against the inhabitants of Jerusalem is reminiscent of Manasseh, as YHWH announces in 2 Kgs 21:13–14 to punish Jerusalem so that it shall become booty (וְהָיָה לִמְשִׁסָּה). The people sinned because they did not expect that the announcement may become true: YHWH will do nothing. The editor may also have had in mind the coming eschatological judgment, the conquest of Jerusalem providing the model. "The way the wicked are characterized is noteworthy. It is reminiscent of the Psalms and the book of Job."[43]

Much later the threat was expanded by the futility curse v. 13b which is quoted word for word from Amos 5:11. Now the horizon is definitely eschatological as it is in vv. 2–3a. In the book of Amos the curse is directed against the wicked who oppress the pious poor.[44] This is true of the book of Zephaniah also, as can be seen from 1:18aα; 2:3 and 3:12. Verses 10–11 possibly share the level of v. 13b. These two verses certainly came in between later, as

---

[42] See Martin Beck, *Der "Tag Yhwhs" im Dodekapropheton: Studien im Spannungsfeld von Traditions- und Redaktionsgeschichte* (BZAW 356; Berlin: de Gruyter, 2005), 93; Wöhrle, *Die frühen Sammlungen*, 203.

[43] Wellhausen, *Die kleinen Propheten*, 152.

[44] Cf. Christoph Levin, "Das Amosbuch der Anawim," *ZTK* 94 (1997): 407–36 (429), repr. in idem, *Fortschreibungen*, 265–90 (284).

they tear the connection of vv. 8–9 and vv. 12–13a.⁴⁵ The language is borrowed from the book of Jeremiah:⁴⁶ קוֹל צְעָקָה מִשַּׁעַר הַדָּגִים וִילָלָה מִן־הַמִּשְׁנֶה וְשֶׁבֶר גָּדוֹל מֵהַגְּבָעוֹת "Sound of a cry from the Fish Gate and wailing from the Second Quarter, and a loud crash from the hills" (v.10). The saying's model is to be found in Jer 51:54: קוֹל זְעָקָה מִבָּבֶל וְשֶׁבֶר גָּדוֹל מֵאֶרֶץ כַּשְׂדִּים "Sound of a cry from Babylon, and a loud crash from the land of the Chaldeans." The editor of Zeph 1:10–11 applied the threat against the foreign nation to the inhabitants of the merchant's quarter of Jerusalem. See also the threat against Moab in Jer 48:3: קוֹל צְעָקָה מֵחֹרוֹנָיִם שֹׁד וָשֶׁבֶר גָּדוֹל "Sound of a cry from Horonaim, desolation and a loud crash." With these sayings the late editors of the book of Jeremiah adapted the prophet's laments about the enemy from the north (שֶׁבֶר גָּדוֹל "loud crash" Jer 6:1 [4:6]) to the nations, Babylon or Moab. From this it can be seen that the phrase of Zeph 1:10 had its roots in the book of Jeremiah and not in the book of Zephaniah. The topographical details of Jerusalem given here are witnessed in the Persian era only, see for the "second quarter" (הַמִּשְׁנֶה) 2 Kgs 22:14⁴⁷ par. 2 Chr 34:22; Neh 11:9, for the "Fish Gate" (שַׁעַר הַדָּגִים) Neh 3:3; 12:39; 2 Chr 33:14.

THE DAY OF YHWH (ZEPH 1:14–16a)

The original sequence of v. 7 is to be found in v. 14a:

קָרוֹב יוֹם־יְהוָה הַגָּדוֹל
קָרוֹב וּמַהֵר מְאֹד

The great Day of YHWH is near,
near and coming very fast.

Initially this has been the first instance the motive of the Day of YHWH was mentioned, which is so predominant a theme of the present shape of the book.

---

⁴⁵ Wöhrle, *Die frühen Sammlungen*, 203–4, after Langohr, "Le livre de Sophonie," 7–10, and idem, "Rédaction et composition," 57 (who however argued only by the content).

⁴⁶ Cf. Ben Zvi, *Historical-Critical Study*, 105–6.

⁴⁷ The oracle of the prophetess Huldah (2 Kgs 22:12–20) was secondarily inserted into the report about King Josiah, cf. Christoph Levin, "Josia im Deuteronomistischen Geschichtswerk," *ZAW* 96 (1984): 351–71 (364–8); repr. in idem, *Fortschreibungen*, 198–216 (209–13). Its emphasis is on כנע niph. "to humble oneself" which belongs to the favorite theological concepts of the Chronicler.

The text supposes the reader was familiar with what the Day of YHWH was. It tells no more than that the Day of YHWH is great and impending. Whether this is a cause of fear or of joy remains open. גָּדוֹל "great" could also be a positive attribute. Taken the connection with v. 7, we may understand the Day of YHWH as the given date of YHWH's sacrifice mentioned there. From this follows that the Day of YHWH was an important date in the cultic calendar, probably a regular event; and of course this event can only have been a positive one, very much in contrast to the meaning developed in the book of Zephaniah as it reads today.

We know from the book of Amos that the Israelites originally desired for the Day of YHWH as a positive event. In Amos 5:18–20 there is a woe-oracle against those who expect the Day of YHWH. The original shape of the oracle was as follows:[48]

הוֹי הַמִּתְאַוִּים אֶת־יוֹם יְהוָה...
הוּא־חֹשֶׁךְ וְלֹא־אוֹר... וְאָפֵל וְלֹא־נֹגַהּ לוֹ

Woe to those who desire the Day of YHWH! ...
It is darkness, and not light, ... and gloom with no brightness in it!
(Amos 5:18a, bβ, 20b)

This is probably the oldest reference to the Day of YHWH preserved in the Old Testament. The negative statement makes it fairly sure that the Israelites expected the day an occasion of joy. There is however no indication in Amos 5 what the original meaning of the event may have been. We are able to fill in this gap by means of Zeph 1:7a, bβ, 14a, 15bγ–16a.

Zeph 1:14b forms a parenthesis relating to the *sound* of the Day of YHWH. Here we find the eschatological concept of the Day of YHWH as it was common in the late tradition: the noise of that day is bitter, so that even the warrior cannot escape (cf. Amos 2:14–16). Because the definition of the Day of YHWH given in v. 15 relates to v. 14a, this part of the verse was added later.

The definition of the Day of YHWH in vv. 15–16a is closely reminiscent of Amos 5:18a, bβ, 20b:

---

[48] The saying was later illustrated in 19 by a traditional proverb about the fate of the unlucky. The phrase "Why do you want the Day of YHWH" in 18bα and the introduction כַּאֲשֶׁר "it is like ..." at the beginning of 19 as well as the resumptive repetition "Is not the Day of YHWH darkness, not light" in 20a serve to connect the insertion with the transmitted oracle. See Reinhard Müller, "Der finstere Tag Jahwes: Zum kultischen Hintergrund von Am 5,18-20," *ZAW* 122 (2010): 576–92.

יוֹם עֶבְרָה הַיּוֹם הַהוּא יוֹם צָרָה וּמְצוּקָה
יוֹם שֹׁאָה וּמְשׁוֹאָה יוֹם חֹשֶׁךְ וַאֲפֵלָה
יוֹם עָנָן וַעֲרָפֶל יוֹם שׁוֹפָר וּתְרוּעָה

That day is a day of wrath, a day of distress and stress,
a day of destruction and devastation, a day of darkness and gloom,
a day of clouds and thick darkness, a day of trumpet blast and cry.

As in v. 14a, the meaning of the term Day of YHWH is supposed to be familiar to the reader or listener. This makes us wonder why it has been felt necessary to illustrate it explicitly afterwards.

We may suggest that the definition given here is directed against an originally positive understanding—no different than it is done in Amos 5. A close look however shows that the list of paired attributes is not a negative one throughout. Besides חֹשֶׁךְ וַאֲפֵלָה "darkness and gloom" as in Amos 5:18bβ, 20b, at the end of the list of attributes we read עָנָן וַעֲרָפֶל "clouds and thick darkness" and שׁוֹפָר וּתְרוּעָה "trumpet blast and cry." These expressions are ambivalent, to say the least. The combination עָנָן וַעֲרָפֶל is to be found in Deut 4:11; 5:22; Joel 2:2; and Ps 97:2. Of these, only Joel 2:2 is to be understood as a threat. This instance is not decisive for the original meaning because it is probably quoting from Zeph 1:15 and Amos 5:18.[49]

The cultic origin of the terminology used in Zeph 1:15 comes out clearly in the core of Ps 97 (vv. 2a, 3–5) which had its *Sitz im Leben* in the temple of Jerusalem, probably at the festival of the new year when YHWH was ascending to his throne:

עָנָן וַעֲרָפֶל סְבִיבָיו...
אֵשׁ לְפָנָיו תֵּלֵךְ וּתְלַהֵט סָבִיב צָרָיו
הֵאִירוּ בְרָקָיו תֵּבֵל רָאֲתָה וַתָּחֵל הָאָרֶץ
הָרִים כַּדּוֹנַג נָמַסּוּ ... מִלִּפְנֵי אֲדוֹן כָּל־הָאָרֶץ

Clouds and thick darkness are round about him.
Fire goes before him and burns his adversaries round about.
His lightnings lighten the world; the earth sees and trembles.
The mountains melt like wax before the Lord of all the earth.[50]

---

[49] Cf. Hans Walter Wolff, *Joel and Amos: A Commentary on the Books of the Prophets Joel and Amos* (Hermeneia; trans. W. Janzen, S. D. McBride and C. A. Muenchow; Philadelphia: Fortress, 1977), *sub loco*.

[50] For the supposed original shape of Ps 97 see Reinhard Müller, *Jahwe als Wettergott: Studien zur althebräischen Kultlyrik anhand ausgewählter Psalmen* (BZAW 387; Berlin: de Gruyter, 2008), 86–102.

The hymnic description of the theophany of the weather-god is close to the Ugaritic myths. The expression אֲדוֹן כָּל־הָאָרֶץ "Lord of all the earth" was also applied to the Baal. It is highly probable that this piece of cultic poetry was used in the pre-exilic temple of Jerusalem besides ancient Psalms like 29 and 93.

The term "clouds and thick darkness" (עָנָן וַעֲרָפֶל) serves as a description of the epiphany of the deity which is performed by a hidden revelation, revealing and veiling the deity at one and the same time. This theophany is ambivalent: terrifying on the one hand, and beneficent on the other, i.e., threatening to the enemies and assisting their own king.

In Zeph 1:15 the ambivalence was originally understood positivly. This is shown by the pair of terms that stands at the end: שׁוֹפָר וּתְרוּעָה "trumpet and cry." The term תְּרוּעָה expresses the cry of battle as well as one of joy, especially victory and on occasion of the enthronement of the king or deity. In the psalms we frequently find the root רוע hiph. used in this way, for example in Ps 98:4–6:

הָרִיעוּ לַיהוָה כָּל־הָאָרֶץ פִּצְחוּ וְרַנְּנוּ וְזַמֵּרוּ
זַמְּרוּ לַיהוָה בְּכִנּוֹר בְּכִנּוֹר וְקוֹל זִמְרָה
בַּחֲצֹצְרוֹת וְקוֹל שׁוֹפָר הָרִיעוּ לִפְנֵי הַמֶּלֶךְ יְהוָה

Cry joyful to YHWH, all the earth;
break forth into joyous song and sing praises!
Sing praises to YHWH with the lyre,
with the lyre and the sound of melody!
With trumpets and the sound of the Shofar
make a joyful noise before the king YHWH.[51]

This hymnic invitation to rejoice has a variation in Ps 100:

הָרִיעוּ לַיהוָה כָּל־הָאָרֶץ
עִבְדוּ אֶת־יְהוָה בְּשִׂמְחָה
בֹּאוּ לְפָנָיו בִּרְנָנָה

Cry joyful to YHWH, all the earth,
serve YHWH with gladness,
come before him with singing!

The genre of Psalm 100 is the invitation to participate in the cult.[52] We can easily see how close it is also to Zeph 1:7. Both texts deal with the cultic presence of YHWH. The shout of the horn (שׁוֹפָר) is also part of the ritual of the enthronement, as can be seen in Ps 98:6 (and relating to human kings in 2 Sam

---

[51] Cf. Müller, *Jahwe als Wettergott*, 168–80.
[52] This is best seen from the parodistic use of the genre in Amos 4:4–5.

15:10; 1 Kgs 1:39; 2 Kgs 9:13). See also 2 Sam 6:15, which says: "David and the house of Israel brought up the ark of YHWH with joyful cry and with the sound of the horn (בִּתְרוּעָה וּבְקוֹל שׁוֹפָר)." The best example is probably Ps 47:6: עָלָה אֱלֹהִים בִּתְרוּעָה יְהוָה בְּקוֹל שׁוֹפָר "God has gone up with a joyful cry, YHWH with the sound of the horn." This is very close to Zeph 1:16. "Such language reflects both theophany and holy war traditions—God is present in the natural order and is portrayed as a holy warrior."[53] Such language is no prophecy.

These observations indicate that Zeph 1:14–16a originally read (and was heard!) as follows:

קָרוֹב יוֹם־יְהוָה הַגָּדוֹל קָרוֹב וּמַהֵר מְאֹד
יוֹם עָנָן וַעֲרָפֶל יוֹם שׁוֹפָר וּתְרוּעָה

The great Day of YHWH is near! Near and coming very fast:
a day of clouds and thick darkness, a day of trumpet blast and cry.

The announcement that the Day of YHWH is near and coming very fast is a cause of joy. People should hasten to prepare themselves, that is, to consecrate themselves for the sacrificial meal celebrated on that occasion.

Prophetic Interpretation (Zeph 1:15abαβ)

It was in a second step only, that this cultic saying was changed into a prophecy of doom by inserting in v. 15abαβ an allusion to Amos 5:18bβ, 20b:

יוֹם עֶבְרָה הַיּוֹם הַהוּא יוֹם צָרָה וּמְצוּקָה
יוֹם שֹׁאָה וּמְשׁוֹאָה יוֹם חֹשֶׁךְ וַאֲפֵלָה

That day is a day of wrath, a day of distress and stress,
a day of destruction and devastation, a day of darkness and gloom.

Now the Day of YHWH is explicitly defined, and in a negative way. Taken as such, the concept of the Day of YHWH served to announce/explain the conquest of Jerusalem.

Exegetes suggested that the prophet Zephaniah himself was quoting the cultic proclamation and using it in an ironical and even satirical way to address his prophetic message to his seventh-century audience.[54] Of course we cannot exclude this possibility. However we should take in account that the

---

[53] Petersen, *Prophetic Literature*, 204.
[54] See especially Seybold, *Satirische Prophetie*, 66–72.

interpretation of the Day of YHWH, as it is given here, is dependent on the book of Amos. The author of Zeph 1:15abαβ was no prophet in the proper meaning, but a Bible reader and exegete.

The Pious Poor Shall be Saved in the Coming Catastrophe (Zeph 1:16b–2:3)

In the final section of the first part of the book, the eschatological focus given to the book in the motto 1:2–3, is applied to the Day of YHWH. "This unit is best understood as an universal-eschatological interpretation added to the sayings of punishment."[55] "The expansion of the catastrophe to 'all the earth' is characteristic for the framework which in vv. 2–3 and vv. 17–18 is given to the sayings of Zephaniah."[56]

The passage is also heterogeneous. Verse 16b applies the threat of punishment to the capture of fortified cities. Probably the editor had in mind the conquest of Jerusalem. Like vv. 8a, 9b and 12–13a this can again be read as announcing the coming disaster as well as justifying the defeat of Judah that occurred in the past.[57]

The next step is formed by v. 18αβγb: Here the Day of YHWH is interpreted as a cosmic catastrophe in the same way as in vv. 2–3aα: "And by the fire of his jealousy, all the earth shall be consumed because destruction, indeed, sudden devastation, he will make of all the inhabitants of the earth." These are the ideas of late eschatology of doom, as they are to be found, e.g., in the Isaiah-Apocalypse and in the book of Joel. In v. 17aα, b, the same idea as in v. 3b was added: the cosmic catastrophe is restricted to humankind. This addition differs from the rest of the sayings because it is uttered in divine speech: "And I shall afflict humankind, and they shall walk like the blind, and their blood shall be spilled out like dust, and their guts like dung." Verse 17aβ which returns to prophetic speech, was later inserted in-between. "The glossator did not take into account that in v. 17a YHWH is speaking."[58] Here the punishment is restricted to the wicked only—as in v. 3aβ and v. 6. Duhm

---

[55] Irsigler, *Gottesgericht und Jahwetag*, 430.

[56] Perlitt, *Nahum, Habakuk, Zephanja*, 116.

[57] Later this application was taken up in Isa 2:15 as part of the poem on the Day of YHWH (Isa 2:12–17). Otto Kaiser, *Das Buch des Propheten Jesaja: Kapitel 1–12* (ATD 17; 5th ed.; Göttingen: Vandenhoeck & Ruprecht, 1981), 75: "In terms of religion history the expectation of the coming Last Judgement expressed here does not belong to the eighth century B.C.E. but to the Persian Era."

[58] Perlitt, *Nahum, Habakuk, Zephanja*, 116.

concludes: "This favourite sentence of the glossators must be set back to the margin."[59] His conclusion however is not adequate, for in v. 18aα the prophecy against the rich and wicked continues. Finally in 2:3 the positive equivalent follows in form of the admonition of the godly *humble of the land* (עַנְוֵי הָאָרֶץ)[60] to hide themselves and to seek for humility for to be saved in the coming catastrophe.[61] "Here the late post-exilic piety is speaking, that was discernible already in 1:6 and lingers in 3:12: The punishment shall not hit all, in any case not the pious."[62] On this level the book of Zephaniah has become an eschatological tractate.

Verses 2:1–2 have been added even later. They take up the admonitions of v. 3 for to vary them in face of the coming day of the wrath of YHWH. The linguistic state of these verses is rather weak.

CONCLUSION: THE GROWING PROCESS OF ZEPH 1:1–2:3

At the beginning of the literary process that produced step for step the first part of the book of Zephaniah, there was a cultic proclamation pronounced on occasion of the celebration of the Day of YHWH:

Silence! from before my Lord YHWH!
For YHWH has prepared a sacrifice, he has sanctified his invitees.
The great Day of YHWH is near! Near and coming very fast:
a day of clouds and thick darkness, a day of trumpet blast and cry.
(Zeph 1:7a, bβ, 14a, 15bγ–16a)

Read without the supposed secondary additions, this piece of liturgy is the best example to be found in the Old Testament for the originally positive meaning of the term יוֹם־יְהוָה. The positive meaning is much clearer than in Amos 5:18–20 where it is only to be understood by negation of the negative.

---

[59] Duhm, *Anmerkungen*, 57; cf. Marti, *Dodekapropheton*, 366.
[60] The term occurs also in Isa 11:4; Amos 8:4; Ps 76:10; Job 24:4; cf. Ps 37:11; Prov 30:14. Cf. Levin, "Das Amosbuch der Anawim," 270–1.
[61] See also Zeph 3:8bβγ, 12a, and cf. Levin, "Das Amosbuch der Anawim," 411–4 (repr. 268–71); idem, "The Poor in the Old Testament: Some Observations," *R&T* 8 (2001): 253–73 (259–60); repr. in idem, *Fortschreibungen*, 322–38 (327).
[62] Perlitt, *Nahum, Habakuk, Zephanja*, 119.

The Day of YHWH is the day of his theophany when he shall ascend to the throne after successfully defeating the powers of chaos. The command to be silent, on the one hand, and the invitation to play the שׁוֹפָר and to shout in joyful cry, on the other, is no contradiction. In religious terms it is the appropriate twofold reaction of humankind in the face of the twofold revelation of the deity as *tremendum et fascinosum*.

The cultic proclamation was later interpreted as a prophecy of doom, quite in line with the description of the Day of YHWH found in the book of Amos. The definition יוֹם עֶבְרָה הַיּוֹם הַהוּא "that day is a day of wrath" was inserted, quoting the negative determination חֹשֶׁךְ וְאֲפֵל of Amos 5:18bβ, 20b and expanding it with two similar paired terms: צָרָה וּמְצוּקָה "distress and stress" and שׁאָה וּמְשׁוֹאָה "destruction and devastation."

There had to be a reason for the announced punishment; finding one was the task of the next editor. He added the *sin of Manasseh*, which in post-exilic times was seen as the main reason why Jerusalem was conquered by the Babylonians. The details were to be found in the edited form of the book of Jeremiah as well as in the record of 2 Kgs 23. By this revision the book of Zephaniah received its alleged historical setting in the time of King Josiah. However, because the editor depended on the language of the book of Ezekiel, he could not have written in the seventh century.

Later editors attributed to the Day of YHWH the meaning of the eschatological doomsday. No doubt, this was done in postexilic times. The motto 1:2–3 that introduces this thematic layer alludes to the flood story of the Yahwistic source of the Pentateuch. This interpretation formed a framework, vv. 17–18 serving as the backward frame (with an appendix in 2:1–3). The Day of YHWH is given the meaning of the final judgment: "The sound of the Day of YHWH is bitter, a warrior cries out there" (v. 14b). The impending dangerous force of the Day of YHWH is stressed. Now it is definitively clear that the sound of the Day of YHWH is not the sound of joy but of grief and fear.

The godly poor shall be saved for their obedience to the Torah. The impious and rich, on the other hand, shall be exterminated by the impending chaos. Thus, in its final shape the book of Zephaniah grew to become the favorite reading of the pious in the Second Temple period. It was this form of the book that served Thomas a Celano in the thirteenth century CE as a model for his famous hymn *Dies irae*: "*quantus tremor est futurus, quando iudex est venturus, cuncta stricte discussurus!*" "What great trembling shall be in those days when the judge will come to investigate strictly all things." The dimension of apocalypticism cannot be overlooked, and we may easily imagine the religious milieu in which those visions came into being: "I will leave in the midst of you a people humble and lowly. They shall seek refuge in the name of YHWH, for they shall pasture and lie down, and none shall make them afraid" (Zeph 3:12, 13b).[63]

---

[63] Many thanks to Lester L. Grabbe for improving the English style.

THE SHAPE OF THINGS TO COME
Redaction and The Early Second Temple Period Prophetic Tradition

Jill Middlemas

INTRODUCTION

Western critical research on the prophetic books has undergone significant changes in the last century.[1] Early investigations of prophecy concentrated to a large extent on extracting glosses and editorial additions from the *ipsissima verba* of the prophetic figures. Once the actual words of the prophet were isolated a variety of discussions ensued about the nature of Hebrew poetry (e.g., Bernhard Duhm, but see also Robert Lowth), the forms of oral speech (e.g., Hermann Gunkel), the process of the transmission of the oral tradition (e.g., Ivan Engnell), and its social context (e.g., Sigmund Mowinckel). The pendulum has swung in quite the opposite direction in that over the last fifty years or so analyses of prophetic literature concentrated more attention on questions of redaction. Concomitantly, the editorial activity that shaped the prophetic books was seen also to be inspired. Although Mowinckel's analysis of the material considered to be inauthentic in Jeremiah led to a greater appreciation of the circles in which the traditions of prophecy were transmitted, it was with the work of Hans Walter Wolff on Amos that even greater attention would be given to the more intrinsic nature of the editorial material and its ability to convey how the words of the prophet were preserved and understood to be fulfilled. Editorial additions were subsequently analyzed with a view towards what they might tell

---

[1] For a comprehensive review of especially the earlier phases of this, see R. E. Clements, *A Century of Old Testament Study* (Guildford: Lutterworth, 1976), 51–75.

us about how and in which communities the biblical books took shape. Moreover, the process of the transmission of the Minor Prophets as a unit of material has received increasing attention. A significant amount of ongoing research is being conducted on the shaping of the so-called Book of the Twelve, the order in which the individual books evolved as groups, and the *Stichwörter* and other devices used to link them.[2]

When taking the long view of the history of Western approaches to the study of the prophetic books of the Old Testament it is possible to observe that the inquiry is inverted in that the current state of the discussion concentrates more on the editorial activity and strategies apparent in prophetic books than on the words thought to stem directly from the prophets themselves.[3] This is due in no small part to the nature of the presentation of the biblical prophetic books, which Michael Floyd has helpfully characterized with the following statement: "each prophetic book presents itself as a document about a particular prophet, written by someone else looking back on the prophet from a (short or long) historical distance."[4] The following inquiry seeks to consider more carefully the form of editorial additions, taking Haggai and Zech 1–8 (also referred to as First

---

[2] A convenient entry point appears in Paul L. Redditt, "The Formation of the Book of the Twelve: A Review of Research," *SBL Seminar Papers* (2001): 58–80. Otherwise, consult Paul R. House, *The Unity of the Twelve*, (JSOTSup 97; Sheffield: Sheffield Academic, 1990), James D. Nogalski, *Precursors to the Book of the Twelve* (BZAW 217; Berlin: de Gruyter, 1993), idem, *Processes in the Book of the Twelve* (BZAW 218; Berlin: de Gruyter, 1993). Ehud Ben Zvi presents a cogent objection to some of the underlying arguments for the unity of the Book of the Twelve in "'Twelve Prophetic Books or 'The Twelve': A Few Preliminary Considerations," in *Forming Prophetic Literature: Essays on Isaiah and the Twelve in Honor of John W. D. Watts* (ed. James W. Watts and Paul R. House; Sheffield: Sheffield Academic, 1996), 125–56.

[3] This brief introduction concentrates on one very particular aspect of research on prophecy. There are many other topics that could form a part of this discussion, e.g., the law and the prophets, the prophets in their ancient Near Eastern context, and true and false prophecy. Consider, for example, how the categories that appeared in Wolff's summary of this topic continue into more recent discussions, e.g., Gene M. Tucker, "Prophecy and the Prophetic Literature," in *The Hebrew Bible and Its Modern Interpreters* (ed. Douglas A. Knight and Gene M. Tucker; Chico, Calif.: Scholars Press, 1985), 325–68, and Reinhard G. Kratz, *Die Propheten Israels* (Munich: C. H. Beck, 2003).

[4] Michael H. Floyd, "Traces of Tradition in Zechariah 1–8: A Case-Study," in *Tradition in Transition: Haggai and Zechariah 1–8 in the Trajectory of Hebrew Theology* (ed. Mark J. Boda and Michael H. Floyd; New York: T&T Clark, 2008), 222.

Zechariah) as test cases, in order to think more fully about differences in technique and what such an inquiry offers to the future of analyses of prophetic literature. An analysis of editorial activity in Haggai and First Zechariah is followed by a brief consideration of the collection of prophecies in Isaiah 56–66, more generally referred to as Trito-Isaiah, in order to point towards the need for greater consideration of shape (what I refer to as centric shaping) as an editorial strategy in the current discussions of prophetic material.

REDACTION AND HAGGAI AND ZECHARIAH 1–8

An analysis of the shape and transmission of the prophetic words of Haggai and First Zechariah profits from the type of form analysis more readily associated with Hermann Gunkel and Claus Westermann supplemented by more recent thoughts by James Muilenburg.[5] By focusing to a large extent on the oral tradition of the prophets, Gunkel, and even more so Westermann, sought to define, classify, and analyze the forms of prophetic speech (*Gattungsforschung*). The emphasis on Form was moved forward positively by James Muilenburg who argued in his presidential address to the Society of Biblical Literature that there was a need to accept the insights of Form Criticism, but understand patterns of biblical literature more carefully.[6] In his address he promoted Rhetorical Criticism, a type of analysis that in his view would give more attention to the words found in units of material and how their linguistic patterns and formulae revealed something about the author's thought and when he thought it. Further, Muilenburg sought to move analysis beyond the mere examination of forms of speech to include an awareness of rhetorical patterns in poetic units and even narrative.[7] Form and patterning, thus, become important indicators of editorial techniques in Haggai and First Zechariah.

A significant part of the discussion of the books of Haggai and Zechariah has followed the lead of Willem Beuken who carefully distinguished prophetic material from editorial additions and noted that the framing material shared

---

[5] See ch. 4 of Hermann Gunkel, *Die Propheten* (Göttingen: Vandenhoeck & Ruprecht, 1917); Claus Westermann, *Grundformen prophetischer Rede* (Munich: Kaiser, 1960); James Muilenburg, "Form Criticism and Beyond," *JBL* 88 (1969): 1–18.

[6] Muilenburg, *Form Criticism*, 18.

[7] Ibid., 10.

certain similarities with the language found in the books of Chronicles.[8] Beuken categorized the milieu of the editors as Chronistic (similar to that used by the Chronicler, but not representing the same author) and his classification and thoughts on how the collections took shape have been refined, debated, even refuted, in further studies of the material produced by Rex Mason, David Petersen, and Janet Tollington.[9] The groundwork for the application of this type of examination on the books of Haggai and Zechariah was established already by Peter Ackroyd, who in a series of articles carefully distinguished edited material and glosses from the prophetic words of Haggai and Zechariah.[10] In more recent years, the question of the applicability of this procedure to the book of Haggai, at least, has come under question.[11] Nevertheless, editorial material can be discerned and characterized.

Editorial material clearly distinguishable from glosses appears in the prophetic collections of Haggai and Zech 1–8. A framework around the oracles of the prophet Haggai has been delineated at 1:1, 3, 12, 13a, 14–15; 2:1–2, 4–5, 10, 13–14, 20, with 2:2, 4–5, 13–14 remaining disputed.[12] There is also edited material that has no direct connection with the framework as with 2:5a. Clear editorial activity occurs to a lesser extent in Zech 1–8. In certain material the

---

[8] W. A. M. Beuken, *Haggai-Sacharja 1–8: Studien zur Überlieferungsgeschichte der frühnachexilischen Prophetie* (SSN 10; Assen: Van Gorcum, 1967).

[9] Rex Mason, "The Purpose of the Editorial Framework of the Book of Haggai," *VT* 27 (1977): 413–21; idem, *Preaching the Tradition: Homily and Hermeneutics after the Exile* (Cambridge: Cambridge University, 1990); David L. Petersen, *Haggai, Zechariah 1–8: A Commentary* (OTL; London: SCM Press, 1985); Janet Tollington, *Tradition and Innovation in Haggai and Zechariah 1–8* (JSOTSup 150; Sheffield: Sheffield Academic, 1993).

[10] Peter Ackroyd, "Studies in the Book of Haggai," *JJS* 2 (1951): 163-76; idem, "Studies in the Book of Haggai (Continued from Vol. II—No. 4)," *JJS* 3 (1952): 1-13; idem, "The Book of Haggai and Zechariah I-VIII," *JJS* 3 (1952): 151-56; idem, "Some Interpretive Glosses in the Book of Haggai," *JJS* 7 (1956), 163-7.

[11] See Michael H. Floyd, "The Nature of the Narrative and the Evidence of Redaction in Haggai," *VT* 45 (1995): 470–90; John Kessler, *The Book of Haggai: Prophecy and Society in Early Persian Yehud* (VTSup 91; Leiden: Brill, 2002), 53–55; idem, "Tradition, Continuity and Covenant in the Book of Haggai: An Alternative Voice from Early Persian Yehud," in Boda and Floyd (ed.), *Tradition in Transition*, 8 n. 28.

[12] Ackroyd, "Studies"; idem, "Studies cont."; idem, "Haggai and Zechariah"; Mason, "Editorial Framework"; idem *Preaching the Tradition*, 191-4; cf. Beuken, *Haggai-Sacharja 1–8*; Tollington, *Tradition and Innovation*.

prophet is referred to in the third person (Zech 1:1, 7; 7:1, 8), in 1:1 and 7 the title "the prophet" is added after his name, and a chronological framework organizes the material. In addition, redactional activity is thought to appear in Zech 1–8 in material where explanatory oracles have been attached to the night visions (Zech 3:6–10; 4:6b–10a; 6:9–15). These appear as corrections to prior interpretation as well as in historical narrative like that found in Zech 7:1–3 that forges a link to the book of the Twelve.[13]

The edited material falls into four different categories of type. First there is evidence of an intermediary formula (also regarded as a revelatory formula) where an individual is represented as one who conveys the divine message.[14] The prophet himself is recognized as an intermediary or there is a third party— an angelic messenger—who intervenes between the deity and the prophet. Haggai contains an example of the first, while Zech 1–8 evidences both types. The agency of the prophet Haggai is conveyed by the most basic form of an intermediary formula, "The word of Yahweh came by the hand (בְּיַד) of Haggai the prophet saying" (Hag 1:3). Although of Zechariah, it is said that, "The word of Yahweh came to (אֶל) Zechariah saying" (Zech 7:8).

The main difference between the intermediary formulae is the choice of בְּיַד to convey the sense of delivery of the divine message to Haggai (Hag 1:1, 3; 2:1). Rex Mason is probably correct that not too much can or should be made of its applicability to Haggai in that the alternative "to (אֶל) Haggai" also occurs (2:10, 20). Nevertheless, it is a distinctive expression that is found rarely elsewhere in prophetic literature. It appears in Deuteronomic literature, Chronicles, and the Priestly Work. Mason traces its applicability here to the Priestly tradition about Moses as law giver and tabernacle builder. In the Priestly tradition Moses instructed the building of the Tabernacle as well as its ritual practices.[15] The appearance of the prepositional phrase in conjunction with the

---

[13] John D. W. Watts, "Prophetic Genre in the Book of the Twelve," *Vision and Prophecy in Amos* (expanded ed.; Macon: Mercer University, 1997), 124–5.

[14] The classification of the framing material as found here is due in no small measure to the careful examination of the phenomenon of prophecy in the books of Chronicles carried out by Schniedewind, where he sets out helpful criteria for what is and is not prophetic. See William M. Schniedewind, *The Word of God in Transition: From Prophet to Exegete in the Second Temple Period* (JSOTSup 197; Sheffield: JSOT, 1995).

[15] Mason, "Editorial Framework"; idem, *Preaching the Tradition*, 192–3. Kessler has shown that the expression is more commonly found in the Deuteronomic tradition (including the book of Jeremiah), but his findings do not

prophet Haggai could reflect a conscious decision to appeal to the tradition of Moses and to his role as conveyor of divine instructions for the Tabernacle and its rituals or the temple as would be appropriate to the context of Haggai. The particular use of בְּיַד with Haggai seen in the light of Moses the Tabernacle builder is appropriate because the prophet's most pressing mission is to rejuvenate interest in and encourage the reconstruction of the Second Temple.

A different type of intermediary formula appears in conjunction with Zechariah that sets him apart from Haggai and other prophets more generally. Zechariah receives messages from Yahweh through an interpreting angel (Zech 1:9–14; and throughout the visions, e.g., 2:3; 4:1; 5:5; 6:4) in addition to those that come directly from Yahweh (e.g., 4:8; 6:9).[16]

Although Haggai is not found with an intermediary, he is called one in 1:13 where he fulfils such a role in speaking to the people, "And said Haggai the messenger (מַלְאַךְ) of Yahweh with the message (בְּמַלְאֲכוּת) of Yahweh to the people saying." The intermediary formula in this instance is being applied to the prophet in a unique way. Mason has explored the startling application of this idiom, which more frequently connotes an angelic messenger.[17] He notes that it is found elsewhere of prophets only in Isa 44:26[18] and Mal 1:1 and 3:1 (although it is also used of a priest in Mal 2:7) and suggests a link to 2 Chr 36:15–16, who understood this term in the context of the divine spokespeople for the Second Temple Community.[19] Its use here of Haggai certainly underscores his authority.[20]

In addition to the intermediary formulae, historical information appears among the edited material. In Hag 1:15, for instance, a certain oracle is delivered on the twenty-fourth day of the sixth month in the second year of Darius the king."[21] These two types of expressions, intermediary formula and historical dating, provide the two simplest forms of editorial activity discernible in prophetic literature more generally. They are distinguishable from other types of formulae in which these elements are found together.

---

discredit Mason's association with the Priestly Moses. See John Kessler, *Book of Haggai*, 118–9.

[16] The interpreting angel also assures Jehoshua the priest in ch. 3.

[17] Mason, *Preaching the Tradition*, 191–2.

[18] It also appears in Isa 42:19, but there it seems to refer to Israel.

[19] So also Kessler, *Book of Haggai*, 148.

[20] See also Petersen, *Haggai, Zechariah 1–8*, 56.

[21] The second part of the date formula giving the regnal year is often transposed to begin the second chapter. Meyers and Meyers have argued that it can serve double duty and that is the understanding adopted here. See Carol L. Meyers and Eric M. Meyers, *The Book of Haggai: Prophecy and Society in Early Persian Yehud* (VTSup 91; Leiden: Brill, 2002).

More common than the appearance of intermediary or historical formulae alone is a third type of formulae in which the two are combined. This is found, for example, in Hag 2:1, "In the second year of King Darius, in the seventh month, on the twenty-first day of the month, came the word of Yahweh by the hand of Haggai the prophet, saying." The same type of combined introduction appears also in Zechariah (1:1, 7: 7:1). A further variation of editorial framing appears in the instances when an intermediary formula is combined with a dating scheme as well as historical information. This type of formula has been termed *Wortereignisformel* or a word-event formula.

Wortereignisformeln contain additional details about those acting alongside the prophet and the event that inspires the prophetic word. For instance, the beginning of Haggai locates his prophetic activity in the reign of the Persian king Darius and with Zerubbabel and Jehoshua, the leaders of the community:

> In the second year of King Darius, in the sixth month, on the first day of the month, the word of Yahweh came by hand of Haggai the prophet to Zerubbabel son of Shealtiel, governor of Judah, and to Jehoshua son of Jehozadak, the high priest, saying (לֵאמֹר). "Thus says Yahweh of hosts (כֹּה אָמַר): These people say the time has not yet come to rebuild Yahweh's house." (Hag 1:1–2, cf. 2:1–3).[22]

A similar type of construction is found in Zechariah as well, but with much more detailed historical background,

> It was in the fourth year of Darius the king the word of Yahweh came to Zechariah on the fourth day of the ninth month in Kislev, Bethel sent to Sharezer and Regem-melech and their men to entreat the favor of Yahweh saying (לֵאמֹר) to the priests of the house of Yahweh of hosts and the prophets, "Should I mourn and practice abstinence in the fifth month, as I have done for so many years?" (Zech 7:1–3)

This is another word-event formula where the prophetic response will follow the description of the events. It is a complicated passage which I have dealt with elsewhere, understanding it as an inquiry from the priests of Bethel to those in Jerusalem about a cultic matter.[23] What is important in this context is

---

[22] A more extensive discussion of this phenomenon with attention to indicators of continuity and discontinuity in tradition with reference to Hag 1:1–2 can be found in Kessler, "Tradition, Continuity and Covenant," 1–39.

[23] See Jill Middlemas, *The Troubles of Templeless Judah* (OTM; Oxford: Oxford University Press, 2005), 134–6; eadem, *The Templeless Age: An*

again we find a type of editorial addition where the prophetic word is being placed in a very secure historical context and thereby responding to a particular situation.

Floyd has drawn attention to the fact that the beginning of Haggai distinguishes it from other prophetic literature because of the appearance of the word-event formula.[24] John Kessler provides a helpful interpretation of this literary strategy as a means to establish continuity in the book of Haggai, "From the very outset, then, the redactor weaves together the date and setting, the cast of characters, and the initial dramatic conflict and sets them before the readers/hearers."[25] The people's concern or reticence to rebuild the temple forms part of the book's framework and is the impetus for the prophetic word. A similar phenomenon is also found in First Zechariah. In Zechariah, the third section of the collection is begun with exactly the same structure, where a concern is expressed about whether or not fasting should be continued. Its answer will supply the conclusion of Zech 1–8. It is the historical setting that motivates the exposition of various regulations to and about the community in chs. 7–8.

Finally, the editorial material supplies interpretive detail. In Haggai, for example, it provides an indication of the efficacy of the prophet's words, "Then Zerubbabel, son of Shealtiel, and Jehoshua, son of Jehozadak, the high priest, with all the remnant of the people, obeyed the voice of Yahweh, their God, and the words of the prophet, Haggai, as Yahweh, their God, had sent him, and the people were in awe of (literally, feared) Yahweh" (1:12, cf. 1:14). Interpretive edited material appears in Zechariah, but in large blocks of text inserted alongside the visions. The most famous addition is that which speaks of the cleansing of Jehoshua in 3:6–10, but two other passages are thought to be later as well; the address to Zerubbabel in 4:6b–10a and an appendix to the series of visions in 6:9–15.

From these, it is possible to suggest, tentatively, five chief reasons for editorial activity of this sort:

(1) To preserve a historical context (or to provide one, given your viewpoint)
(2) To give legitimacy to the prophet and to lend authority to the tradition of the prophet (especially the written record)
(3) To link books— editorial intervention linked the books of Haggai and First Zechariah by a chronological framework in which their

---

Introduction to the History, Literature, and Theology of the "Exile" (Louisville: Westminster John Knox, 2007), 33–4.

[24] Floyd, "Nature of the Narrative," 476.
[25] Kessler, "Tradition, Continuity and Covenant," 10.

prophetic activity overlapped and through ideological motivation in which the two prophets were portrayed as seeking to attain the same goal (rebuilding the temple). The appearance of the *Wortereignisformel* at the beginning of Haggai and close of First Zechariah provides another means to associate the collections.

(4) To clarify and explain—the editorial framing indicates the divine origin of the words of Haggai and positive reactions to his words. In Zechariah, the added interpretive material further adds to how the prophet foresees the community as well as explaining the necessity of human response and clarifying human responsibility.

(5) To indicate the immediacy with which the prophetic words were transmitted.[26]

It can be seen that there is some truth to the claim made by John Watts who speaks of the function of the editorial framework as a skeleton.[27] The isolation and classification of the various forms of editorial material would subsequently lead the redaction critic to analyze the material more closely in order to determine the social setting, milieu, and/or concerns of the editor/author as has been expertly accomplished by Beuken with his Chronistic milieu and Mason with his concept of the Levitical sermon. However, the use of the material in Haggai for this purpose has drawn criticism in recent years exactly because of its rhetoric.

DISTINGUISHABLE FRAMING IN HAGGAI?

Although it is possible to extract editorial material and analyze its form, Michael Floyd has raised an important challenge to the ability to do so particularly in conjunction with the book of Haggai. In a more recent examination of the question of redaction and the book of Haggai, Floyd has argued successfully that what tends to be regarded as editorial material is actually an integral part of the oracles themselves.[28] In this regard he examines three factors used to determine

---

[26] Watts notes further that the historical interlude in Zech 7 functions as a type of parallel to the only historical interjection in the prophetic book of Amos (7:10–17) and may serve as a link between them, but pursuing this point would take us too far afield from the present analysis.

[27] Watts, "Prophetic Genre."

[28] Floyd, "Nature of the Narrative." See also Kessler, *Book of Haggai*, 53–55; idem, "Tradition, Continuity and Covenant," 8 n. 28.

what is redactional material and what is not in prophetic literature: the linguistic elements of superscriptions, prophetic and authorial viewpoint, and diction. In the first place Floyd finds that the superscriptions in the book of Haggai appear similar to those of other prophetic books (sharing linguistic elements, for example), but are actually unlike them in that they are expressed as complete sentences that function as narration, not just as introduction.[29] Another feature that marks the book of Haggai as distinct among the prophetic books is that the viewpoint expressed in the edited material is very like that of the prophet.[30] Finally, a third observation relates to diction. The vocabulary and phraseology of the edited material and the speeches of the prophet are closely aligned suggesting that the two underwent the same process of composition.[31] These observations about the framework of Haggai reveal that it functions as an authoritative part of the prophet's message rather than as introductions or classifications of the prophetic speech.

Floyd has effectively shown that it is less helpful to examine the prophetic book of Haggai according to criteria applied to other prophetic books, whereby the words of the prophet and those of the edited material are separated out to discern the social context of each as well as the compositional process of the book as a whole. The framework and the speeches in Haggai are inextricably intertwined. It is not that a separation of redacted material in Haggai has been accomplished in vain, however. As the analysis has shown it is possible to isolate and categorize editorial material. What is special about the book of Haggai as Floyd has shown is that the editor assumes the viewpoint of the prophet so it is more difficult to ascertain a separate social context for the author and editor. The editorial additions in Haggai alert the reader to a different reading strategy. It is not a prophetic book plus accretions, but rather a unified composition with a unity in outlook and purpose.[32]

Floyd has provided a helpful and illuminating examination of what has been discerned as the edited material and the prophetic speeches in the book of Haggai. Traditio-historical approaches have failed to do justice to a particular feature of Haggai by which the framework and the prophetic oracles are intertwined. The editor has claimed the prophetic authority of Haggai for himself and his own time. The appearance of this type of editorial strategy in the book of

---

[29] Floyd, "Nature of the Narrative,"475–6.

[30] Ibid., 477–9.

[31] Ibid., 481–2.

[32] This impacts how one understands the genre of the piece and Floyd argues that the book of Haggai represents a prophetic history (historiography) which avails the interpreter the possibility only to "make a critical assessment of what the author tells us in the present text." For more discussion, see Floyd, "Nature of the Narrative," 470–90.

Haggai begs the question of other ways awareness of rhetoric can enable a reassessment of redaction and the prophetic literature.

DISTINGUISHING FRAMING IN ZECHARIAH

Rex Mason already remarked that "Zechariah cc. 1–8 presents questions of structure quite different from those of the book of Haggai."[33] Although it clearly contains a framework, in comparison with Haggai, and indeed, other books of the Twelve, the existing editorial activity is much less concentrated in attributive or chronological details—occurring only at 1:1, 7 and 7:1, 8. In one respect, Zechariah is like Haggai with its straightforward chronological presentation, where the frame provides a skeleton for the prophetic message. In contrast to the shaping of Haggai, however, the dating scheme appears only in three places to demarcate the framework from the visions (1:1, 7; 7:1).[34] The effect achieved is a three-fold division where a series of otherworldly night visions in 1:7–6:25 are encapsulated by an introductory call to obedience in 1:1–6 and a conclusion that restores the centrality of Jerusalem and extends future hope to ancient Israel and the nations in 7:1–8:23.

Zechariah is more complex still in that the vision sequence is itself punctuated by interpretive material. Carol Meyers and Eric Meyers have understood the interpolation of a scene about the cleansing of Jehoshua as a key to the organization of the night visions. In their analysis, they argue that the night visions are shaped according to a concentric structure, where the first three visions parallel the last three. At the heart of the visions is the fifth about the lampstand and olive trees as well as the inserted fourth about the cleansing of the high priest. By placing these two visions in the center, the editorial shaping, in their view, focuses attention on the temple and the leadership of the community.[35] The centering of the night visions provides important information about how the editor envisioned community in the early Second Temple community.

However, it is not just the night visions that are shaped concentrically. The entire collection stemming from Zech 1–8 is structured similarly with the night visions forming the core encapsulated in material of a more regulatory nature. The chronological scheme divides the visions from regulations applicable to the

---

[33] Mason, *Preaching the Tradition*, 197.

[34] The fourth framing formula in 7:8 represents that of an intermediary type alone.

[35] Meyers and Meyers, *Book of Haggai*, lv.

community, creating the effect of a frame around a center. The introduction in 1:1–6 holds forth a renewed call to obedience. Cognizant of Yahweh's restorative actions, Zechariah upbraids the community to renew their relationship. The concluding chapters (chs. 7–8) clarify the central role of Jerusalem in the new age, extend Yahwistic promises to Yehud and the nations, and provide additional regulations concerning behavior to indicate how the new community has access to divine promises. Zechariah distinctively contains a dating scheme and a shaping scheme where a center is surrounded and clarified. Demarcated from the night visions by framing editorial insertions, the introductory and concluding passages in First Zechariah indicate more clearly how the community should respond to the prophetic message and the divine plans as well as how divine instruction can be interpreted more concretely.

CENTRIC CRITICISM AND ITS IMPLICATIONS

In addition to providing interpretive detail the editorial material in Zech 1–8 functions to create the effect of a center and a periphery. Another prophetic collection that is thought to stem from around the time of the early second temple also displays this shape. Similar to First Zechariah the prophecies of Trito-Isaiah (Isa 56–66) contain a nucleus of visionary material surrounded by a frame that provides regulations and explanations. Unlike First Zechariah (and indeed Haggai and most of the other prophetic books) it is less helpful to discuss a chronological or attributive framework in Trito-Isaiah. There is no evidence of one. Rather than editing in this way, Trito-Isaiah contains interpretive activity only. It has a special shape in which a series of explanatory details gather around a core nucleus of oracles very similar to those of Deutero-Isaiah in chs. 60–62.[36] Placed around this nucleus of purely positive prophecies can be found one or more redactional layers at 56–59 (made up of three sections of material, 56:1–8; 56:9–57:21; 58:1–59:20) and 65:1–66:17, with which I would include 63:7–64:11. Supplementary material appears in 66:18–24 as well.[37]

---

[36] Claus Westermann, *Das Buch Jesaja: Kapitel 40–66* (ATD 19; Göttingen: Vandenhoeck & Ruprecht, 1966); more naturally extended to 63:6, see Paul A. Smith, *Rhetoric and Redaction in Trito-Isaiah: The Structure, Growth and Authorship of Isaiah 56-66* (VTSup 62; Leiden: Brill, 1995).

[37] For an introduction to issues of redaction, see Karl Pauritsch, *Die neue Gemeinde: Gott sammelt Ausgestossene und Arme (Jesaja 56–66): Die Botschaft des Tritojesaia-Buches literar-, form-, gattungskritisch und redaktionsgeschichtlich untersucht* (AnBib 47; Rome: Biblical Institute, 1971); Paul D. Hanson, *The Dawn of Apocalyptic* (Philadelphia: Fortress, 1975); Seizo Sekine, *Die Tritojesajanische Sammlung (Jes 56–66) redaktionsgeschichtlich untersucht* (BZAW 175; Berlin: de Gruyter, 1989); Klaus Koenen, *Ethik und*

A link to Deutero-Isaiah is not made through a chronological framework like that found joining the prophetic activities of Haggai and Zechariah, but rather through the recapitulation of the main prophecies of Isa 40–55 within a core nucleus. Since Westermann's *Das Buch Jesaja* (1966), a core nucleus of prophecies in Isa 60–62 either by or in the style of Deutero-Isaiah and consisting entirely of salvation oracles to the city and the people of Jerusalem has been generally agreed. The rhetorical shape of the collection functions as an editorial strategy on par with the application of a chronological or attributive framework. As such, an editor provides interpretive details around a text in order to comment upon it. With the case of Trito-Isaiah, the effect results in an explanation of why the prophecies of Deutero-Isaiah have failed to materialise and subsequently projects them into the future. Moreover, the oracles outside the nucleus specify suitable and unsuitable practices for the restoration community.[38]

Shaping a book in a concentric pattern as an editorial strategy has not received as much attention as have the type of chronological and attributive framing devices found in Haggai and Zechariah, but it is an equally important redactional strategy. Greater consideration to the rhetorical patterns of the material in Zech 1–8 and Trito-Isaiah could even form the basis of a new type of criticism, centric criticism, if you will, i.e., analysis of the form of a book or collection of oracles in a concentric pattern and how the center functions in relation to the whole. Does a nucleus of material provide the point of departure for elaboration, comment or modification or does it provide an alternative perspective to the outer material as a correction or exposition perhaps?

There are a few other collections that seem to reflect this shaping strategy. Jörg Jeremias has argued that the book of Amos is redacted with a central core

---

Eschatologie im Tritojesajabuch: Eine literarkritische und redaktionsgeschichtliche Studie (WMANT 62; Neukirchen-Vluyn: Neukirchener, 1990); Odil H. Steck, *Studien zu Tritojesaja* (BZAW 203; Berlin: de Gruyter, 1991); Smith, *Rhetoric and Redaction*, and Reinhard G. Kratz, "Tritojesaja," *TRE* 34 (2002): 124–30. The number of redactional layers is not yet agreed upon, but for a careful and thorough argument for one main redaction see Smith, *Rhetoric and Redaction*, 1995.

[38] For a more extensive treatment of these practices with particular attention to the community, see Jill Middlemas, "Trito-Isaiah's Intra- and Internationalization: Identity Markers in the Second Temple Period," in *Judah and the Judeans in the Achaemenid Period: Negotiating Identity in an International Context* (ed. Oded Lipschits, Gary N. Knoppers and Manfred Oeming; Winona Lake, Ind.: Eisenbrauns, 2011), 105–25.

section of prophecies.³⁹ It is also a feature of collections that appear in the *Ketubim*, including the book of Lamentations, Proverbs (where a center of regulations, i.e., proverbial maxims is surrounded by imprecation or advice for living), and the book of Job (where the framework sets the foundation for the explanation and drama of the center).

This list of works with a center focus draws attention to the fact that writing around a core nucleus may be a feature of composition and/or redacting activity found in ancient Israel from the period of the downfall of the temple in the sixth century BCE and onwards. The situation is otherwise with the Book of the Twelve, of which Haggai and Zechariah form a part. Recent studies on the book of the Twelve have shown how the linking of prophetic books existed before the fall of Jerusalem. Indeed, Nogalski in his *Literary Precursors to the Book of the Twelve*, has argued that a Deuteronomistic corpus of Hosea, Amos, Micah, and Zephaniah pre-dated what is conventionally known as the Exile.⁴⁰ Since a circular editing strategy distinct from the types of literary features that categorize the shaping of the book of the Twelve appears to take place from the sixth century BCE onwards, a question arises about whether centric redaction is related practically and/or ideologically to the events that took place at that time.

There has been a flurry of attention in recent years on scribes, scribal activity, and the actual production of biblical texts.⁴¹ There are four chief areas of discussion: likely chronological periods of scribal activity (when the societal conditions were conducive to writing—the monarchical period, late in the

---

³⁹ Jörg Jeremias, *The Book of Amos* (trans. Douglas W. Stott; OTL; Louisville: Westminster John Knox, 1995), 5–9.

⁴⁰ Nogalski, *Literary Precursors*; idem, *Redactional Processes*.

⁴¹ E.g., Ehud Ben Zvi, "The Urban Center of Jerusalem and the Development of the Literature of the Hebrew Bible," in *Urbanism in Antiquity: From Mesopotamia to Crete* (ed. Walter E. Aufrecht, Neil A. Mirau, and Steven W. Gauley; JSOTSup 244; Sheffield: Sheffield Academic, 1997), 194–209; Philip R. Davies, *Scribes and Schools: The Canonization of the Hebrew Scriptures* (London: SPCK, 1998); Raymond F. Person, *The Deuteronomic School: History, Social Setting, and Literature* (SBL Studies in Biblical Literature 2; Atlanta: SBL, 2002); William M. Schniedewind, *How the Bible Became a Book: The Textualization of Ancient Israel* (Cambridge: Cambridge University, 2004); David M. Carr, *Writing on the Tablet of the Heart* (New York: Oxford University, 2005); Martti Nissinen, "How Prophecy Became Literature," *SJOT* 10 (2005): 154–72; Reinhard G. Kratz, "The Growth of the Old Testament," in *The Oxford Handbook of Biblical Studies* (ed. John W. Rogerson and Judith M. Lieu; Oxford: Oxford University, 2006); Karel van der Toorn, *Scribal Culture and the Making of the Hebrew Bible* (Cambridge: Harvard University, 2007); Floyd, "Traces of Tradition," 223–30.

Persian period, or even in Hellenistic times), the locations of scribal activity (temples, the royal court, and households), the number of scribal schools at any given time (many, a few, or even one), and the purpose (to enable memorization and recitation and/or to educate the meaning of texts). Redaction criticism has of course formed a natural part of this type of inquiry by delineating editorial additions and expansions. Related to redaction is the increased importance given to scribes and the production of biblical texts. A new feature of the discussion would include distinguishing scribal techniques, such as centric shaping. Would a certain group of scribes indicate their activity by the inclusion of particular features such as shaping, diction, and phraseology? A focus not only on the phenomenon of editorial activity as a means to assess the tradition(s) in which it grew, i.e., the social context of the various authors (here an editor is being understood as an author), but also on the shaping or rhetorical patterning of material forms a necessary step in assessments of textual transmission and scribal practice.

Conclusions

Returning to the survey of the way research on the prophets has developed over the last century or so, it is possible to say that the emphasis on Form and Redaction Criticisms has resulted in fruitful study of the context in which the transmission of authoritative texts took place. Further examination of the editorial strategies in Haggai and Zech 1–8, with a brief consideration of Trito-Isaiah, suggests, however, their limitations as well as the importance of an awareness of shaping as an editorial practice. Further work needs to be done on centric shaping and its importance in order to consider such questions as: How is a concentric shape achieved? Why does it occur? How prevalent an enterprise is it? Does is appear more consistently with certain types of literature? What are its purposes and who are its proponents? The title of this article, "The Shape of Things to Come," has a dual meaning. It looks forward from the period of the sixth century BCE onwards at an emerging literary strategy. In addition, a close consideration of the interrelation between a core nucleus and outer material when a collection of biblical material has a concentric shape provides a new and likely profitable direction for study, especially with regards to the nuts and bolts of the transmission of biblical material. It might even give us an insight into those elusive scribes and their practices.

ISRAEL AND THE NATIONS IN THE LATER LATTER PROPHETS

David L. Petersen

It is an honor to participate in this session devoted to prophetic texts and their ancient contexts. The invitation to present a paper devoted to the second half of the book of the twelve was both enticing and challenging. How might one think creatively about the social contexts represented by Nahum, Habakkuk, Zephaniah, Haggai, Zechariah, and Malachi? The challenges were, essentially, these. Three of the books (or at least major portions thereof)—Nahum, Habakkuk, and Zephaniah—may be rather firmly set in the Neo-Babylonian period; two—Haggai and First Zechariah—belong to the early Persian period; finally, Deutero-Zechariah and Malachi are of indeterminate age, though most scholars date that literature to later on in the Persian period. What sort of test probe might help us understand the ways in which these contexts affected the nature of prophetic activity and the literature associated with it?

To answer this question, I decided to examine the discourse concerning foreign nations in the future as it appears in these books, especially since those nations comprised one of the important contexts for Israel's prophets. One might reasonably begin with the assumption that Israel's prophets were very much aware of other nations. Each of the three so-called Major Prophets includes lengthy collections of oracles against the nations. The first six of the Minor Prophets include comparable material. Collections known as "oracles against the nations" appear as early as the book of Amos. In Amos, the oracles against the nations involve only Levantine states. Joel 3–4 includes rhetoric directed against both Syro-Palestinian cities and nations (Tyre, Sidon, Philistia, and Edom) along with reference to larger empires (Egypt and Greece). Obadiah and Jonah focus on Edom and Nineveh (Babylonia) respectively. Micah envisions an attack against Assyria.

These six books also refer in summary fashion to Yahweh's actions vis-à-vis "the nations" (e.g., Joel 4:2; Obad 15–16; Mic 4:1–3; 5:7–9). With the exception of the text in Obadiah, most of this literature appears to be redactional. Put another way, the earlier books in the Book of the Twelve tend to speak of particular cities and nations. Later editors tended to refer to "the nations," and not to particular states.[1]

One may postulate then that the prophetic discourse concerning international affairs can take place in at least two different ways: references to specific cities or nations and general comments about "all the nations." If it is licit to construe the international discourse of the first half of the Book of the Twelve in this way, how does it appear in the second half of that Book? To what extent do oracles against specific nations appear? How prominent is more general language about *haggôyim* or *'ammîm*. Does one or another of these options become more or less prominent?

At the outset, it is clear that specific nations do receive attention. Nahum, like Jonah, focuses on Nineveh. Habakkuk refers to the Chaldeans (1:6). Neither case, however, presents something comparable to the oracles against nations in Amos or the three major prophetic books. To find such material, one must turn to Zephaniah and Zechariah.

Zephaniah 2:5–15 offers something similar to earlier oracles against the nations, referring to at least ten entities (e.g., Ashkelon, Assyria, Nineveh, Cush, and Cheret). The large number of countries in such a small number of verses is striking. The rhetoric is one of vast destruction, though with minimal indictment. And the indictments, when they occur, are vague. For example, when referring to Moab and Ammon, the poet writes, "they have taunted my people and made boasts against their territory" (Zeph 2:8). More typical are reports of future disaster: "You also, O Cushites, shall be killed by my sword" (Zeph 2:12). One might read these verses and suggest that Zephaniah is covering a vast geographic swath with this list of nations, though he does so by listing specific nations, not by referring to nations in a more general way.

Neither Haggai nor First Zechariah refer to a particular nation as a part of Yahweh's future activity, though First Zechariah does include allusive language

---

[1] For an assessment of portions of this literature, see Martin Roth, *Israel und die Völker im Zwölfprophetenbuch: Eine Untersuchung zu den Büchern Joel, Jona, Micha, und Nahum* (FRLANT 210; Göttingen: Vandenhoeck & Ruprecht, 2005).

such as "daughter Babylon" (2:7) "the land of Shinar" (5:11), "the north country" (6:8) or "the west country" (8:7).

Deutero-Zechariah also refers to specific nations. Zechariah 9:1–8 are rather like Zeph 2:5–15; they are chock full of individual cities and nations. The poem includes at least eleven toponyms, all of which are located in Syria-Palestine. All the toponyms specify territory to either the north or west of Judah. And, as was the case with Zephaniah, the language of indictment is vague. Zechariah 9:7, when referring to Philistia, reads, "I will take away blood from its mouth and its abominations from between its teeth." The nature of this bloody abomination remains unclear. Then, later in Deutero-Zechariah, one hears about the destruction of Greece (9:13), the degradation of Assyria and Egypt (10:11), fire in Lebanon (11:1), and possible punishment of Egypt (14:19). With the exception of the punishment of Egypt, no indictments occur along with these judgments.[2] Finally, I observe that Malachi refers to only one foreign nation, Edom (Mal 1:4), reaffirming that past destruction will be repeated, if necessary, but presenting no indictment of that country.

In sum, prophetic discourse concerning specific foreign nations becomes less prominent as one moves into the later Latter Prophets. In all of Haggai, First Zechariah, and Malachi, Yahweh interacts with only one specific foreign nation in the future.

What may one say about more general discourse concerning "the nations" or "peoples"? I want to suggest that such diction is strikingly different from language about individual nations. Future action concerning "the nations" is absent in Nahum and Habakkuk. It is, however, present twice in Zephaniah, twice in Haggai, multiple times in Zechariah, and twice in Malachi. Clearly there has been a shift in diction about foreign nations. The latter books speak increasingly about the nations in general terms. Is the change simply lexical? I don't think so. Rather, when one reviews the presence of the phrase "the nations" or "the peoples" in the latter six prophetic books, it seems clear that the phrase belongs to a larger set of expectations involving what will happen to the nations. Those expectations are of two basic sorts: Yahweh fighting against the nations and the nations (subsequently) venerating Yahweh.

First, a number of the texts speak of Yahweh's attack against or the destruction of the nations. Zephaniah 3:8 reads, "…for my decision is to gather nations, to assemble kingdoms, to pour out upon them my indignation, all the

---

[2] I find it particularly interesting that Egypt and Greece appear in both Deutero-Zechariah (Greece [Zech 9:13]; Egypt [Zech 14:18–19]) and Deutero-Joel (Greece [Joel 4:6]; Egypt [Joel 4:19]).

heat of my anger; for in the fire of my passion all the earth shall be consumed." In this strongly eschatological passage, there is a move toward treating the nations as a totality, as befits the hyperbolic notion of the entire earth being destroyed. Haggai 2:7 is similar, though less violent, "I will shake all the nations, so that the treasure of all nations shall come, and I will fill this house with splendor." This motif of the despoliation of the nations appears in Zech 14:14 as well, coming immediately after a scene of international combat. (Several other texts attest to God's destructive posture toward the nations [Hag 2:7; Zech 1:15; 2:4; 2:12; 12:2–4].)

This battle is, in several texts, localized; it takes place at and against Jerusalem, so Zech 12:9, "on that day I will seek to destroy all the nations that come against Jerusalem" or Zech 14:2, "I will gather all the nations against Jerusalem to battle...." (Needless to say there are comparable texts in other prophetic books and the Psalms [Isa 60:5–7, 11, 16; 61:6; 66:12; Mic 4:11; Joel 4:11–12; Ps 72:10 et al.].)

Second, a striking, new element emerges in three of the later, latter prophetic books—Zephaniah, Zechariah, and Malachi. In these books, "the nations" are occasionally viewed in a positive way. Each of these books depicts the nations venerating Israel's deity. Interestingly, this positive view does not occur when an individual nation is named. The books depict this "religious" behavior of the nations in several distinctive ways.

a. The nations will venerate Yahweh at a distance; Zeph 2:11 exemplifies this notion: "to him shall bow down each in its place all the coasts and islands of the nations." Malachi 1:11 seems to belong to this same vein; "For from the rising of the sun to its setting my name is great among the nations, and in every place incense is offered to my name, and a pure offering; for my name is great among the nations." (Mal 1:14 reiterates this same perception.)

b. The nations will make a pilgrimage to Jerusalem, as in Zech 8:22 "many peoples and strong nations shall come to seek the Lord of hosts in Jerusalem and to entreat the favor of the Lord." (Cf. Mic 4:1–2//Isa 2:3; Isa 60:6; 66:18; not much in Psalter). Zechariah 14:16 specifies the moment for such a pilgrimage to be Sukkot, "Then all who survive of the nations that have come up against Jerusalem shall go up year after year to worship the King, Yahweh of hosts, and to keep the festival of Sukkot."

c. The nations will venerate Yahweh in diverse ways, as in Zephaniah 3:9, "all of them will call on the name of Yahweh and serve him with one accord" (a number of texts refer to the "name" of the deity). Moreover, nations and/or peoples will become affiliated with Yahweh, as found in Zech 2:15 (Engl 11), "Many nations shall join themselves to Yahweh on that day, and shall be my people." Zechariah 8:23 strikes a similar tone, "In those days, ten men from nations of every language shall take hold of a Jew, grasping his garment and saying, 'Let us go with you, for we have heard that God is with you.'"

How may one explain this new language about and views concerning the nations? Here one must draw back and ask about both the putative contexts that lie behind the oracles against the nations during the monarchic period and the new contexts that lie behind the language regarding "the nations" in the Persian period.

The oracles against the nations during the monarchic era appear to be rooted in the theo-political world of Jerusalem. Much of the discourse found in them is associated with Yahweh's imperial rule from Zion. There can be little doubt that this imperial rule was integrally linked with the Davidic imperium. That linkage may explain the configuration of the earliest oracles against the nations, namely, those found in the book of Amos. Many years ago, George Ernest Wright argued that the nations indicted in Amos 1–2 had violated certain norms present in the treaty relationship that they would have had with the greater Israel of the united monarchy.[3] Further, many if not most of the oracles in the nations in prophetic books betray detailed knowledge of foreign and political relations of a sort that would have been current at the Jerusalem court. As a result, I think we may postulate that the setting for the oracles concerning specific nations was prophetic utterance at the Davidic court, which of course, included the royal chapel, the temple in Jerusalem.

During the Persian period, there was no longer a Judahite court at which foreign ambassadors could speak to local officials. Judah no longer made treaties or engaged in diplomatic relations; it was a subprovince of the Persian Empire. Put simply, the discourse in which singly named nations were important became far less important. However, foreign nations as such were, in principle, of increasing importance to Yahwists, because after the dispersals of Judahites in the early sixth century, Yahwists now lived among the nations—with Egypt and Babylonia as the most important centers (the book of Nehemiah can, when referring to the context in which Nehemiah is working, refer to "the nations" [e.g., Neh 6:16], without specifying any particular city or people).

With the end of Judah as an independent state, the social context of the Davidic court had vanished, but the temple had not. Further, there are clear indications that, in the Persian period, things prophetic were associated explicitly with the world of ritual. The characterization of the Levitical singers as prophets is perhaps the clearest example of this new situation. As a result, it makes sense to examine briefly the literature associated with the temple—the

---

[3] George Ernest Wright, "Nations in Hebrew Prophecy," *Encounter* 26 (1965): 225–237.

Psalms—to see how the nations are understood there. Is what one reads in the later Latter Prophets similar to or different from the way in which the nations appear in the Psalter?

The following texts are suggestive:

Ps 22:28
All the ends of the earth shall remember
    and turn to the Lord;
and all the families of the nations
    Shall worship before him

Ps 67:3–4
Let the nations praise you, O God;
    let all the peoples praise you.
Let the nations be glad and sing for joy

Ps 68:32
Sing to God, O kingdoms of the earth;
    sing praises to the Lord

Ps 72:17
May all nations be blessed in him;
    may they pronounce him happy

Ps 86:9
All the nations you have made shall come
    and bow down before you, O Lord
        and shall glorify your name

Ps 102:16
The nations will fear the name of the Lord
    and all the kings of the earth your glory
    (cf. Mic 7:17, in a more negative light)

Ps 117:1
Praise the Lord, all you nations!
    Extol him, all you peoples!

The new element in late prophetic discourse concerning foreign nations, namely, the nations' veneration and/or praise of Yahweh, also appears in Psalms. One may therefore theorize that this setting, the world of the worship, was the origin for this motif present in late prophetic language about "the nations."

To identify the ritual world as the source for this motif has further explanatory power. These Psalmic texts offer a rationale for that praise, a rationale that is not routinely present in the late prophetic texts: the nations will/should praise Yahweh because that deity "rules over the nations" (Ps 22:29), because that deity "judges the peoples with equity" (Ps 67:4), because Yahweh has "made" the nations (Ps 86:9), and because of Yahweh's steadfast love for his people (Ps 117:2). The prophetic texts typically do not include these reasons but they do, as we have seen, include the expectation that the nations will, indeed, worship Yahweh. In fact, the late prophetic texts offer more particular language about how and where such veneration will take place, issues absent from the psalmic language about such praise.

Now, of course, the psalter itself almost certainly reflects more than one social context, particularly in the Second Temple period. Worship, as Rainer Albertz and Erhard Gerstenberger have argued, occurred in the temple at Jerusalem and elsewhere, such as homes, early synagogues, and sectarian settings.[4] It is, of course difficult to know in which setting or settings the aforementioned psalms had their origin or were used. Similarly, it is difficult to know if Levitical prophets or other non-Levitical prophetic tradents were active in both contexts, though there is evidence to suggest that they were both out in the country and at the temple (Neh 12:27). These uncertainties, however, do not preclude the more general hypothesis that the discourse of psalms has influenced prophetic language about the nations in the Second Temple period.

What then may one suggest by way of tentative conclusions when examining the place of the nations in the later Latter Prophets?

1. Oracles concerning specific nations in the later Latter Prophets are primarily a phenomenon of the monarchic period. They are either pre-exilic, so Zeph 2, or rooted in pre-exilic historical realities (Zech 9). In the oracles about the nations, there is little if any evidence of positive rhetoric concerning specific cities or nations.

2. With few exceptions and with the end of the state of Judah, oracles against specific nations become a less important part of prophetic literature than had earlier been the case. Instead, the "international" dimension appears in discourse concerning "the nations." This almost certainly reflects a change in social context. Prophets were no longer related to the royal court, which is

---

[4] Erhard Gerstenberger, *Psalms, Part 1 with an Introduction to Cultic Poetry* (FOTL XIV; Grand Rapids: Eerdmans, 1988), 30–33; Rainer Albertz, *A History of Israelite Religion in the Old Testament Period, Vol. 2: From the Exile to the Maccabees* (OTL; Louisville: Westminster John Knox, 1994), 503–7.

where they almost certainly would have heard about and commented about foreign nations in an earlier time.

3. Post-exilic, prophetic discourse about "the nations" includes diverse traditions: judgment and/or war against the nations, a pilgrimage of nations to Jerusalem, veneration of Yahweh by the nations (some of these elements may be related to the so-called Zion tradition, but the motif of the veneration of Yahweh does not seem integral to the Zion tradition).

4. The veneration of Yahweh by the nations is a new element in the later Latter Prophets. That discourse concerning "the nations" finds its closest literary companion in Psalms. This literary similarity probably attests to the interplay between the prophetic activity and the ritual world. In the Second Temple period, the books of Chronicles attest to a close connection between prophets and Levitical singers. Those scribes and/or prophets who continued to pen literature found in prophetic books were utterly familiar with the world of psalmody and far less informed about the status of individual nations than had been their pre-exilic forbears. As a result, international discourse had become "de-historicized." As a result, prophetic literature used increasingly the more general language of "the nations," which appears rooted in the Psalms.

5. This paper, which has examined only the second half of the Book of the Twelve, needs to be complemented by a study of the three major prophetic books as well as the first half of the Book of the Twelve (especially Joel and Micah). Only then could one hypothesize about the prophetic discourse concerning "the nations" in a comprehensive fashion.

SAMUEL'S INSTITUTIONAL IDENTITY IN THE DEUTERONOMISTIC HISTORY *

Marvin A. Sweeney

I

Samuel is well-recognized in the Deuteronomistic History (DtrH) as the primary leader of Israel during its transition from the period of the Judges to the period of the early monarchy. Nevertheless, his institutional identity is unclear, insofar as he functions as a visionary prophet, priest, and judge in the narratives of 1 Samuel. In this respect, he is very much like Moses, who embodies a similar set of roles in Exodus–Numbers and Deuteronomy, and he resembles to a degree Elijah and Elisha, who are identified as prophets and yet carry out priestly functions in the narratives devoted to their activities in 1–2 Kings. Although 1 Chr 6 includes Samuel and his father Elkanah in the Levitical genealogies, the narratives in 1 Samuel make it quite clear that Elkanah is an Ephraimite and that Samuel is the first born son to Elkanah's wife Hannah. Most scholars identify Samuel as a prophet or judge, and explain his priestly actions by arguing that he lived in a time when the Levitical priesthood had not been fully institutionalized.[1]

---

* In this article the divine names "G-d" and '$ĕlōqîm$ are used as a traditional Jewish form of respect.

[1] For overview discussions concerning Samuel's institutional identity, see Aelred Cody, *A History of Old Testament Priesthood* (AnBib 35; Rome: Pontifical Biblical Institute, 1969), 72–80; George W. Ramsey, "Samuel," *ABD* 5:954–7; Joseph Blenkinsopp, *Sage, Priest, Prophet: Religious and Intellectual Leadership in Ancient Israel* (Library of Ancient Israel; Louisville: Westminster

This paper examines the question of Samuel's institutional identity, and argues he represents a model of priest known in northern Israel, but not in Jerusalem and perhaps southern Judah where the Levitical priesthood was dominant. Insofar as the DtrH is committed both to the notion of a Levitical priesthood as YHWH's cultic representatives in the temple and prophets as YHWH's mouthpieces to Israel, it constructs Samuel as a prophet so that he might function as one of the spokespersons of YHWH that play such key roles throughout its presentation of Israel's history.[2] Insofar as statements by YHWH in Num 3 indicate that the first-born sons of Israel originally served as priests before being replaced by the Levites, it would seem that Samuel represents an early example of such a priest, first-born to his mother and deposited in the Shiloh sanctuary to be raised as a priest.

II

The first task is to examine Samuel's identity as a prophet as presented in 1 Samuel. First Samuel and the DtrH always refers to Samuel as a prophet, but never refers to him as a priest, judge, king, or other institutional identity although he functions in all of these capacities.

A key text is 1 Sam 3:20–21, which identifies Samuel as a prophet for YHWH, "And all Israel from Dan to Beer Sheba knew that Samuel was truly a prophet for YHWH (*ne'ĕmān šĕmû'ēl lĕnābî' lyhwh*), and YHWH again appeared in Shiloh, for YHWH was revealed to Samuel in Shiloh by means of the word of YHWH." This text is crucial for several reasons. First, it employs the standard Hebrew term for a prophet, *nābî'*, to identify Samuel's institutional identity. Second, it associates Samuel's identity as a prophet with the experience

---

John Knox, 1995), 132–4; Lester L. Grabbe, *Priests, Prophets, Diviners, Sages: A Socio-Historical Study of Religious Specialists in Ancient Israel* (Valley Forge, Penn.: Trinity, 1995), 44, 67–8, 122–3.

[2] For the roles of prophets as mouthpieces of YHWH in the DtrH and its underlying works, see Martin Noth, *The Deuteronomistic History* (JSOTSup 15; Sheffield: JSOT, 1981); Walter Dietrich, *Prophetie und Geschichte: Eine redaktionsgeschichtliche Untersuchung zum deuteronomistischen Geschichtswerk* (FRLANT 108; Göttingen: Vandhoeck & Ruprecht, 1972); idem, *David, Saul und die Propheten: Das Verhältnis von Religion und Politik nach den prophetischen Überlieferungen vom frühesten Königtum in Israel* (BWANT 122; Stuttgart: Kohlhammer, 1992); P. Kyle McCarter, *1 Samuel* (AB 8; Garden City: Doubleday, 1980), 18–23; Antony F. Campbell, *Of Prophets and Kings: A Late Ninth-Century Document (1 Samuel 1–2 Kings 10)* (CBQMS 17; Washington: Catholic Biblical Association of America, 1986).

of a vision in the narrative of 1 Sam 3 that inaugurates his career as a prophet of YHWH. Third, this narrative begins in 1 Sam 3:1 with a notice that, "The boy Samuel was serving YHWH before Eli, and the word of YHWH was rare (precious) in those days; visionary experience (*ḥāzôn*) was not widespread." When read in relation to 1 Sam 3:20–21, the notice in 1 Sam 3:1 forms a literary enclosure that presents the means by which the dearth of prophecy in the land was resolved by Samuel's visionary experience of YHWH.

Subsequent narratives in 1 Samuel either explicitly or implicitly identify Samuel as a prophet. Indeed, the following introduction in 1 Sam 4:1 to the Ark Narrative of 1 Sam 4–6 states, "and the word of Samuel was to all Israel," signals that Samuel's identity as a prophet will underlie all of the following material.

The narrative in 1 Sam 8 concerning YHWH's decision to grant the people's request for a king indicates that Samuel consulted YHWH on the matter and reported all of YHWH's words to the people. Other scholars have noted that Samuel's role in designating Saul as king is analogous to the roles of other prophets, such as Nathan, Ahijah, Elijah, and Elisha, who designate David, Jeroboam, and Jehu.[3]

The narrative in 1 Sam 9:1–10:16 concerning Samuel's designation of Saul as king identifies Samuel as a "man of G-d" (*'îš hā'ĕlōqîm*) and as a "seer," (*rō'eh*) throughout. Both terms are commonly employed to designate a prophet in the Hebrew Bible,[4] and 1 Sam 9:9 explains, "Formerly in Israel thus said a man when he went to inquire of G-d, 'come, and let us go to the seer (*rō'eh*),' for today's prophet (*nābî'*) was formerly called a seer."

The narrative in 1 Sam 10:17–27 concerning the selection of Saul as king by lot likewise presents Samuel as a prophet when he summons the people to Mizpah and begins his speech to them with a version of the classical prophetic messenger formula, "Thus says YHWH, G-d of Israel" (*kōh 'āmar yhwh ĕlōqê yiśrā'ēl*).

Both narratives concerning YHWH's rejection of Saul as king in 1 Sam 13–14 and 15 likewise present Samuel as a prophet. In 1 Sam 13:13–14 Samuel delivers a classical prophetic word of judgment against Saul which lays out both the basis for divine judgment and the proclamation of judgment itself by charging that because Saul has failed to observe the commandments of YHWH, his dynasty will not endure. First Samuel 15 begins with Samuel's prophetic word of judgment against Amalek in v. 2, which again begins with an example

---

[3] See Ramsey, "Samuel," 955; Campbell, *Of Prophets and Kings*.

[4] See David L. Petersen, *The Roles of Israel's Prophets* (JSOTSup 17; Sheffield: JSOT, 1981), 35–50.

of the prophetic messenger formula, "Thus says YHWH of Hosts, I am punishing what Amalek did to Israel when he (Amalek) attacked him (Israel) on the road when he (Israel) went up from Egypt." Later, 1 Sam 15:10–11 employs the classical prophetic word formula, "And the word of YHWH came to Samuel, saying…" (*wayĕhî dĕbar-yhwh 'el šĕmû'ēl lē'mōr*), to introduce YHWH's instructions to Samuel concerning Saul. And 1 Sam 15:17–19, 20–23, 28–29 presents Samuel's condemnation of Saul in the form of a classical prophetic judgment speech.

The narrative concerning Saul's inquiry of the dead Samuel by means of the witch of Endor once again presents Samuel's condemnation of Saul in the form of a prophetic judgment speech in vv. 17–19.

Finally, although 1 Chr 6:7–13 identifies Samuel as a Levite, 1 Chr 9:22; 26:28; and 29:29 follow 1 Sam 9:1–10:16 in identifying Samuel as a seer (*rō'eh*), and 2 Chr 35:18 follows 1 Sam 3:20–21 by identifying him as a prophet (*nābî'*).

All of these cases point to Samuel's role as a prophet of YHWH, but there is ample evidence of Samuel's roles as judge and priest as well. The presentation of Samuel as judge of Israel appears in 1 Sam 7:2–17 and 8:1–3. The term, *šōpēṭ*, "judge," is never applied to Samuel, but the verb *wayyišpōṭ*, "and he judged," is twice applied to Samuel's "judging" Israel in 1 Sam 7:6, 15, and *šāpaṭ*, "he judged," is employed in 1 Sam 7:17. Both senses of the term, i.e., to rule, and, "to decide judicial cases," are applied to Samuel in this section insofar as he presides over Israel in its conflict with the Philistines and hears legal cases. When he is old, he appoints his sons as judges, Hebrew, *šōpĕṭîm*, according to 1 Sam 8:1–3, but they are inadequate for the task.

Although many scholars argue that Samuel's basic identity is that of a judge as in the book of Judges,[5] we must observe that his judgeship has priestly dimensions. When Samuel leads Israel against the Philistines, the narrative does not portray him as participating directly in battle; rather, he officiates over the offerings that are made to YHWH and makes appeals to YHWH on the people's behalf before they actually went to battle. We may observe that Eli, Hophni, and Phineas did not accompany Israel to battle initially against the Philistines in 1 Sam 4, and Hophni and Phineas only joined Israel later to carry the Ark of the Covenant in a failed effort to rally the Israelites after initial setbacks. We may also observe that Deut 20:1–4 presents the priest's role in war as a figure who exhorts the soldiers prior to the battle, but does not lead them in actual combat. Moses, the Levite, plays a similar role in battle against Amalek in Exod 17:8–16 when his extended rod aids Israel in overcoming the Amalekites, and he later builds an altar to mark the victory. We may observe that judicial functions are part of the purview of the priests, although not exclusively so, according to Deut

---

[5] Ramsey, "Samuel," 955.

16:18–17:13 in which the Levitical priests serve as the chief magistrates of Israel. We may note also that Moses the Levite establishes and oversees judges in Israel according to Jethro's advice in Exod 18. With these considerations in mind, it appears that Samuel's functions as judge coincide with his identity and functions as a priest.

When we turn to Samuel's functions as priest, we see ample attestation to his priestly role. He is never labeled as *kōhēn* or as *lēwî* in the 1 Samuel narratives, but his actions are frequently those of a priest. The most obvious indicator of priestly identity for Samuel is the role that he plays in offering sacrifices to YHWH. Although there are instances in which non-priests offer sacrifice in the Bible, such an act is generally reserved for the priesthood. We have already observed Samuel's actions as a priest in conjunction with his role as judge. When he gathers the people at Mizpah for war against the Philistines in 1 Sam 7:2–17, libation offerings are made before YHWH in v. 6 as the people fast and confess their sins. Nevertheless, Samuel's role in presenting the libation offerings is not made clear, although the text suggests that he presided over the ceremony. In vv. 9–10, however, the text makes it quite clear that Samuel made an *'ōlâ*, i.e., a whole burnt offering, to YHWH. The *'ōlâ* is the basic offering made to YHWH in the temple each day by the priests, and it frequently serves as the basic offering outside of the temple as well.[6] A second instance of Samuel's association with sacrifice appears in 1 Sam 9:1–10:16 when he presides over the *zebaḥ*, sacrifice, in Ramah as Saul and his servant enter the city. The *zebaḥ* would likely refer to the *zebaḥ šĕlāmîm*, the so-called "peace offering" or "sacrifice of well-being," that was generally offered in addition to the *'ōlâ* to implore YHWH to ensure the well-being of the community or individual making the offering.[7] Samuel's role is to bless the *zebaḥ* of the city, according to 1 Sam 9:13, which allows the people to eat it. Furthermore, Samuel seats Saul at the head of table and gives Saul the *šôq* or thigh portion of the *zebaḥ*, which is the *šôq hattĕrûmâ* or the thigh of consecration normally granted to the priests and their families (Exod 29:27; Lev 7:34; 10:14–15; Num 6:20).[8] Such an act on Samuel's part presumes priestly authority. Later in the same narrative, Samuel instructs Saul to wait for him at Gilgal where he (Samuel) will offer *'ōlôt*, whole burnt offerings, and *zibḥê šĕlāmîm*, "sacrifices of well-being," before Israel goes to battle against the Philistines. Again, the narrative presumes Samuel's priestly

---

[6] Gary A. Anderson, "Sacrifice and Sacrificial Offerings (OT)," *ABD* 5 (1992): 870–86, esp. 877–8.

[7] Anderson, "Sacrifice and Sacrificial Offerings," 878–9.

[8] See Jacob Milgrom, *Leviticus 1–16* (AB 3; Garden City: Doubleday, 991), 473–81.

authority. Indeed, when Samuel finally arrives at Gilgal in 1 Sam 13:8–14, he condemns Saul for having offered the *'ōlâ* without having waited for him (Samuel) to arrive so that he might officiate. Saul also intended to offer the *zebaḥ šĕlāmîm*, again, a priestly prerogative. Saul's failure to observe YHWH's commands, not simply to wait for Samuel to arrive but to allow him to perform the priestly functions of sacrifice, cost him his throne in this passage. Finally, 1 Sam 16:15 portrays Samuel's role as officiant over sacrifice when he travels to Beth Lehem to anoint David ben Jesse as the next king of Israel. The narrative employs the verb *zbḥ* to describe Samuel's intended actions, which suggests that he intended to offer the *zebaḥ šĕlāmîm*, in which the priests and people share in eating the sacrifice, in Beth Lehem.

All of these instances presume Samuel's right to officiate or offer sacrifice on behalf of Israel. Such prerogative is normally reserved for a priest in ancient Israel.

But there is one more indicator of Samuel's priestly status, viz., his role as a visionary. Visionary experience is hardly confined to the priesthood. Indeed, clearly non-priestly figures such as Jacob ben Isaac (Gen 28), Amos of Tekoa (Amos 7–9), and Isaiah ben Amoz (Isa 6) have visionary experiences, although all are associated with temples. Likewise, figures identified as both priests and prophets, such as Moses ben Amran (Exod 33), Jeremiah ben Hilkiah (Jer 1; 24), Ezekiel ben Buzi (Ezek 1–3; 8–10; 40–48), Zechariah ben Berechiah ben Iddo (Zech 1–6), and possibly Habakkuk (Hab 2–3), all engage in visionary experience. But we must note that visionary experience is not associated exclusively with prophets. It is part of the priestly purview as well as indicated in Lev 16:2, which states that the high priest may not enter the Holy of Holies of the temple where YHWH appears at will. Rather, he comes only to make expiation for the people on Yom Kippur, the Day of Atonement, when he presents the various offerings before YHWH. The priest is the only person allowed to enter the Holy of Holies and visionary experience of YHWH is therefore possible for him there as well.

Indeed, such revelatory experience of YHWH plays a role in defining the holy garments of the high priest. He is to wear an ephod or breast plate inlaid with twelve precious stones to represent the tribes of Israel. Insofar as the background of the ephod is to be found in oracular inquiry of YHWH,[9] it also points to the priest's revelatory experience of YHWH and his role in communicating the will of YHWH based on that experience to the people. We may observe that the ephod appears in different forms, such as a linen ephod, and that it is employed by persons who are not explicitly identified as priests, such as Gideon (Judg 8) and David (2 Sam 6), but it does point to the capacity of the priests for revelatory or visionary experience.

---

[9] Raphael I. Panetz, "Ephod," *ABD* 2 (1992): 550–1.

It is at this point that we must note the setting of Samuel's initial visionary or revelatory experience of YHWH in 1 Sam 3, i.e., his initial visionary experience occurs while he is sleeping in the Shiloh Temple where the Ark of the Covenant is located. We may also note that Samuel is described as serving YHWH, (*měšārēt 'et-yhwh*), before Eli in the temple at the time of his vision. The expression, *měšārēt 'et-yhwh*, is normally, although not exclusively, reserved for priestly service,[10] and access to the temple and the Ark of the Covenant is normally reserved for priests. Although we must observe that non-priests might have had access to the temple and the Ark at this early time in Israel's history and that the literary framework of the present form of the narrative clear portrays Samuel's experience to inaugurate his role as a prophet (*nābî'*), Samuel's priestly associations are clear.

One makes similar observations about Samuel's visionary experience in 1 Sam 9:1–10:16, i.e., Samuel is clearly in communication with YHWH throughout the account of his encounter with Saul, but he does so as a figure who officiates over sacrifice in Ramah and assigns to Saul the *šôq hattěrûmâ* normally reserved for priests.

When taken together with our earlier observations concerning the priestly associations of Samuel's actions in his role as judge, we must come to a conclusion, viz., although the 1 Samuel narratives clear identify Samuel as a prophet, seer, and man of G-d, he also very clearly functions as a priest even though he is never labeled as such. Indeed, the Chronicler appears to have faced this question as well and resolved the issue by labeling Samuel as both prophet and seer as we noted above, but the Chronicler also makes sure to work Samuel and his family line into the genealogy of the Levites in 1 Chr 6:7–13. In essence, the Chronicler resolved the issue by identifying Samuel as both prophet and Levite.[11] Indeed, traditional Jewish exegetes, such as Radak and Rashi, accept the Chronicler's decision and interpret the identification of Samuel's father Elkanah as an Ephraimite in 1 Sam 1:1 as an indication of his residence, not of his tribal identity.[12]

III

---

[10] Cody, *A History*, 74.

[11] Cf. Sara Japhet, *1 and 2 Chronicles: A Commentary* (OTL; Louisville: Westminster John Knox, 1993), 155–6.

[12] For the commentaries of Radak (R. David Kimḥi) and Rashi (R. Solomon ben Isaac), see any standard edition of the Mikraot Gedolot.

These observations demand that we press the question farther, i.e., why does 1 Samuel identify Samuel only as a prophet when it is so clear that he functions as a priest as well? Three major considerations come into play.

First, we may observe that northern traditions frequently ascribe prophetic identity to leading authority figures. The patriarchs Abraham and Jacob are both credited with visionary experiences in the EJ accounts of Gen 15 and 28 respectively even though neither is ever identified as a prophet. The elders of Israel are granted prophetic status in Num 11 even though the function of the elders is to play a role in the governance of Israel rather than to act as prophets. Even in the Samuel traditions, Saul is credited with prophetic experience even though he is not a prophet. And Elijah and Elisha are identified as prophets, even though so many of their own actions are those of priests, e.g., offering sacrifice at Mt. Carmel, experiencing divine revelation on Mt. Horeb much like the priest in the Holy of Holies, and playing music while delivering an oracle much like the later prophets identified as Levitical temple singers.

Second, we must observe that although many if not all of Samuel's priestly actions identified above are ascribed to the Levitical priesthood in the priestly portions of the Pentateuch, the P portions of the Pentateuch themselves are aware that the Levites were not always the priesthood of ancient Israel. The books of Exodus and especially Numbers emphasize the means by which the Levites emerged as YHWH's divinely chosen priestly tribe during Israel's sojourn in the wilderness. But statements made by YHWH in Num 3:11–13 and 3:40–51 clearly indicate that the first-born sons of Israel served as priests for YHWH before the tribe of Levi was chosen for this role; for example:

> YHWH spoke to Moses, saying "And I, behold, I, have taken the Levites from among the people of Israel in place of all the first-born, the first issue of the womb among the people of Israel: the Levites shall be Mine. For every first-born is Mine. At the time that I struck the first-born in the land of Egypt, I consecrated every first-born in Israel, human and animal, to Myself to be Mine, YHWH's." (Num 3:11–13)

And

> And YHWH said to Moses, "Record every first-born male of the people of Israel from the age of one month up, and make a lists of their names, and take the Levites for Me, YHWH, in place of every first-born among the people of Israel, and the cattle of the Levites in place of every first-born among the cattle of the people of Israel." (Num 3:40–41)

Indeed, vestiges of the practice of dedicating first-born sons (first-born to the mother) appear elsewhere in the Bible as well. Exod 34:19–21 indicates that every first issue of the womb belongs to YHWH, including all the first-born of cattle and sheep. The legal paragraph goes on to declare that every first-born ass and human being must be redeemed, i.e., the owner or parent must present some sort of an offering at the temple in place of first-born ass or human being. Such a conception stands behind the Aqedah narrative in Gen 22, in which Isaac, first-born to his mother Sarah, is redeemed from sacrifice by a ram that is sacrificed in his place. Exodus 34:19–21 appears also to be an elaboration on Exod 22:28–29, which requires Israelites not to put off the skimming of their vats, to give their first-born sons to YHWH, and also to give the first-born of cattle and flocks to YHWH.

Most interpreters presuppose that the command to give the first-born sons to YHWH entails their sacrifice, as illustrated by the Aqedah narrative and the analogy of giving first-born cattle and sheep to YHWH as offerings.[13] But can we presuppose the practice of child sacrifice in ancient Israel—even at an early period—when biblical tradition is adamant that the sacrifice of children is abhorrent to YHWH? Perhaps the tradition reacts against a time when child sacrifice was practiced in Canaan or the surrounding regions by Israel's ancestors or predecessors, but such an act is considered foreign to Israel's self-understanding—and the texts cited here aid in making sure that Israel does not engage in such practice.

But YHWH's statements to Moses in Num 3:11–13 and 3:40–51 suggest another possibility, viz., that Israel's earliest priesthood was constituted by the dedication of first-born sons to the service of YHWH, but whereas first-born cattle and sheep were sacrificed to YHWH, the first-born sons served as priests to offer sacrifices and serve in other holy capacities instead of serving as sacrifices themselves. Only later did the Levitical priesthood develop as a priestly, hereditary tribe or caste to undertake such functions, especially in Jerusalem and perhaps in Judah as well. Such a development might well explain the condemnation of Jeroboam ben Nebat, the first king of northern Israel, for his practice of appointing anyone to be a priest rather than Levites. Perhaps his practice represents an earlier Israelite practice of designating the first-born sons as priests, whereas the Judean-oriented DtrH affirmed the role of the Levites as YHWH's priesthood and condemned other practices as antithetical to the true will of YHWH for holy service in Israel's and Judah's temples.

---

[13] But see William H. C. Propp, *Exodus 19–40* (AB 2A; Garden City: Doubleday, 2006), 263–72; Jon D. Levenson, *The Death and Resurrection of the Beloved Son: The Transformation of Child Sacrifice in Judaism and Christianity* (New Haven: Yale, 1993), esp. 4–17.

Samuel's circumstances certainly appear to fit this model. He is the first-born son of his mother Hannah and his Ephraimite father Elkanah. He is deposited in the Shiloh sanctuary to be raised for priestly service by the high priest Eli. He develops into a visionary prophet and oracle diviner who speaks on behalf of YHWH, much like other Levites or priests, such as Moses, Jeremiah, Ezekiel, Zechariah, and perhaps others. And when he offers sacrifice or engages in other priestly functions, no objection is made because his right to do so is unquestioned.

Such considerations return us to the issue addressed at the outset of this paper, i.e., the institutional identity of Samuel in the DtrH. Clearly, the DtrH affirms Samuel's identity as a prophet (*nābî'*), but it never refers to him as a Levite or priest as it does with Eli and his sons Hophni and Phineas. But we have also noted how 1 Sam 3:1 and 3:20–21 (see also 1 Sam 4:1) frames the narrative concerning Samuel's inaugural visionary experience while sleeping before the Ark of the Covenant in the Shiloh sanctuary with language that indicates that this experience makes Samuel a prophet. We have also seen how 1 Sam 9:9 explains that Samuel's role as a seer (*rō'eh*), would be understood in contemporary times (of the author of the narrative) as a prophet (*nābî'*). Given the commitment to the temple and the Levitical priesthood evident throughout the DtrH, the DtrH editors must have edited the earlier underlying Samuel narrative to characterize him as a prophet, *nābî'*, rather than as an earlier form of priest by virtue of his status as a first-born son dedicated to divine service in the Shiloh sanctuary by his parents. In this manner, DtrH resolves a problem in the presentation of the institutional identity of Samuel. For its own part, Chronicles corrects a problem that it perceives in the DtrH account by identifying Samuel as a Levite as well as a prophet.

IV

In sum then we may note several conclusions or implications: (1) historically speaking, Samuel was an early type of Israelite priest by virtue of his identity as a first-born son to his mother who was dedicated for holy service to the Shiloh Temple; (2) Samuel's holy service as a priest included both his role as visionary prophet and his role in presiding over the offering of sacrifices to YHWH; (3) the DtrH, given its commitment to the holy temple and its Levitical priesthood, made sure to identify Samuel as a prophet, *nābî'*, to conform to its sense of sacred propriety while condemning northern Israel for its use of non-Levitical priests; and (4) the Chronicler resolved a problem perceived in the DtrH by designating Samuel as a Levite and providing a Levitical genealogy for his family.

EZEKIEL: A COMPROMISED PROPHET IN REDUCED CIRCUMSTANCES

Lena-Sofia Tiemeyer

INTRODUCTION

Personifications are common to all literature, although the form in which they occur differs. Sometimes entirely fictive characters are presented as historical persons, sometimes historical persons are hidden behind a screen of fiction, and sometimes personifications are made deliberately recognizable as literary fiction.[1] This realization has highlighted the need to differentiate between the author of a prophetic text and the prophetic "I" within that same text. As a result, several recent scholarly treaties focus on the literary aspects of the presentation of prophets, asking less about the (prophetic) author(s) behind the text and more about the prophetic persona as presented in the text.[2] Scholars

---

[1] Johannes C. de Moor (ed.), *The Elusive Prophet: The Prophet as a Historical Person, Literary Character, and Anonymous Artist* (OTS 45; Leiden: Brill, 2001), vii.

[2] See especially Matthijs J. de Jong, "Ezekiel as a Literary Figure and the Quest for the Historical Prophet," in *The Book of Ezekiel and its Influence* (ed. Henk Jan de Jonge and Johannes Tromp; Aldershot: Ashgate, 2007), 1–16, who states clearly that the only Ezekiel that we know is that Ezekiel presented in the book bearing his name. (p. 5). See also Corrine L. Patton, "Layers of Meaning: Priesthood in Jeremiah MT," in *The Priests in the Prophets: The Portrayal of Priests, Prophets, and Other Religious Specialists in the Latter Prophets* (ed. Lester L. Grabbe and Alice O. Bellis; JSOTSup 408; London: T&T Clark, 2004), 149–76, Corrine L. Patton, "Priest, Prophet, and Exile: Ezekiel as a Literary Construct," in *Ezekiel's Hierarchical World: Wrestling with a Tiered*

range between those who see a given prophetic book as based, at least in part, upon the sayings of a historical character, and those who regard the prophetic literature as un-historical presentations of prophets.[3]

In line with this research, the present article will look at the literary persona of Ezekiel. What ways and to what extent does the book of *Ezekiel* portray Ezekiel as a prophet? Moreover, what purpose does this portrayal serve and who benefits from it? Furthermore, does this portrayal differ from the portrayal of prophets in earlier biblical texts? Questions regarding the historical Ezekiel will be set aside. In order to avoid confusion between the book and the character that appears in the same book, I shall italicize the book titles. Moreover, it should be understood that whenever I refer to the prophet Ezekiel or to any other prophet by name, I am referring to the literary personae within the biblical texts.

My study is based on the portrayal of Ezekiel as presented by the final form of the MT of *Ezekiel*. It is possible that the present text is the result of literary activity over a longer period of time and it is equally possible that the LXX may, in some cases, present an earlier reading. This means that a close reading of *Ezekiel* may reveal conflicting portrayals of the character of Ezekiel, as one textual/redactional layer may characterize Ezekiel differently from another textual layer. Nonetheless, as the final redactor has arranged and contextualized the various strands of material, I maintain that the final form of the MT yields a distinct and unified portrayal of Ezekiel.

Along the same lines, I shall read *Ezekiel* as literature, accepting the claims that the book makes regarding its speakers. I shall therefore distinguish between Ezekiel's and God's first person utterances. When doing so, we shall discover that there is considerable tension with regard to the understanding of Ezekiel's prophetic office between, on the one hand, Ezekiel's words and actions and, on the other hand, the divine oracles. I shall look at two specific areas of conflict. First, I shall explore Ezekiel's role as God's marionette and argue that Ezekiel deplores his loss of personal freedom. Secondly, I shall investigate Ezekiel's role as God's spokesman and suggest that Ezekiel is reluctant to forego the traditional prophetic role as mediator between God and the people of Israel. I shall also briefly touch upon Ezekiel's success in maintaining his priestly purity.

Reality (ed. Steven L. Cook and Corrine L. Patton; Atlanta: Society of Biblical Literature, 2004), 73–89. In the latter article, Patton focuses on Ezekiel's role as priest and argues that the book of *Ezekiel* presents us with an idealized picture of a priest.

[3] See further discussion in Yehoshua Gitay, "The Projection of the Prophet: A Rhetorical Presentation of the Prophet Jeremiah," in *Prophecy and Prophets: The Diversity and Contemporary Issues in Scholarship* (ed. Yehoshua Gitay; SBL Semeia Studies; Atlanta, Ga.: Scholars Press, 1997), 41–55.

Finally, I shall look at the result of these changes: who benefits from them and who loses?

EZEKIEL: GOD'S APPOINTED MARIONETTE

As noted by many scholars, Ezekiel is portrayed as God's ultimate tool to the degree that he lacks a distinct personality.[4] In fact, Ezekiel emerges from the pages less as a historical person than as the embodiment of a particular theological perspective.[5] In this section, I shall explore these claims further. On the one hand, I shall show that the persona of Ezekiel most of the time embodies the theodicy that Israel is absolutely guilty of sin and that God's destruction of his people is an act of divine justice. Ezekiel represents God's side of the issue and his words and his actions reveal a theocentric theology. It is therefore apt to call him God's marionette. On the other hand, as I hope to demonstrate, a few passages demand a more nuanced way of understanding what the persona of Ezekiel represents. In these cases, Ezekiel rejects his assigned role as God's spokesperson and instead embodies Israel's view.

The book of *Ezekiel* opens with a dual superscription. The third person superscription in Ezek 1:3 states that Ezekiel is of priestly descent.[6] The latter description fits both the prophet Ezekiel and the content of *Ezekiel* well as both are permeated with priestly theology and priestly concerns. At the same time, the first person statement in Ezek 1:1 provides Ezekiel's perspective on his call to ministry. He defines himself as one who sees "visions of God" (מראות אלהים).

---

[4] C.f., Karin Schöpflin, *Theologie als Biographie im Ezechielbuch: Ein Beitrag zur Konzeption alttestamentlicher Prophetie* (FAT 36; Tübingen: Mohr, 2002), 187–8, and Robert R. Wilson, "Prophecy in Crisis: The Call of Ezekiel," in *Interpreting the Prophets* (ed. James L. Mays and Paul J. Achtemeier; Philadelphia: Fortress, 1987), 157–69 (165). See also Daniel I. Block, *The Book of Ezekiel Chapters 1–24* (NICOT; Grand Rapids: Eerdmans, 1997), 27, who states that "in spite of the autobiography form, one wonders if the real Ezekiel is ever exposed."

[5] Andrew Mein, "Ezekiel as a Priest in Exile," in de Moor (ed.), *The Elusive Prophet*, 199–213. See also Schöpflin, *Theologie als Biographie*, 127, who states that "Dem Ezechielbuch hingegen ist die Titelgestalt als solche nur insofern wichtig, als sie in einem besonderen Verhältnis zu YHWH steht."

[6] It is unclear whether the word כהן in the expression יחזקאל בן בוזי הכהן refers to Ezekiel or to his father Buzi.

In either case, Ezekiel identifies himself as a prophet in that he describes himself as a person with whom God communicates and whose oracles he conveys.[7]

Nonetheless, Ezekiel's self-portrayal differs in significant ways from the way other prophets are described or describe themselves. First, Ezekiel portrays himself as a man completely overpowered or even stunned by God. Notably, in his visionary reports, rather than conversing with God within the visions, as Amos, Isaiah, Jeremiah, and Zechariah do, Ezekiel depicts his verbal interaction with God as extremely limited. His only responsive act is falling to the ground in awe (e.g., Ezek 1:14–28a; cf. 44:4).[8]

Secondly, in a manner not shared by other accounts of prophets, Ezekiel describes himself as a person lacking control over his own body. Instead, God/the Spirit controls it. In Ezek 1:28b–2:2, as Ezekiel hears a voice commanding him to stand up, God's spirit enters into him and raises him up. Likewise, at the end of the oracle, the Spirit removes Ezekiel. Ezek 8:1–8 contains similar imagery. Ezekiel describes how God takes him by the hair and transports him in a vision to Jerusalem (v. 3) and even telling him where to look (v. 5). Moreover, although God asks him a question ("do you see what they are doing"), this is no more than a rhetorical question as God responds himself.

Thirdly, Ezekiel depicts himself as lacking control over any outward show of feelings. In contrast to Jeremiah who laments spontaneously, God is in command of at least the outward expression of Ezekiel's feelings. For instance, God commands Ezekiel to lament several times (Ezek 21:6, see also 32:2 שא קינה על פרעה מלך־מצרים and 32:18 והורדהו נהה על המון מצרים).[9] Along similar lines, when God brings about the death of Ezekiel's wife, God forbids Ezekiel to show any outward signs of mourning (Ezek 24:15–27). Ezekiel complies without uttering a word.

---

[7] See further Baruch J. Schwartz, "A Priest Out of Place: Reconsidering Ezekiel's Role in the History of the Israelite Priesthood," in Cook and Patton (ed.), *Ezekiel's Hierarchical World*, 61–71, who argues that Ezekiel is a visionary rather than a legislator, and what he reports is a *prophet's* account. We may thus do an injustice to the text if we assume that Ezekiel performed priestly duties in exile or if we assumed that he ever served as a priest in Jerusalem before the exile. See also Patton, "Layers of Meaning," 151, who highlights that the same is true for the book of *Jeremiah*. While the superscription in Jer 1:1 announces that Jeremiah is a priest, the book presents him as a prophet.

[8] For exceptions, see especially Ezek 9:8 and 11:13 discussed below.

[9] Ezek 21:6 is best understood as a sign act rather than as a true lament. The purpose is to get the people around Ezekiel to ask for the reason of his crying. See further Kelvin G. Friebel, *Jeremiah's and Ezekiel's Sign Acts: Rhetorical Nonverbal Communication* (JSOTSup 283; Sheffield: Sheffield Academic, 1999), 289–90.

Fourthly, Ezekiel often describes himself as someone akin to a robot that automatically fulfils God's commands without pausing to reflect and/or to question. Ezekiel's report of his vision of the valley of the dry bones is typical in this respect (Ezek 37:1–14). God and Ezekiel have something resembling a conversation, although what Ezekiel does is in fact merely throwing the conversational ball back to God. God asks him whether the bones that he sees can receive life again (v. 3). Ezekiel, refusing to make an independent statement, responds that God alone knows this (אדני ה' אתה ידעת). God then commands him to prophecy over the bones, giving him the exact words to say (vv. 9–10), and, without further ado, the bones receive life. The closest parallel to this, yet standing in sharp contrast, is Jeremiah's complaint in Jer 20:9. Although being unable to resist God's commands, he nonetheless reflects over this inability and wishes for the situation to be otherwise.

The account in Ezek 40–48 belongs in this category as well. Ezekiel informs us that he is brought to Israel in a vision and that he is commanded to "use his eyes and his ears and to pay attention" (ראה בעיניך ובאזניך שמע ושים לבך) so that he can report everything (40:4; 44:5). He is even to write it down (43:10–11). And indeed, Ezekiel remembers all the rooms and their measurements but offers no comment about them. God speaks directly to him once, asking whether he sees the flood (47:6 הראית בן אדם), but Ezekiel offers no response. God then guides him back to the flood bank. There Ezekiel offers, not a spoken phrase but a thought: "As I came back, I saw a great number of trees on both sides of the river" (בשובני והנה אל־שפת הנהר עץ רב מאד מזה ומזה). This is one of the very few personal remarks of the entire book, and in its blandness and in its insignificance the remark serves as a rather poignant symbol of Ezekiel's lack of independent thoughts.

This picture that Ezekiel paints of himself is rather unpalatable, at least for most modern readers, as it is totally devoid of initiative and independence. Moreover, at first sight, we may easily assume that Ezekiel himself agrees with this picture. A closer look, however, reveals a tension within Ezekiel's portrayal between what he obediently *does* and what he really *feels*. Ezekiel describes himself as *bitter* and *angry* (3:14 מר בחמת רוחי) during his first visionary journey, and that the hand of the Lord was "*heavy* upon him" (3:14 ויד ה' עלי חזקה). Upon arrival in Tel Aviv among the exiles, Ezekiel further states that he sat "*appalled* in their midst" (משמים בתוכם) for seven days (3:15). Furthermore, as Block points out, the account of Ezekiel's calling in Ezek 1–3 "leaves one with nagging questions about his disposition towards his calling." Why is the prelude to his commissioning so overwhelming (1:4–28), why does the Spirit need to command him to stand up and then to set him to his feet when presumably he could have stood up by himself (2:1–2), why does God need to warn him not to be rebellious like the rest of the people (2:8)?[10] Taken together, Ezekiel's description of the way he feels about God's/the Spirit's ways of taking control over his body and his outward feelings, in conjunction with the very fact that he does not or is not given the opportunity to move by his own volition, paints a picture of inner tension. Ezekiel hardly ever voices openly his opposition to his role as God's compliant tool, but he records his feelings of unease.

EZEKIEL: GOD'S APPOINTED SPOKESMAN

Turning to the divine oracles, a similar image emerges. Ezekiel is commissioned to be God's spokesman, to the exception of everything else. This one-sided definition of the prophetic role is attested elsewhere (e.g., Exod 7:1–2), although not to the same extent and not with the same constancy. I shall therefore argue that the oracles in the book of *Ezekiel* redefine the prophetic office. Three factors support this claim. First, much of the literature of ancient Israel associated prophets with intercession. Secondly, intercession was regarded to be a prophetic task in the sixth century BCE. Thirdly, as the character of Ezekiel is consciously modelled after Moses, intercession was expected of him. However, in appointing him as a watchman, God forced him to break with this tradition. Finally, in the light of these observations, I shall evaluate Ezekiel's own response to this redefinition of his prophetic office.

To What Extent Are the Prophets of Ancient Israel Portrayed as Intercessors?

The traditions we have about prophets in the Hebrew Bible are not descriptions of what actual prophets in ancient Israel did but reflections of prophecy based on later perceptions.[11] This means that we have to be careful not to simply equate the tasks ascribed to a prophetic figure within the Hebrew Bible with the tasks of the prophets of ancient Israel. My focus here is therefore not so much to

---

[10] Block, (*Ezekiel*, 1, 11–12), argues that Ezekiel is a reluctant prophet. He acknowledges (n. 13) that his interpretation was stimulated by private conversation with Mark Bryan following the latter's paper titled "The Force Behind and Within Ezekiel: Didn't You Hear?" (paper presented at the annual meeting of the SBL in Chicago, 1994).

[11] Matthijs J. de Jong, *Isaiah Among the Ancient Near Eastern Prophets: A Comparative Study of the Earliest Stages of the Isaiah Tradition and the Neo-Assyrian Prophecies* (VTSup 117; Leiden: Brill, 2007), 323.

determine whether the prophets of ancient Israel interceded, but rather whether they were commonly portrayed as doing so.

The Hebrew Bible does not describe all prophets as intercessors, and people other than prophets are sometimes described as intercessors. Nonetheless, several texts clearly associate intercession with prophetic figures (1 Kgs 14; 2 Kgs 1:2–8, 17a; 8:7–15; Amos 7:1–8:3; Jer 7:16; 11:14; 14:11–12) and portray prophets as intermediaries, i.e., people whose task was to stand between the deity and the people. Based on these texts, many scholars argue that intercession was one of the duties of the prophetic office in ancient Israel.[12] As such, Israelite prophets had a twofold role, on the one hand representing God to the people by proclaiming divine oracles, and, on the other hand, representing the people

---

[12] See, e.g., A. B. Rhodes, "Israel's Prophets as Intercessors, in Scripture in History and Theology," in *Essays in Honor of J. Coert Rylaarsdam* (ed. Arthur L. Merrill, Dikran Y. Hadidian, and Thomas W. Overholt; Pittsburgh: Pickwick, 1977), 107–28; Henning Graf Reventlow, *Gebet im Alten Testament* (Stuttgart: Kohlhammer, 1986), 239–246; see also idem, *Das Amt des Propheten bei Amos* (FRLANT 80; Göttingen, Vandenhoeck & Ruprecht, 1962), 30–56, and idem, *Liturgie und prophetisches Ich bei Jeremia* (Gütersloh: Gerd Mohn, 1963), 140–3; Shalom M. Paul, "Prophets and Prophecy," *EncJud* 13: 1170–1; Nahum M. Sarna, *Exodus* (JPSTC; Philadelphia: Jewish Publication Society, 1991), 205; Daniel Bodi, *The Book of Ezekiel and the Poem of Erra* (OBO 104; Göttingen: Vandenhoeck & Ruprecht, 1991), 262; Patrick D. Miller, *They Cried to the Lord: The Form and Theology of Biblical Prayer* (Minneapolis: Fortress, 1994), 262–5. For an up-to-date overview of scholarly opinions, see Michael Widmer, *Moses, God, and the Dynamics of Intercessory Prayer* (FAT II/8; Tübingen: Mohr Siebeck, 2004), 28–56. This view has been challenged by primarily Hans Wilhelm Hertzberg, "Sind die Propheten Fürbitter?" in *Tradition und Situation: Studien zur alttestamentlichen Prophetie. Artur Weiser zum 70. Geburtstag am 18.11.1963 dargebracht von Kollegen, Freunden und Schülern* (ed. Ernst Würthwein and Otto Kaiser; Göttingen: Vandenhoeck & Ruprecht, 1963), 63–74, and Samuel E. Balentine, "The Prophet as Intercessor: A Reassessment," *JBL* 103 (1984): 161–73, esp. 162–4. See also Uwe Becker, "Der Prophet als Fürbitter: Zum Literarhistorischen Ort der Amos-Visionen," *VT* 51 (2001): 141–65, who argues that, in the case of Amos, there are compelling literary arguments for reading all the four visions together. In doing so, it becomes clear that the main message of the text is not that Amos is a successful intercessor but rather that God reaches out in grace while the people are unwilling to repent.

before God through lamenting and/or intercessory prayer.[13] Yochanan Muff, for example, regards the prophets as both messengers of the divine court, i.e., instruments of God's will, and "independent advocates," i.e., agents of the defendant who attempted to mitigate the divine decree.[14] One of their key tasks was thus to establish an ongoing dialogue between God and Israel, and to find a balance of God's emotions between divine justice and divine love and God's need to control and restrain his anger.[15]

Likewise, Miller argues that intercession was considered to be an integrated part of God's decision making. As such, intercession was expected, indeed required, of the prophet.[16] This is best illustrated by the fact that in nearly all cases, the Hebrew Bible speaks of a change of God's mind (*Niphal* of נחם) as the result of intercessory prayer.[17] In this way, both intercessory prayer and God's corresponding ability to change his mind are interlinked and fully consistent with each other.[18] We may thus conclude that intercession was held to be a prophetic task, although not restricted to the prophets.

Looking more specifically at Abraham's and Moses's intercession, Balentine categorizes intercessory prayers as prayers of crisis. This type of prayer has three essential features: (1) a crises between the person praying and God, (2) a response to the crisis in the form of a prayer that raises questions about divine justice and divine intervention, and (3) some resolution or at least explanation of the crisis. These types of prayers represent the tradition of piety of "loyal opposition" to God and to his ways of executing justice.[19] In addition, they belong in the lament tradition, together with especially the prayer of Jeremiah, Habakkuk and Job. They share the characteristics of denying their own guilt and placing it on God: the lament does not only call God's attention to what is wrong but seeks to secure its correction. In that way, they are prayers "to God against God." [20] Abraham and Moses, together with Jeremiah and Job,

---

[13] See further my discussion in Lena-Sofia Tiemeyer, "God's Hidden Compassion," *TynBul* 57 (2006): 193–4.

[14] Yochanan Muff, *Love and Joy: Law, Language and Religion in Ancient Israel* (New York: Jewish Theological Seminary of America, 1992), 9.

[15] Muff, *Love and Joy*, 33.

[16] Patrick D. Miller, "Prayer and Divine Action," in *God in the Fray: A Tribute to Walter Brueggemann* (ed. Tod Linafelt and Timothy K. Beal; Minneapolis: Fortress, 1998), 211–32 (esp. 216–21).

[17] With the exception of Gen 6:6–7; 1 Sam 15:11, 35.

[18] Miller, "Prayer and Divine Action," 217–21, and *They Cried to the Lord*, 277–8.

[19] Samuel E. Balentine, *Prayer in the Hebrew Bible: The Drama of Divine-Human Dialogue* (OBT; Minneapolis: Fortress, 1993), 118–20.

[20] Ibid., 146–50, 195–96.

represent this need, from the victim's perspective, in that they, on the one hand, assume that God is reliable and committed to justice, and, on the other hand, needs to correct or to adjust the way justice is meted out. The balance of power between God and God's human partners needs to be shifted.[21]

I see no inherent difficulty with this characterization of Israel's prophets. At the same time, I wish to stress that it is no more (and no less) than a literary and a theological construct. What we thus have is a firm textual tradition, attested primarily in Amos, Jeremiah and 1–2 Kings, that describes prophets as intercessors and depicts them as middle-men/women who represented the human perspective to God and who were given the task to stand up to God in order to vouchsafe the survival of the people of Israel.

Did Intercession Originate within the Context of Prophecy?

This brings us to the issue of the (literary) origin of intercessory prayer: did the idea of a spokesperson representing the people to God originate within literature connected with prophets or did it come from elsewhere and only later came to be associated with the prophetic office? As we discussed above, many texts associate intercessory prayer with the prophetic role. At the same time, there are other texts that associate intercession with non-prophets. Finally, there are texts that describe intercessors and that call these intercessors prophets but where these intercessors do not display any (other) characteristic that is normally associated with the prophetic role. I shall center my discussion on Moses as he, alongside Abraham and Samuel, is described as involved in intercession and as he is referred to as a prophet, and ask whether he is called a prophet because he is an intercessor or, *vice versa*, whether he is described as interceding because he is a prophet.

Most scholars have approached this issue from a historical-critical perspective, with the aim of determining whether the prophets of ancient Israel were the first intercessors or whether they took over the idea of intercession from others. My task here is simpler: through this overview of scholarly opinions, I merely wish to demonstrate that intercession was considered a prophetic task at the time of writing *Jeremiah* and *Ezekiel*.

Moses is without doubt the intercessor *par excellence* in the Hebrew Bible, as he intercedes on behalf of Pharaoh,[22] his own sister,[23] and on behalf of the

---

[21] Ibid., 195–6.
[22] Exod 8:28; 9:28; 10:17, using the verb העתירו.

people of Israel,[24] reaching the climax in Exod 32:10, 32 where he successfully pleads with God to avert the divine punishment of Israel. Samuel takes second place.[25] Together, Moses and Samuel are noted as frequent intercessors[26] and they are both referred to as prophets.[27] Abraham is finally called a prophet in the very context where he intercedes for Abimelech.[28] Yet none of these three personae perform tasks that the rest of the Hebrew Bible would ascribe to a prophet. They utter no oracles of doom or salvation, nor do they serve kings with their predictions, and they share few if any characteristics with the itinerant miracle workers Elijah and Elisha. This seems to suggest that intercession originated outside the prophetic context and that only at a later time, when intercession had became associated with the prophetic office, the attribute "prophet" was added to the Pentateuchal narratives.

Along these lines, Reventlow regards Moses's role as intercessor as primary and the depiction of him as a prophet as secondary. In this way, there is no genuine connection between Moses's task as intercessor and his title "prophet."[29] From a different perspective, yet reaching a similar conclusion, Petersen argues that a tradition of Moses as a prophet was neither known nor influential in prophetic circles, as no passage in the later prophets relate to Moses as a prophet.[30] The Pentateuch represents him as a wonder-worker with priestly prerogatives and immediate access to God that sets him apart and above other prophets. It would follow that we cannot use the Pentateuchal material pertaining to Moses as an argument for an original connection between prophets and intercession. Rather, Moses is first and foremost described as an intercessor, and only later, in retrospect when intercession had come to be associated with the prophetic role, as a prophet. In other words, Moses is called a prophet because he intercedes.

---

[23] Num 12:13–15.

[24] Exod 8:4–9; 9:27–33; 10:16–19; 17:8–13; Num 12:11–14; 21:7.

[25] E.g., 1 Sam 7:12, 15.

[26] Jer 15:1; Deut 34:10; Ps 99:6.

[27] Moses in Num 12:7; Deut 18:15 [indirectly]; 34:10; Samuel in 1 Sam 3:20; 2 Chr 35:15.

[28] See Gen 20:7 (ויתפלל בעדך), 17 (ויתפלל אברהם). It is questionable whether we can relate to Abraham's dialogue with God in Gen 18:16–33 as intercession. See, e.g., the discussion in Reventlow, *Gebet im Alten Testament*, 263–64.

[29] Reventlow, *Gebet im Alten Testament*, 230, 237–38. He makes the same argument regarding Samuel.

[30] David L. Petersen, *The Prophetic Literature: An Introduction* (Louisville, Kentucky: Westminster John Knox, 2002), 220–6; Mic 6:4; Jer 15:1; Isa 63:11–12; Mal 4:5–6 do not refer to Moses as a prophet. The possible exception is Hos 12:13.

In contrast, Balentine argues that that the narrative about Abraham's bargaining in Gen 18:22–33 and Moses's intercession in Exod 32:7–14, among other texts, are to be assigned to the Deuteronomistic editor and thus of exilic or post-exilic origin.[31] Aurelius draws similar conclusions from his tradition-historical treatment of the narratives relating to Moses's intercession, and argues that the motif of Moses's intercession in Exod 32:30–34 is influenced by Amos 7:1–6.[32] Even later, Exod 32:7–8, 10–14 was inserted, with its motifs taken from especially the account of the prophet Micah's successful intercession on behalf of the people of Israel (Jer 26:18–19) but also from Amos 7 and other passages.[33] For Balentine and Aurelius, the prophets were thus the original intercessors while Moses gradually becomes an intercessor as later traditions and/or redactors make their mark on the narratives surrounding his character. In other words, Moses is portrayed as interceding because he is remembered as a prophet.

Widmer holds a middle position. He argues that the portrayal of Moses in the Pentateuch is coherent with that of prophets. First, by interceding, Moses is portrayed as the archetypical prophet.[34] Secondly, the language of Moses's commission (Exod 3:10–15) is reminiscent of the prophetic call narratives (they are all "sent" [שלח], cf. Isa 6:8; Jer 1:7; Ezek 2:3). Thirdly, the expression "thus says YHWH" which signifies an oracle conveyed by a prophet, is used in the Pentateuch only in connection with Moses (e.g., Exod 3:14–15; 4:22; 5:1; 32:27).[35] At the same time, Moses is distinguished from and supersedes all other prophets in his intimacy with God (Num 18:18; Deut 34:10).[36] Moses is thus being portrayed simultaneously and independently from each other as an intercessor and as a prophet. This in turn suggests that, at least from the perspectives of the authors of the Pentateuch, intercessory prayer and prophet-hood walked hand in hand from the very beginning.

Weighing the various propositions, we can see that much depends on the relative dating of the various texts. In particular, do the traditions of Moses the intercessor[37] predate those of Amos the prophetic intercessor[38] or *vice versa*? It

---

[31] Balentine, Prayer in the Hebrew Bible, 119–20.
[32] Erik Aurelius, *Der Fürbitter Israels: Eine Studie zum Mosebild im Alten Testament* (ConBOT 27; Stockholm: Almqvist & Wiksell, 1988), 82–83, 203–4.
[33] Aurelius, *Der Fürbitter Israels*, 92–93, 205.
[34] Widmer, *Dynamics of Intercessory Prayer*, 29.
[35] Ibid., 76, with supporting bibliography.
[36] Ibid., 73–75.
[37] Exod 5:22; 8:8, 12, 28–39; 9:28, 33; 10:17–18; 17:8–16; 32:10–14, 30–32; Num 11:1–3; 12:1–15; 14:13–16; 16:22–17; Deut 9:12–29.

is not possible in the present context to provide an in-depth answer. What we can say, however, is that at the times of the composition of the various strands of the books of *Jeremiah* and *Ezekiel*, i.e., from the first quarter of the sixth century and onwards, intercession had come to be firmly associated with the prophetic office. Likewise, the traditions surrounding Moses, as well as those surrounding Abraham and Samuel, that combined the roles of prophet and intercessor, were in all probability known in some form, oral and/or literary, at this time.[39]

Ezekiel: A Prophet unlike Moses

We can thus assume that, at the time shortly prior to the fall of Jerusalem, i.e., the *terminus post quem* for the material in the books of *Jeremiah* and *Ezekiel*, the idea of an interceding prophet was a distinct theological and literary construct. Furthermore, the figure of Moses had become identified as an ideal, successfully interceding prophet. Against this background, it is distinctly possible that the literary portrayals of Jeremiah and Ezekiel were modelled after Moses. However, as I shall argue shortly, this modelling of Moses and Ezekiel is one of contrast: both men fall short of the ideal of a prophetic intercessor as they are both, in different ways, prohibited by God to fulfil this task.

Scholars have long noted the similarities between the portrayal of Jeremiah and that of Moses.[40] Notably, Seitz highlights that Jeremiah is consciously modelled as a new Moses by those who held views on prophecy that might be called Deuteronomistic and who viewed intercession as an integral part of Moses's prophetic vocation.[41]

Two factors favor this position. First, *Jeremiah* sees intercession as one of the most important aspects of the prophetic ministry (e.g., Jer 27:18; 42:2, 4) and, secondly, *Deuteronomy* regards intercession as an integral part of Moses's prophetic vocation (Deut 9:22–29). At the same time, the idea of intercession is toned down in other parts of *Deuteronomy*. In fact, the portrayal of the ideal prophet in Deut 18:9–22 does not include intercession. I would therefore like to stress that the image of the interceding prophet is unlikely to have originated in the circles responsible for *Deuteronomy*, and that other factors, alongside that of

---

[38] Amos 7:1–9; 8:1–3.

[39] See further my discussion in "God's Hidden Compassion," 193–4.

[40] See, e.g., the discussions by William L. Holladay, "The Background of Jeremiah's Self-Understanding: Moses, Samuel and Psalm 22," *JBL* 83 (1964): 153–64, and Widmer, *Dynamics of Intercessory Prayer*, 76.

[41] Christopher R. Seitz, "The Prophet Moses and the Canonical Shape of Jeremiah," *ZAW* 10 (1989): 3–27 (esp. 4).

Deuteronomistic influence, helped shape the portrayal of Jeremiah as an intercessor. As we noted above, it is reasonable to assume that the vision account in Amos 7:1–8:3 that portrays the prophet as an intercessor was known in the beginning of the sixth century BCE.[42] Furthermore, as we also noted, it is likely that traditions of the interceding Moses as found in *Exodus* and *Numbers* were known, although possibly not in the form in which we have them today. Notably, Deut 9:19 is likely to be a revised version of the accounts of Moses's intercession in Exod 32:11–14,[43] and Deut 9:25–29 may be a revised version of the account in Num 13–14.[44]

Jeremiah, however, is no new Moses but rather a failed one. As Luis Alonso Schökel argues, Jeremiah is presented as an anti-Moses. Notably, while Moses managed to successfully convince God not to destroy the people of Israel, God banned Jeremiah's intercession before he had even begun (Jer 7:16; 11:14; 14:11; 15:1).[45]

Turning to the book of *Ezekiel*, there is again evidence to suggest that the portrayal of Ezekiel is influenced by that of Moses. Levenson notes that the concept of Ezekiel as a "new Moses" fits the theology of *Ezekiel*. In particular, he notes that Ezek 20:32–44 speaks of a "new Exodus," the goal of which is a properly functioning liturgy, and that Ezekiel 40–48 is the only corpus of legislation that is not placed in the mouth of Moses. In a sense, Mt. Zion becomes a new Mt. Sinai in Ezek 40–48.[46] Along similar lines, McKeating argues that the activities attributed to Ezekiel in Ezek 40–48 correspond to those of Moses. He also proposes that Ezekiel functions as a new Moses in the account in Ezekiel 37: while Moses created the people of Israel through his prophetic and lawgiving activities, Ezekiel awakened the new Israel after the

---

[42] See further Jörg Jeremias, *The Book of Amos* (OTL; trans. Douglas W. Stott; Louisville, Ky.: Westminster John Knox, 1998), 2. Most recently, Jason Radine, *The Book of Amos in Emergent Judah* (FAT II/45; Tübingen: Mohr Siebeck, 2010), 37–8, dates most of the book of Amos, including the vision report in Amos 7–8, to the seventh century BCE, i.e., prior to the fall of Judah in 586 BCE.

[43] See, e.g., Moshe Weinfeld, *Deuteronomy 1–11* (AB 5; New York: Doubleday, 1991), 411.

[44] See, e.g., Weinfeld, *Deuteronomy 1–11*, 414.

[45] See, e.g., Luis Alonso Schökel, "Jeremías como anti-Moisés," in *De la Tôrah au Messe* (ed. Maurice Carrez, Joseph Doré, and Pierre Grelot; Paris: Desclée, 1981), 245–54 (esp. 251). See also Seitz, "Prophet Moses," 9–12.

[46] Jon D. Levenson, *Theology of the Program of Restoration of Ezekiel 40–48* (HSM 10; Missoula, Montana: Scholars Press, 1976), 38–45.

exile through prophesying.⁴⁷ Finally, Kohn detects Deuteronomistic influence in *Ezekiel*. She points out that Ezekiel, like Moses, is warned by God before being given his mission that it will fail owing to the hardened heart of others (Ezek 2:4; Exod 7:3). Furthermore, the statement in Deut 18:18 is alluded to in several ways in relation to Ezekiel. First, the idiom "a prophet among them" is repeated in Ezek 2:5, and secondly, the idea of God putting words in the prophet's mouth is found in Ezek 2:10–3:3.⁴⁸

I do not doubt the Deuteronomistic influence in the book of *Ezekiel*, and I see a clear link between Ezekiel's prophetic role as presented in the divine oracles and Deut 18:18 in that both regard prophethood as a one-sided endeavor: the prophet is God's spokesperson rather than his counterpart in the decision making. At the same time I detect a distinct contrast in the presentations of Moses and Ezekiel pertaining to intercession. Therefore, alongside Schökel, I shall argue that in this particular regard the book of *Ezekiel* presents Ezekiel as an anti-Moses. Ezekiel, in sharp contrast to the interceding Moses of *Exodus* and *Numbers*, is forbidden to fulfil the prophetic intercessory role. Instead, Ezekiel is forced into a reduced prophetic role as God's spokesman only.

Two key themes contribute to this reduction/redefinition of the prophetic office, namely God calling Ezekiel to be a watchman (צפה) and God rendering Ezekiel mute. First, in Ezekiel's call to be a watchman, God ascertains that Ezekiel is only allowed to speak when God has spoken to him and to say only what God has said.⁴⁹ Ezekiel's prophetic office is thus reduced to conveying God's will *verbatim*.⁵⁰ The watchman metaphor, although clearly related to the idea of the prophet as an intercessor, is distinct from it.⁵¹ The two roles are instead complementary in that the watchman is God's representative towards the people, while the intercessor is the people's representative towards God.⁵²

---

⁴⁷ H. McKeating, "Ezekiel the 'Prophet like Moses'?" *JSOT* 61 (1994): 97–109.

⁴⁸ Risa Levitt Kohn, "A Prophet Like Moses? Rethinking Ezekiel's Relationship to the Torah," *ZAW* 114 (2002): 236–54 (esp. 249, 253–54).

⁴⁹ Ezek 3:16–21, 26–27; 33:7–20.

⁵⁰ See further Lena-Sofia Tiemeyer, "The Watchman Metaphor in Isaiah 56–66," *VT* 55 (2005): 378–400 (esp. 379–83).

⁵¹*Contra* Daniel Bodi, *The Book of Ezekiel and the Poem of Erra* (OBO 104; Göttingen: Vandenhoeck & Ruprecht, 1991), 263–4, who concludes, based on this comparative study, that "Both Išum and Ezekiel are present in order to placate and reason the wrathful divinity and they both watch over the love relationships of Erra and Yahweh respectively" (277). This may be true for Erra, but it can definitely not be said of Ezekiel as portrayed in the book bearing his name.

⁵² Cf. Tiemeyer, "The Watchman Metaphor," 394.

Secondly, through rendering Ezekiel mute, God hinders him from uttering anything beyond what God tells him to say (until the fall of Jerusalem—Ezek 24:27; 33:22).

The picture of Ezekiel's eating of the scroll (Ezek 2:9–3:3)[53] concurs with this impression. By eating the scroll, Ezekiel is transformed from being the free agent that his prophetic predecessors were, to becoming God's mouthpiece alone, his "human idol" whose mouth God opens only when he wishes Ezekiel to speak God's words.[54]

The main consequence of this redefinition of Ezekiel's prophetic office is his inability to function as an איש מוכיח (Ezek 3:26), a term best translated as "a man who intervenes."[55] Ezekiel is thus barred from intervening in the present situation. God can speak through him but Ezekiel himself cannot take any

---

[53] For an interesting take on the eating of the scroll, see Margaret S. Odell, "You Are What You Eat: Ezekiel and the Scroll," *JBL* 117 (1998): 229–48, esp. 244–5, who argues that by eating the scroll, Ezekiel internalizes God's judgment. As a priest, he thus identifies with the people.

[54] Block, *Ezekiel*, 1, 159.

[55] The term was long held to signify a person whose main task was to "reprove" another party. See, e.g., Walther Eichrodt, *Der Prophet Hesekiel* (ATD 22; Göttingen: Vandenhoeck & Ruprecht, 1966), 21 ("Wahner"); John W. Wevers, *Ezekiel* (NCB; London: Marshall, Morgan & Scott, 1969), 58 ("reprover"). Yet as this interpretation disagrees with the content of the rest of the book of Ezekiel, Robert R. Wilson, "An Interpretation of Ezekiel's Dumbness," *VT* 22 (1972): 98–101; followed by, among others, Margaret S. Odell, "The Inversion of Shame and Forgiveness in Ezekiel 16,59–63," *JSOT* 56 (1992): 101–12, esp. 106; and G. A. te Stroete, "Ezekiel 24,15–27: The Meaning of a Symbolic Act," *Bijdragen* 38 (1977): 163–75, esp. 173–74, proposes the translation "mediator" or as "arbitrator." The function of the איש מוכיח would then be to promote dialogue between two parties rather than to reprove one of them. Accordingly, after having been told not to be an איש מוכיח, Ezekiel would still be able to fulfil his task as a watchman by warning the people of the coming doom, but he would be unable to initiate communication between the two parties or to intercede with God on behalf of the people. Along the same lines, Pietro Bovati, *Re-establishing Justice: Legal Terms, Concepts and Procedures in the Hebrew Bible* (trans. Michael J. Smith; JSOTSup 105; Sheffield: JSOT, 1994), 44–48, demonstrates that the root יכח carries shades of "arbitrating" or "taking sides." See also Thomas Renz, *The Rhetorical Function of the Book of Ezekiel* (VTSup 298; Leiden: Brill, 1999), 157–62.

initiative, either to intercede or to proclaim repentance.[56] This redefinition of the prophetic role continues in Ezek 24:24 where Ezekiel is called a sign/portent (מופת; cf. Ezek 12:6, 11).[57] Instead of being a person who promotes communication between God and the people, Ezekiel is thus being reduced to a one-sided sign-post that points to God. This breaking down of the prophetic role began already in the book of *Jeremiah* when Jeremiah is forbidden to intercede.[58] Now, in the book of *Ezekiel*, it reached its full fruition.

Ezekiel's Protests to the Redefinition of His Prophetic Role

As in the previous description of Ezekiel as God's marionette, this portrayal of Ezekiel's prophetic role is unsatisfactory in many respects. Ezekiel is a prophet curtailed and compromised. Moreover, Ezekiel is aware of this and hints at his own frustration. As noted by Block, why does God need to command Ezekiel *three* times to eat the scroll and then in the end God ends up *feeding* it to him?[59] An eager prophet surely would have eaten the scroll himself at God's first command. This suggests a reluctance of Ezekiel's part of giving up his prophetic freedom in order to become God's spokesman alone. Moreover, why does God need to shut him up in his house, mute and bound with ropes (3:24–27)? This seems like either a precaution of or the repercussion of a spirit/act of rebellion. Finally, God's imposing one year of speechlessness for every day that Ezekiel sat with the people of Israel (3:15) sounds like an act of divine punishment as well as a preventative measure: God forcibly distances Ezekiel from those amongst whom he sat, i.e., from those with whom he might side. From now on, Ezekiel must stifle every impulse to adopt their perspective and/or to intercede for them.[60] Further support for this image of a silently rebelling Ezekiel can be detected in the references to intercession in Ezek 9:8; 11:13; 13:5 and 22:30, as well as in Ezek 8:1; 14:1 and 20:1–3.

---

[56] Tiemeyer, "God's Hidden Compassion," 208–9,

[57] See also Jacqueline E. Lapsley, *Can These Bones Live? The Problem of the Moral Self in the Book of Ezekiel* (BZAW 301; Berlin: de Gruyter, 2000), 115–16, who points out that Ezekiel is thus not so much a messenger as he is a sign to the people, a sign that will bring them knowledge about who God is and how he acts in the world. Ezekiel's sign acts are as important as the divine oracles that he speaks, in that both types of actions point to God.

[58] Seitz, "Prophet Moses," 11.

[59] Block, *Ezekiel*, 1, 12.

[60] Block, *Ezekiel*, 1, 157–58.

Ezekiel 9:8

It has been argued that intercession is a central motif in the book of *Ezekiel*, as, in fact, Ezekiel is portrayed as interceding twice (Ezek 9:8; 11:13).[61] A closer look at these two passages, however, reveals again a tension in the portrayal of Ezekiel between the way in which Ezekiel describes his prophetic role, and what he, on another level, wants to do.

The reference to intercession in Ezek 9:8 occurs in the context of Ezekiel's visionary journey to Jerusalem (8:3). Ezekiel reports that, as he is led through the temple precincts, God informs him about the *coming* destruction. In response, Ezekiel falls on his face and asks God whether he is going to destroy all of Israel (9:8). God answers him matter-of-factly that as the guilt of Israel and Judah is enormous, he will not have any compassion for them. This message is confirmed by the appearance of a man who, while God speaks, returns to report that he has *already carried out God's command*. In this way, Ezekiel conveys his own willingness to intercede—as a prophet should[62]—only to be thwarted by God. Rather than telling his prophet what he is going to do beforehand, God tells him of his plans only as they are being carried out. On one level, this stresses the inescapable character of God's punishment of Jerusalem. On another level, it indicates that, from God's perspective, the time when his prophets served as his partners in decision-making is definitely over.

Ezekiel 11:13 and Ezekiel 8:1; 14:1 and 20:1–3

Ezekiel reports a similar event in Ezek 11. The Spirit moves Ezekiel to another part of the Jerusalem temple (11:1), falls upon him, and commands him to prophecy against the people that he sees (11:4 הנבא עליהם). As Ezekiel realizes the result of his prophesying—Pelatiah, the son of Benaiah dies—Ezekiel falls upon the ground and cries out to God, asking him whether he plans to annihilate all that remains of Israel (11:13 אהה אדני ה' כלה אתה עשה את שארית ישראל). Again, as in Ezek 9, it is *too late*. The reality of God's judgment hits Ezekiel only after he has carried it out, leaving him desperately trying to save what is left.

---

[61] Bodi, *Poem of Erra*, 262–4. In particular, Bodi argues that the motif of the watchman as well as that of the person standing in the gap is to be equated with intercession.

[62] Cf. Bodi, *Poem of Erra*, 262, states that "when Ezekiel breaks out in a cry of intercession to Yahweh at the carnage commencing in the midst of the temple he is acting as a true prophet."

God then responds in the following passage with words of comfort (Ezek 11:14–21), something that can easily cause the reader to regard Ezekiel's intercession as having been successful.[63] However, this impression cannot be substantiated. Instead of addressing the people of Jerusalem, one of which Ezekiel just saw die, the divine oracle in Ezek 11:14–21 states that they remain condemned—for the benefit of the exiles. It thus appears that God does not really respond to Ezekiel's intercession.[64]

In addition, Ezek 8:1; 14:1 and 20:1–3 depict Ezekiel together with the elders of Israel. In Ezek 8:1 Ezekiel states that the elders are simply sitting together before him (וזקני יהודה יושבים לפני). Likewise, in 14:1 Ezekiel tells that the elders have come to sit before him (ויבוא אלי אנשים מזקני ישראל וישבו לפני). Finally, in 20:1–3 Ezekiel informs the reader that the elders have come to ask for his advice (באו אנשים מזקני ישראל לדרש את ה' וישבו לפני). What should we make of this information? Running the risk of reading too much into silence, I nevertheless would like to follow Reventlow's suggestion and argue that the elders' acts hint at their expectation that Ezekiel would function as their spokesman before God.[65] Likewise, I wish to maintain that Ezekiel's explicit mention of these circumstances allude to his own silent willingness to serve as their mediator. However, God rejects the elders' plea, as he intervenes in each instance before Ezekiel has said anything. In 8:1b, God's hand falls upon Ezekiel and Ezekiel is taken in a vision to Jerusalem (8:2–3). In 14:2 and in 20:2, God tells Ezekiel about the sins of the elders, thus effectively foreclosing any potential intercession (14:3; 20:3–4).

Ezekiel 13:5 and 22:30

Finally, the famous reference to God's search for a man who would repair the wall and who would stand in the breach on behalf of the people in order to prevent its destruction in Ezek 22:30 (cf. 13:5) is pertinent to our inquiry. Is God searching for an intercessor, as some scholars have advocated,[66] or is he

---

[63] See, e.g., Bodi, *Poem of Erra*, 263.

[64] The same conclusion is born out by text-critical study. As noted by Walther Zimmerli, *Ezekiel*, 1 (trans. R. E. Clements; Hermeneia; Philadelphia: Fortress, 1979), 256; Block, *Ezekiel*, 1, 342, the material in Ezek 11:14–21. bears all the marks of being an independent unity, originally unattached to the preceding section.

[65] Reventlow, *Gebet im Alten Testament*, 245.

[66] Miller, *They Cried to the Lord*, 276–77, including note 46, uses Ezek 22:30–31, as well as Ezek 13:5, as a proof text that God expects a prophet to

searching for someone to appeal for repentance and to announce God's coming judgement?[67] None of the options is ideal, as much of the book of *Ezekiel* insists that neither repentance nor intercession can prevent the coming destruction of Jerusalem. Nonetheless, the latter option makes the least sense as God already has an exemplary person in Ezekiel who calls to repentance and announces God's judgement. Why, then, would God lament the absence of such a person? The former option, i.e., that God laments the absence of an intercessor to "stand in the breach on behalf of Israel," makes more sense because God truly does not have an intercessor. God himself has invalidated the single eligible person, namely Ezekiel. This underlines the tragic character of God in the book of *Ezekiel*: ironically, God has rendered his prophet unable to fulfil his proper God-ordained role as intercessor.

THE PROPHET WHO GAVE UP

Two more issues contribute to our picture of Ezekiel's compromised prophetic role. The only time when God lets Ezekiel get away with his own will is in an area that has nothing to do with Ezekiel's prophetic role. In Ezek 4:12–15, as Ezekiel objects to cooking his food on a fire of human excrements, God allows him to use animal dung. In this way, Ezekiel is allowed to maintain his priestly purity, while his prophetic role remains curtailed and compromised. It is furthermore noteworthy that Ezek 40–48 does not contain the words "to prophesy" or "prophet."[68] This gives the impression that Ezekiel saw no future continuation of his prophetic office and thus gave it up.[69]

CONCLUSION: WHO GAINS?

Who, then, gains from this redefinition of the prophetic role? It could be argued that God gains: he can drive through his will unimpeded. It could also be argued

---

stand up and intercede, thus serving as a counter force in his decision making. See also Reventlow, *Gebet im Alten Testament*, 246.

[67] E.g., Block, *Ezekiel*, 1, 728; Paul Joyce, *Ezekiel: A Commentary* (JSOTSup 482; London: T&T Clark, 2007), 160, who connects the question with that in Ezek 9:11, i.e., the man that God is looking for is someone who sighs and groans over all the abominations committed in Jerusalem.

[68] Iain M. Duguid, *Ezekiel and the Leaders of Israel* (VTSup 163; Leiden: Brill, 1994), 103–9.

[69] See also Patton, "Priest, Prophet, and Exile," 73–89, who argues that in Ezek 40–48 Ezekiel's priestly role supersedes his prophetic role.

that the people gain, as they would be able to relate to Ezekiel's words as God's undiluted words.[70] Finally, it could be argued that Ezekiel gains. He becomes the epitome of prophethood, one where the prophet is so influenced by God that he is wholly his mouth-piece. As his own capacity to act is so effaced, he becomes, to cite Lapsley, "a perfect model for the people because all his actions are the direct consequence of the knowledge of God, which has been directly given by God, and which constitutes the core of his moral self."[71]

Yet I prefer claiming the opposite, namely that everyone involved loses when the prophet fulfills only half of his appointed job description. The prophet loses as he ceases to be a human being. To be lifted back and forth held by the hair, to be denied human emotions, or to be commanded to prophesy against people in such a manner that results in their death (Ezek 11:4-13, above), is not to be envied.

The people also lose as they have no spokesperson left to turn to who would plead their cause.[72] In addition, the book of *Ezekiel* describes how the people lose what defines them as human beings, namely their free will. The people are given a new heart so that they will automatically do what God wants them to

---

[70] Nicholas J. Tromp, "The Paradox of Ezekiel's Prophetic Mission: Towards a Semiotic Approach of Ezekiel 3,22–27," in *Ezekiel and His Book: Textual and Literary Criticism and Their Interrelation* (ed. Johan Lust; BETL: Leuven: Leuven University, 1986), 210, Wilson, "Prophecy in Crisis," 165–66, Renz, *Rhetorical Function*, 15–60, Schöpflin, *Theologie als Biographie*, 128.

[71] Lapsley, *Can These Bones Live?*, 116. Along similar lines, Ellen F. Davis, *Swallowing the Scroll: Textuality and the Dynamics of Discourse in Ezekiel's Prophecy* (JSOTSup 78; Bible and Literature Series 21; Sheffield: Almond, 1989), 83–84, states that "[Ezekiel] is a guide: a model of the human creature who does hear the divine word, who responds fully and appropriately to what YHWH is doing" (24:27). See also de Jong, "Ezekiel as a Literary Figure," 14–15, who argues that the persona of Ezekiel is a literary-theological construct. Written in retrospective after the fall of Jerusalem, the book of *Ezekiel* uses a prophetic figure to give the highest authority to its message of future restoration for Israel.

[72] See, for example, the widow of Sarephath who approached Elijah about the death of her son (1 Kgs 17:18), Naaman who approached Elishah to heal his body (2 Kgs 5:9), Eliakim, the royal servant who approached Isaiah ben Amos at the even of the Neo–Assyrian siege of Jerusalem (2 Kgs 19:2–4). Ezekiel is more of a Jeremiah who produces an oracle of doom as a response to Zedekiah's plea for intercession (Jer 37:3, 17). Jeremiah, however, is still able to give Zedekiah hope, advising him to change his ways so that God might change his (Jer 38:20–21). See also Davis, *Swallowing the Scroll*, 54.

do.[73] In a sense, the new heart parallels the change of the prophetic office in that the ability to oppose God is eliminated. It can, of course, be argued that this development is all positive as the people would be pre-programmed to do what is right in God's eyes. Humankind, together with the world around them, would thus be better off without human free will. At the same time, by losing its ability to make independent moral decisions, humankind would be altered beyond recognition which might be counted as a loss.

Finally, God loses, as there would be no Amos to plead with him to cancel his destructive plans (Amos 7:1–6), and there would be no Moses to bargain with him for Israel's survival (Exod 32:10–14), with the result that God would lose the incentive to let compassion triumph over rage (Hos 11:8). In the words of Balentine, the loss of prayer would forfeit honest covenant interaction and would eventually lead to a "monopoly of divine power."[74]

I would like to conclude that in response to these potential changes, the persona of Ezekiel as emerging from the text of the book of *Ezekiel* is one of mute protest. He submits to God's transformation of his humanity and of his prophetic role. Yet his very behavior forms a protest. His apathy, his lethargy, and his lack of involvement are all pointed indicators of his less than enthusiastic response to God.

Going one step further, could the portrayal of Ezekiel also be the protest of the author(s)/editor(s) of the book of *Ezekiel*? In other words, is it possible that the "I" of Ezekiel serves as the spokesman for the people responsible for the final text of *Ezekiel*? Rather than accepting the theodicy of the text and agreeing with the claim that God is blameless—he had to destroy Israel because they were so sinful—they push the responsibility back to God. If Ezekiel had been given the freedom to intercede, and if he had been able to take up his role as God's partner in his decision-making—something that God deterred him from doing—then people's lives might have been saved. The portrayal of Ezekiel is thus a glimmer of protest against the theodicy of *Ezekiel* within the book itself.

---

[73] See the insightful discussion by Lapsley, *Can These Bones Live?*, esp. 67–107. She argues that the portrayal of a new heart given by God is the result of the author's wrestling with what he perceived to be the incapability of his contemporaries of understanding their moral failings and of transforming themselves.

[74] Balentine, *Prayer*, 197.

THE QUR'ANIC DAVID

Peter Matthews Wright

The language of the Qur'an is richly and densely allusive to prior Near Eastern revelations, oral (we presume) and written. Through the centuries, this aspect of Qur'anic discourse has been a source of inter-sectarian polemic: non-Muslims arguing that such allusions are evidence of the Qur'an's "derivative" or "second-hand" nature;[1] Muslims denying derivation and claiming, instead, that the Qur'an "corrects" prior Scriptures and, in the process, supersedes them.[2] I must confess that I find much about this ongoing argument quite puzzling. On the one hand, given the current development of the literary history of the ancient Near East and the Bible's evidently allusive and actively "appropriationist" place within that history, no astute reader of the Bible and para-biblical literatures can, in good conscience, assert that Biblical discourse is somehow immune to the charge of "derivation" while the Qur'an is not.[3]

---

[1] See Reuven Firestone, "The Qur'an and the Bible: Some Modern Studies of Their Relationship," in *Bible and Qur'an: Essays in Scriptural Intertextuality* (ed. John C. Reeves; SBLSymS 24; Atlanta: Society of Biblical Literature, 2003), 1–22. See also Fazlur Rahman, *Major Themes of the Qur'an* (2d ed.; Minneapolis: Bibliotheca Islamica, 1989), xii–xvi.

[2] See Asghar Ali Engineer's remarks on the "Ulema's theory of Qur'anic supercession," in *Islam in Contemporary World* (Elgin, Ill.: New Dawn, 2007), 46.

[3] Recent studies of the Bible's use of allusion and literary appropriation include Richard B. Hays, *Echoes of Scripture in the Letters of Paul* (New Haven: Yale University, 1989); Benjamin D. Sommer, *A Prophet Reads Scripture: Allusion in Isaiah 40–66* (Stanford: Stanford University, 1998);

On the other hand, while the Muslim contention that the Qur'an attempts to correct aspects of prior Scriptures appears to me to be difficult to dispute, the question remains whether Jews and Christians deem the sort of corrections that the Qur'an offers as palatable or even necessary. Moreover, the rhetoric of the Qur'an's "corrective" agenda must be considered in light of the revelation's own repeated contention that it was revealed to "confirm" (*musaddiq*) precursor scriptures.[4] Muslims who advance the supersessionist thesis conveniently overlook this aspect of the Qur'anic *kerygma* and, in the process, do it a disservice.

My own work on the Qur'an is intended to serve as a reminder that the impulse to correct is not, in all cases, synonymous with an impulse to supersede. An example drawn from every day life may help to illustrate my point. If, in casual conversation with a friend, I discover that she is under the mistaken impression that the nearest convenience store is six blocks from where we happen to be standing, I may correct her impression by saying, "Actually, there is a 7–11 right around the corner." In so doing, I am not attempting to persuade her to abandon the desire to patronize convenience stores—or even the far convenience store, for that matter. I simply want to her to know that, should she not wish to travel the six blocks, there is an alternative close by.

It is true that if I happen to be the proprietor of the nearby 7–11 (but not the farther store), I may be interested in diverting my companion's business from my competitor. In that case, applying a hermeneutics of suspicion, one might infer that I am hopeful that this diversion of my friend's business will result in a level of customer loyalty to my store that will eclipse previous loyalties to any other store. Perhaps I harbor a long term goal of diverting enough customers from my competitors to drive them out of business. This is certainly possible, but it does not necessarily follow from my desire to correct my friend's mistaken impression. Indeed, I may be on very good terms with the proprietor of the far store; we may belong to the same civic or religious organizations; our children may play in the same soccer league; our wives might have been sorority sisters in college; he may be my cousin, etc. In those cases, I might be grieved by the very prospect of his store failing. Yet, this still would not necessarily prevent me from informing my friend of the location of the nearby 7–11.

Ronald Hendel, *Remembering Abraham: Culture, Memory, and History in the Hebrew Bible* (Oxford: Oxford University, 2005); and Robert Alter's introduction to his work *The Book of Psalms: A Translation with Commentary* (New York: W. W. Norton & Co. 2007), xiii–xl.

[4] Qur'an 2:42, 2:89, 2:91, 2:97, 2:101, 3:3, 3:81, 4:47, 5:48, 6:92, 35:31, 46:12, 46:30. References to the Qur'an in this paper are to *Al-Qur'an Al-Karim bir-Rasm al-Uthmani* (Damascus: Uthman Taha, 1993).

When engaged in interpretation, much depends upon context and what we know of the history of the Red Sea basin in Late Antiquity suggests that sectarian competition for adherents among its indigenous populations, while vigorous, was complicated by ancient networks of blood and communal ties. When developing an historical approach to Qur'anic "corrections" of Biblical material, original context must be taken into consideration. Only then can we make sense of the Qur'an's insistence—contrary to the subsequent interpretive tradition—that it is a *confirmation* of previous scriptures. In order to account for the neglect of this particular aspect of the Qur'anic *kerygma* in the subsequent interpretive tradition, scholars must carefully consider the historical changes that took place within the Muslim community in the post-Prophetic period (i.e., the rise of an Arabo-Islamic empire). Once we have made such an adjustment to our thinking, we are also prepared to consider the Qur'an's corrections of Biblical material as *exempla* of a Near Eastern rhetorical mode that has Biblical antecedents.[5]

The Qur'an explicitly places itself in a prophetic lineage that contains figures associated with both the Hebrew Bible and New Testament—this is well known. But often overlooked are the ways in which the Qur'an implicitly locates itself within a broader lineage: that of Near Eastern prophecy more generally. Put another way, the Qur'an belongs to a genre of religious literature produced in the Near East over a period that spans the better part of two millennia (from, say, the twelfth century BCE to the seventh century of our own era, and from the Iranian plateau in the East to the Nile Valley in the West). Included in this genre are the writings associated with Zarathustra, the Tanakh, Christo-centric literature, and the Qur'an. When regarded through the lenses supplied by sectarian gate-keepers and heresiologists, all of these literatures contain evidence of intertextual engagements with materials that lie outside of their respective canonical boundaries. But when regarded through the broader, more inclusive lens of sacred literary genre, the intertextuality that characterizes these writings is intra-mural in nature: there is a "super-canon" that embraces them all and that is identifiable as such through an analysis of their shared rhetorical structures.[6]

---

[5] In my view, the best introduction to this subject remains Marshall G. S. Hodgson, *The Venture of Islam: Conscience and History in a World Civilization*, vol. 1 (Chicago: University of Chicago, 1974), 71–230.

[6] See Morton Smith, "The Common Theology of the Ancient Near East," *JBL* 71 (1952): 135–147 and Norman O. Brown, "The Prophetic Tradition," in *Apocalypse and/or Metamorphosis* (Berkeley: University of California, 1992), 46–68.

Until today, scholarship on the Qur'an has been reluctant to adopt the broader view. There are significant historical and theological reasons underwriting this reluctance—reasons that reflect, on the one hand, the traumas induced by the colonial occupation of majority Muslim societies by non-Muslims and, on the other, the protocols of lost Muslim empire. Both reasons continue to weigh heavily upon the minds of Muslims and call for sensitivity when one is discussing Islamic sacred literature.[7] That said, what must ultimately drive scholarly inquiry is evidence adduced from the materials under scrutiny. My own study of the Qur'an, conducted from the vantage point provided by the broader view, suggests that Islamic Scripture sets its prophetic "seal of approval" upon identifiable streams of Biblical interpretation. In so doing, Qur'anic discourse supports the claim that it represents a "correction" of prior Scriptural traditions while simultaneously (and consistently) asserting that it is a "confirmation" of prior traditions. A look at the Qur'anic David sheds light upon how this works.

The Israelite King David (Arabic: *Dawud*) is mentioned in the Qur'an no less than sixteen times. He appears as a prophetic figure—one of the Prophet Muhammad's ancient precursors (Q. 4:163; 6:84). Like the Prophet Muhammad, Dawud is a bearer of holy writ (the psalms or *az-zabur*) and was endowed by God with some remarkable characteristics. For example, the Qur'an tells us that God subjugated the mountains that they might sing praises to Him with Dawud in the deep of the night and at the dawning of the day (Q. 38:18). The Qur'an provides a number of details about David's life that one also encounters in the Former Prophets: that he killed Goliath (*Jalut*, Q. 2:251), succeeded Saul as King of Israel, and had a son named Solomon who was renowned for his wisdom (Q. 21: 78).

The Qur'an also informs us that Dawud was a penitent—though we do not learn the precise nature of his sin. His repentance is placed within the context of a dispute between two brothers (one rich, the other poor) over the ownership of a single sheep. This story appears to be an allusion to the parable that the Prophet Nathan relates to King David in 2 Sam 12 in order to prompt David to convict himself in the matter of his (David's) machinations with regard to Bathsheba and her unfortunate husband, Uriah the Hittite (2 Sam 11). But no mention is made of Bathsheba, Uriah, or Nathan in the Qur'anic account. Instead, the Qur'an simply asserts that Dawud, upon reviewing the dispute presented him by the two brothers, understands that God has put him to the test; he asks God to forgive him, and God accepts his plea (Q. 38: 21–25).[8]

---

[7] See Peter Matthews Wright, "Modern Qur'anic Hermeneutics" (Ph.D. diss., University of North Carolina at Chapel Hill, 2008), 56–60.

[8] See Isaac Hasson, "David," *Encyclopaedia of the Qur'an*, Vol. 1 (ed. Jane Dammen McAuliffe; Leiden: Brill, 2001), 495–7.

This apparent omission, in a highly allusive text, has occasioned speculation on both sides of the "Borrowed Qur'an/Unborrowed Qur'an" divide. Those who insist on depicting the Qur'an as a "second-hand revelation" regard such an omission as proof that Muhammad (the presumed "author" of the Qur'an) drew upon limited and unreliable Biblical sources when composing his text.[9] On the other hand, those who insist upon depicting the Qur'an as a revelation designed to "correct" the "corrupted information" that allegedly found its way into the Biblical corpus, regard this omission as an instance of Divine editing. According to this view, the Biblical story of Bathsheba does not appear in the Qur'an because it does not belong in the Bible.[10]

These two positions make for wonderfully insoluble and perpetual polemics; they also ignore the history of the interpretation of the King David we encounter in the Former Prophets—the beginnings of which are included in the canon of the Hebrew Bible itself. I am referring here, of course, to the portrait of King David rendered for us in the book of 1 Chronicles. Like the Qur'anic portrait of David, 1 Chronicles is silent on the matter of Bathsheba, Uriah, and King David. Instead, 1 Chr 20 teases us with language that echoes 2 Sam 11—where the David and Bathsheba story is preserved. Second Sam 11 tells us that, at the season of the year when kings were wont to go out to battle, David sent his armies out but remained behind in Jerusalem. It was then and there, with time on his hands and ample opportunity, that David spotted Uriah's wife in her bath. First Chronicles 20 opens with a similar reflection: at the time of the year when kings were wont to go out to do battle, David sent out his troops while remaining behind in Jerusalem; but, the extra-marital mischief that 2 Samuel recounts is absent from the chronicler's tale.[11]

To be consistent, a reader committed to the "Borrowed Qur'an" thesis should feel obliged to regard the Biblical chronicler with a jaundiced eye: such an omission must count as proof that the author of the book of Chronicles drew upon limited and unreliable sources when composing his text. That is certainly one way of reading these books. I am not at all convinced, however, that it is the

---

[9] See, e.g., Rodwell's preface to *The Koran* (trans. J. M. Rodwell; London: J. M. Dent & Sons, 1909), 1–18.

[10] Popular modern Qur'an commentaries such as S. Abul A'la Maududi's *The Meaning of the Qur'an* often purport to be able to distinguish between "corrupted" portions of the canonical books of the Bible and those portions which escaped corruption. See footnote 205 in Maududi, *The Meaning of the Qur'an*, Vol. 1 (16th ed.; Lahore: Islamic Publications, 1997), 192–3.

[11] Biblical references in this paper are to the *JPS Hebrew-English Tanakh* (Philadelphia: Jewish Publication Society, 2000).

best way to read them. After all, the chronicler's use of language that echoes what we find in 2 Samuel appears to be an allusive "flag"—a trope that signals to the reader that the author is well aware of the prior text but intends to engage in a reinterpretation of the received tradition. The Qur'an's appropriation of Nathan's parable of the dispute over a single sheep may be understood to function in the same way. Both 1 Chronicles and the Qur'an employ allusion to alert their readers to the fact that they are aware of the received tradition: they simply refuse to be passive transmitters of it. On the contrary, by means of their allusiveness, the Qur'an and 1 Chronicles activate the knowledge bases of their audiences, empowering them to initiate a fuller engagement with the alluding texts and the precursor Scriptures to which they allude.[12]

By virtue of this hermeneutical process, alluding texts accomplish a crucial social task, for they continue existing traditions while, simultaneously, revising them to suit new audiences and new times. In this manner, the inter-generational continuity that traditional stories supply is strengthened insofar as that continuity is made relevant to current tastes. By tracing the interpretive swerve away from an adulterous and impliedly murderous David to a more chaste (though still penitent) *Dawud*, we can follow (albeit at great distance) the development of the profile of this important figure in the religious imagination of the ancient to late ancient Near East. When we do this, we discover that the revisionist interpretation of the Biblical chronicler is only the beginning of a normative narrative line designed to rehabilitate the image of the Israelite king as we meet him in 2 Samuel.[13]

The Rabbis of the Talmud picked up where the chronicler left off. For them, David was a model of piety who spent his leisure hours, when he could find some, engrossed in study and prayer. Indeed, despite the assertion of the chronicler that Satan was able to induce David to authorize the taking of a census (1 Chr 21:1), later Rabbinic tradition assures us that the king was "one of the few pious men over whom the evil inclination had no power."[14] The Qur'an, by endorsing this particular interpretative trajectory, sets its prophetic "seal of approval" upon it. It then, in turn, becomes a link in a longer chain of Muslim exegesis in which the rehabilitation of the David of 2 Samuel is strengthened

---

[12] My work on scriptural allusion builds on that of many other scholars (John Hollander, M. H. Abrams, Richard B. Hays among them), but I am indebted above all to Joseph Pucci's *The Full-Knowing Reader: Allusion and the Power of the Reader in the Western Literary Tradition* (New Haven: Yale University, 1998).

[13] As Ronald Hendel puts it: "...tradition is itself unstable, and interpretation goes on, without end" (*Remembering Abraham*, 30).

[14] Louis Ginzberg, *The Legends of the Jews*, Vol. 4 (Baltimore: The Johns Hopkins University, 1998), 101–4 (citing *Baba Batra* 17a).

and generalized (in the eighth–ninth centuries) into a doctrine of prophetic impeccability (*'isma*).[15]

The notion that the Qur'an (or any purported collection of prophetic discourses) represents a link in an exegetical chain is disturbing to anyone who insists upon the theory that prophecy and the interpretation of prophecy are two distinct enterprises. According to this theory, works of interpretation are supposedly engaged in a "secondary" or even "parasitical" activity—wholly dependent upon "primary" works for their *raison d'être*. Consequently, some may view my concept of the exegetically allusive Qur'an as simply the latest iteration of the "Borrowed Qur'an" position. But nothing could be further from the truth. What I do in my work is simply take the Qur'an at its word when it places itself and the Prophet who brought it in a lineage of inspired Near Eastern seers that includes (but is not limited to) many of those whom we find in the Bible and cognate literatures.[16] In studying that lineage, I have encountered the opinion of many capable scholars who have remarked both the perceived decline of classical Hebrew prophecy in post-exilic literature and yet, at the same time, the "continuation of the prophetic voice."[17] In the words of one such scholar:

> By most accounts, the exile precipitated the collecting and editing of earlier traditions. With the writing down of tradition comes the inevitable process of interpretation. The exilic redaction of the Deuteronomistic History is one example of the process of collecting and editing earlier traditions that went on in the exilic period. The book of Chronicles follows as an example of the reinterpretation of that tradition. Chronicles is, on the one hand, *an interpretation of ancient prophecy* and, on the other, *a reflection of post-exilic prophecy itself*.[18]

The "Borrowed Qur'an" position can accept the Qur'an as "an interpretation of ancient prophecy"—though its proponents tend to discount (if not completely dismiss) the quality or validity of that interpretation. And they reject the claim that the Qur'an represents, in any way, post-exilic prophecy itself. In my opinion, all people are free to accept, discount, qualify, or reject any claim made by anyone to Divine revelation. Apart from some sort of public, continuous,

---

[15] See Paul E. Walker, "Impeccability," *Encyclopaedia of the Qur'an*, Vol. 2 (ed. Jane Dammen McAuliffe, Leiden: Brill, 2001), 505–7.

[16] See, e.g., Qur'an 5:19.

[17] William M. Schniedewind, *The Word of God in Transition: From Prophet to Exegete in the Second Temple Period* (JSOTSup 197; Sheffield: Sheffield Academic, 1995), 22.

[18] Ibid.

universal visionary experience vouchsafed to all those who make it their business to investigate such matters, I do not know what would count as insurmountable evidence that the Qur'an, the book of Chronicles, or any other scripture produced in the ancient to late ancient Near East is an example of Divine communication with humankind. I am fairly confident, however, that the mere fact that the Qur'an, the book of Chronicles, and other scriptures *interpret* precursor texts is not a compelling reason to reject claims made on their behalf to Divine authority. In fact, the evidence seems to suggest that interpretation of earlier prophecy is a post-exilic (if not pre-exilic) prophetic mode. Such evidence would seem to strengthen—not weaken—the Qur'an's inclusion of the Prophet Muhammad within a lineage of inspired Near Eastern seers that includes many of those familiar to us from the various books of the Bible and cognate literatures.[19]

---

[19] The conceptual shift that I have made in my own appreciation of Near Eastern scriptures and that I advocate for all who would study them seriously is to view Near Eastern prophecy as an ancient genre of religious discourse. A prophet working within that tradition is one who utilizes the established conventions of the genre. Piety-minded individuals (such as the author of the book of Deuteronomy) find such a definition troubling: for if prophetic "authenticity" (i.e., bona fide "messengership" on behalf of the Divine) is simply a matter of conforming one's discourse to generic protocols, then there is no adequate criterion for distinguishing between the "true" prophet and the "false." Not surprisingly, Deut 18:21–22 offers a test for making just such a distinction: "And should you ask yourselves, 'how can we know that the oracle was not spoken by the Lord?'—if the prophet speaks in the name of the Lord and the oracle does not come true, that oracle was not spoken by the Lord; the prophet has uttered it presumptuously: do not stand in dread of him." On its face, this test looks reasonable, until one begins to interrogate what it might mean for ambiguously worded prophetic oracles to "come true." There is also the problem of determining whether or not the *ipsissima verba* of the prophets resides in the oral tradition that lies "behind" the written redactions that have come down to us (see, e.g., Sigmund Mowinckel, *The Spirit and the Word: Prophecy and Tradition in Ancient Israel* [ed. K. C. Hanson, Minneapolis: Fortess, 2002]). Perhaps most problematic of all is the practice of some biblical prophets to revise the oracles of those among their canonical predecessors whom time, in the later prophet's judgment, had proved wrong, e.g., Deutero-Isaiah's revisions of Isaiah's Davidic promises (see Benjamin Sommer, *A Prophet Reads Scripture*, 152–160). In light of these problems, I argue that if the prophetic genre is about "getting things right," it is about getting them right by means of a tradition of continual revision.

Even so, the re-description of the Qur'anic event outlined here runs counter to the narrative that Muslims began to develop about themselves and their role in world history in the first decades following the death of the Prophet Muhammad—decades that witnessed Arab Muslim forces triumph militarily over their Byzantine and Sasanian counterparts. Contrary to a still popular mythology, these campaigns were carried out to acquire wealth, not converts. Minority Muslim rule over large non-Muslim populations was conducted from garrison towns (*amsar*) that enforced a strict separation between the conquerors and their new dominions. Throughout the history of Islamdom—and especially in times of great social and political stress—the "*amsarī*" religious imagination has helped to preserve for the future the distinctively Arab tone of the tradition while weakening the allusive ties that had bound the Revelation to its original, poly-confessional audience. Today, this "*amsarī*" imagination reigns supreme among Muslims—an unfortunate (if understandable) circumstance, in my view, given present political realities.[20]

On a more optimistic note, perhaps, I would like to make a suggestion in closing that I hope will serve as a stimulus to further thought. My argument that revisionary processes of inter-Scriptural interpretation lie as close to the heart of the Qur'anic *kerygma* as they do to biblical and para-biblical literature does not exhaust the possibilities of generic analysis where King David is concerned. I would therefore further suggest that the prophetic moral "rehabilitation" of David belongs to a broader literary genre than even that of Ancient to late Ancient Near Eastern prophecy. I make this assertion on the basis of my study of the literary evolution of the Greek Alexander romance. In Richard Stoneman's succinct summary,

> Each age makes its own Alexander: the Hebrew tradition makes him a preacher and prophet, the later Christian Greek and Syriac versions emphasize his faithful obedience to God; in the European Middle Ages he is an exemplar of the chivalrous knight; for the Persians he is, in one tradition, the arch-Satan because he destroyed the fire-altars of the Zoroastrian religion, while in the epic authors he is the legitimate king of Persia because he really is the son of Darius and not of Philip... [21]

---

[20] See Hodgson, *The Venture of Islam*, Vol. 1, and also Gordon Darnell Newby, *The Making of the Last Prophet: A Reconstruction of the Earliest Biography of Muhammad* (Columbia: University of South Carolina, 1989), 1–25.

[21] *The Greek Alexander Romance* (trans. Richard Stoneman; London: Penguin Classics, 1991), 2. Stoneman might well have added to his list the Qur'an's depiction of the mysterious figure of *Dhul-Qarnayn* ("he of the two-

The different Alexanders to be encountered in various literary traditions appear to correspond to the moral, intellectual, political, or spiritual needs of the interpretive communities that have appropriated this extraordinary figure's legend. That the cultural memories of Alexander should enjoy revisionary interpretation in the process of literary transmission over the course of generations should surprise no one who approaches this subject with what Morton Smith termed the requisite "practical atheism" of the historian.[22] Of course, the application of Smith's practical atheism raises few eyebrows in the case of Alexander—except, perhaps, in the Islamic tradition where Alexander is sometimes viewed as an instrument of God.[23] The case of David, king of Israel, is another matter: for much of David's legend is contained in sacred literature. What makes David's case different, however, is not an identifiable attribute of sacred literature that distinguishes it from secular literature; David's case is deemed to be different by members of religious communities who engage in special pleading on behalf of the bodies of literature they hold sacred. To allow such special pleading to exempt that literature from the canons of sound historical method is to compromise scholarship and, in the event, to impede the development of literary knowledge. This is not a fruitful way to proceed.

Rather than indulge the sectarian passion for special pleading, I would suggest that the developed history of the revisionary interpretations evident among the various extant versions of the Greek Alexander romance warrant the hypothesis that the moral rehabilitation of David (traced above) belongs to a genre (like poetry) that encompasses both sacred and secular literature. For lack of a more elegant term, I will call this genre "the moral rehabilitation of kings," and encourage my colleagues in other branches of literary study to identify similar candidates for inclusion in this field.

---

horns") who is claimed within the Muslim exegetical tradition to be none other than Alexander the Great (see Qur'an 18:83–101).

[22] Morton Smith, "Historical Method in the Study of Religion," in *Studies in the Cult of Yahweh*, Vol. 1 (ed. Shaye D. Cohen; Leiden: Brill, 1996), 3–11.

[23] See footnote 21, *supra*.

BIBLIOGRAPHY

Ackerman, S. A. "At Home with the Goddess." Pages 455–68 in *Symbiosis, Symbolism, and the Power of the Past*. Edited by W. G. Dever and S. Gitin. Winona Lake: Eisenbrauns, 2003.
Ackroyd, P. R. "Some Interpretive Glosses in the Book of Haggai." *JJS* 7 (1956): 163–7.
———. "Studies in the Book of Haggai." *JJS* 2 (1951): 163–76.
———. "The Book of Haggai and Zechariah I-VIII." *JJS* 2 (1952): 1–13.
Ackroyd, Peter R. *I & II Chronicles, Ezra, Nehemiah*. Torch Bible. London: SCM, 1973.
Albertz, Rainer, ed. *From the Exile to the Maccabees*. Vol. 2 of *A History of Israelite Religion in the Old Testament Period*. OTL. Louisville: Westminster John Knox, 1994.
Albright, W. F. *From Stone Age to Christianity: Monotheism and the Historical Process*. 2d ed. Garden City: Doubleday, 1957.
Allen, L. C. *Jeremiah: A Commentary*. OTL. Louisville: Westminster John Knox, 2008.
Alter, Robert. *The Art of Biblical Narrative*. New York: Basic Books, 1981.
———. *The Book of Psalms: A Translation with Commentary*. New York: W. W. Norton & Co. 2007.
Amit, Yairah. "The Role of Prophecy and Prophets in the Theology of the Book of Chronicles." *Beth Mikra* 93 (1983): 3–23.
Anderson, Gary A. "Sacrifice and Sacrificial Offerings (OT)." *ABD* 5 (1992): 870–86.
Arbeitman, Y. I. "Tamar's Name: Or Is It? (Gen 38)." *ZAW* 112. 2000): 341–55.
Arneth, Martin. "Die antiassyrische Reform Josias von Judah: Überlegungen zur Komposition und Intention 2 Reg 23:4–15." *ZABR* 7 (2001): 189–216.
Ash, P. S. "Jeroboam I and the Deuteronomistic Historian's Ideology of the Founder." *CBQ* 60 (1998): 16–24.
Astour, M. C. "Tamar the Hierodule: An Essay in the Method of Vestigial Motifs." *JBL* 85 (1966), 185–196.
Aurelius, Erik. *Der Fürbitter Israels: Eine Studie zum Mosebild im Alten Testament*. CB OT 27. Stockholm: Almqvist & Wiksell, 1988.
Balentine, Samuel E. "The Prophet as Intercessor: A Reassessment." *JBL* 103 (1984): 161–73.
———. *Prayer in the Hebrew Bible: The Drama of Divine-Human Dialogue*. OBT. Minneapolis: Fortress, 1993.
Barrick, W. B. *The Kings and the Cemeteries: Toward a New Understanding of Josiah's Reform*. VTSup 88. Leiden: Brill, 2002.

Beal, Richard. "Hittite Oracles." Pages 59–83 in *Magic and Divination in the Ancient World*. Edited by Leda Ciraolo and Jonathan Seidel. Leiden: Brill/Styx, 2002.

Beck, Martin. *Der "Tag Yhwhs" im Dodekapropheton: Studien im Spannungsfeld von Traditions-und Redaktionsgeschichte*. BZAW 356. Berlin: de Gruyter, 2005.

Becker, U. "Der Prophet als Fürbitter: Zum Literarchistorischen Ort der Amos-Visionen." *VT* 51 (2001): 141–65.

Beentjes, Pancratius C. "Discovering a New Path of Intertextuality: Inverted Quotations and Their Dynamics." Pages 31–50 in *Literary Structure and Rhetorical Strategies in the Hebrew Bible*. Edited by Leonard J. de Regt, Jan de Waard and Jan P. Fokkelman. Assen: Van Gorcum, 1996.

———. *Tradition and Transformation in the Book of Chronicles*. SSN 52. Leiden: Brill, 2008.

Begg, Christopher "'Seeking Yahweh' and the Purpose of Chronicles." *LS* 9 (1982): 128–41.

———. "The Classical Prophets in the Chronistic History." *BZ* 32 (1988), 100–107.

Ben Zvi, E. "'Twelve Prophetic Books or 'The Twelve': A Few Preliminary Considerations." Pages 125–56 in *Forming Prophetic Literature: Essays in Honor of John D. W. Watts*. Edited by James W. Watts and Paul R. House. Sheffield: Sheffield Academic, 1996.

———. "The Urban Center of Jerusalem and the Development of the Literature of the Hebrew Bible." Pages 194–209 in *Urbanism in Antiquity: From Mesopotamia to Crete*. Edited by W. E. Aufrecht, N. A. Mirau, and S. W. Gauley. JSOTSup 244. Sheffield: Sheffield Academic, 1997.

———. "Imagining Josiah's Book and the Implications of Imagining It in Early Persian Yehud." Pages 193–212 in *Berührungspunkte. Studien zur Sozial- und Religionsgeschichte Israels und seiner Umwelt*. AOAT 350. Edited by I. Kottsieper et al.. Münster: Ugarit Verlag, 2008.

———. *A Historical-Critical Study of the Book of Zephaniah*. BZAW 198. Berlin: de Gruyter, 1991.

Ben Zvi, E. and Michael H. Floyd, eds. *Writings and Speech in Ancient Israelite Prophecy*. SBLSS 10. Atlanta: Society of Biblical Literature, 2000.

Bendavid, Abba. *Parallels in the Bible*. Jerusalem: Carta, 1972.

Ben-Dov, Jonathan. "Writing as Oracle and as Law: New Contexts for the Book-Find of King Josiah." *JBL* 127 (2008): 223–39.

Berger, Peter L. "Charisma and Religious Innovation: The Social Location of Israelite Prophecy." *ASR* 28 (1963): 940–950.

Berman, J. A. *Created Equal: How The Bible Broke with Ancient Political Thought*. New York: Oxford University, 2008.

Beuken, W. A. M. *Haggai-Sacharja 1–8: Studien zur Überlieferungsgeschichte der frühnachexilischen Prophetie*. SSN 10. Assen: Van Gorcum, 1967.

Bird, Phyllis A. "The Place of Women in the Israelite Cultus." Pages 81–102 in *Missing Persons and Mistaken Identities: Women and Gender in Ancient Israel*. Minneapolis: Fortress, 1997. Repr., *Ancient Israelite Religion: Essays in Honor of Frank Moore Cross*. Edited by Patrick D. Miller, Jr., Paul D. Hanson and S. Dean McBride. Philadelphia: Fortress, 1987.

Blenkinsopp, Joseph. *Sage, Priest, Prophet: Religious and Intellectual Leadership in Ancient Israel*. Library of Ancient Israel. Louisville: Westminster John Knox, 1995.

———. *Prophecy and Canon: A Contribution to the Study of Jewish Origins*. Notre Dame. University of Notre Dame, 1977.

Block, Daniel I. *The Book of Ezekiel Chapters 1–24*. NICOT. Grand Rapids: Eerdmans, 1997.

Boda, M. J. and M. H. Floyd, eds. *Tradition in Transition: Haggai and Zechariah 1–8 in the Trajectory of Hebrew Theology*. New York: T&T Clark, 2008.

Bodi, Daniel. *The Book of Ezekiel and the Poem of Erra*. OBO 104. Göttingen: Vandenhoeck & Ruprecht, 1991.

Bovati, Pietro. *Re-establishing Justice: Legal Terms, Concepts and Procedures in the Hebrew Bible*. Translated by M. J. Smith. JSOTS 105. Sheffield: JSOT, 1994.

Brettler, Marc Z. "The Structure of 1 Kings 1–11." *JSOT* 49 (1991): 87–97.

Brown, Norman O. "The Prophetic Tradition." Pages 46–68 in *Apocalypse and/or Metamorphosis*. Berkeley: University of California, 1992.

Broyles, C. C. and C. A. Evans. *Writing and Reading the Scroll of Isaiah: Studies of an Interpretive Tradition*. SVT 70/1. Leiden: Brill, 1997.

Bynum, Carolyn W. "Perspectives, Connections & Objects: What's Happening in History Now?" *Daedalus* 138 (2009): 71–86.

Campbell, Antony F. *Of Prophets and Kings: A Late Ninth-Century Document (1 Samuel 1–2 Kings 10)*. CBQMS 17. Washington: Catholic Biblical Association of America, 1986.

———. *The Ark Narrative (1 Sam 4–6. 2 Sam 6): A Form-Critical and Traditio-Historical Study*. SBLDS 16. Missoula: Scholars Press, 1975.

Carr, D. M. *Writing on the Tablet of the Heart*. New York: Oxford University, 2005.

Carroll, Robert P. "Prophets and Society." Pages 203–25 in *The World of Ancient Israel: Sociological, Anthropological, and Political Perspectives: Essays by Members of the Society for Old Testament Study*. Edited by R. E. Clements. Cambridge: Cambridge University, 1989.

———. *From Chaos to Covenant: Uses of Prophecy in the Book of Jeremiah*. London: SCM, 1981).

———. *Jeremiah: A Commentary*. OTL. London: SCM, 1986.

Chavel, S. "'Let My People Go!': Emancipation, Revelation and Scribal Activity in Jeremiah 34:8–11." *JSOT* 76 (1997): 93–95.

Clements, R. E. "Max Weber, Charisma, and Biblical Prophecy." Pages 89–108 in *Prophecy and Prophets*. Edited by Yehoshua Gitay. Atlanta: Scholars Press, 1997.

———. *A Century of Old Testament Study*. Guildford: Lutterworth, 1976.

Cody, Alred *A History of Old Testament Priesthood*. AnBib 35. Rome: Pontifical Biblical Institute, 1969.

Cogan, Mordechai. "A Slip of the Pen? On Josiah's Actions in Samaria (II Kgs 23:15–20)." Pages 3–8 in *Sefer Moshe: The Moshe Weinfeld Jubilee Volume. Studies in Bible and the Ancient Near East, Qumran, and Post–Biblical Judaism*. Edited by Chaim Cohen et al. Winona Lake: Eisenbrauns, 2004.

Collins, John J. *The Bible after Bible: Historical Criticism in a Postmodern Age*. Grand Rapids: Eerdmans, 2005.

Conrad, E. W. "Reading Isaiah and the Twelve as Prophetic Books." Pages 3–17 in *Writing and Reading the Scroll of Isaiah: Studies of an Interpretive Tradition*. SVT 70/1. Leiden: Brill, 1997.

Cook, John Stephenson Frierson (Steve). *Women Prophets in the Omride Court: A Sociohistorical Analysis of Ancient Near Eastern Prophecy*. Ph.D. diss., Vanderbilt University, 2009.

Cook, Stephen L. *The Social Roots of Biblical Yahwism*. Atlanta: Society of Biblical Literature, 2004.

Crenshaw, James L. *Prophetic Conflict: Its Effect upon Israelite Religion*. BZAW 124. Berlin: Walter de Gruyter, 1971.

Cross, F. M. *Canaanite Myth and Hebrew Epic*. Cambridge: Harvard University, 1973.

Curtis, Edward L. and Albert A. Madsen, *A Critical and Exegetical Commentary on the Books of Chronicles*. ICC. Edinburgh: T&T Clark, 1910.

Davies, Philip R. *Scribes and Schools: The Canonization of the Hebrew Scriptures*. London: SPCK, 1998.

———. "Josiah and the Law Book." Pages 65–77 in *Good Kings and Bad Kings*. Edited by Lester L. Grabbe. LHBOTS 393. New York: T&T Clark, 2005.

———. *Memories of Ancient Israel*. Louisville: Westminster John Knox, 2008.

———. ed. *The Prophets*. Biblical Seminar 42. Sheffield: Sheffield Academic, 1996.

Davis, Ellen F. *Swallowing the Scroll: Textuality and the Dynamics of Discourse in Ezekiel's Prophecy*. JSOTS 78. Bible and Literature Series 21. Sheffield: Almond, 1989

Davison, Lisa Wilson. *Preaching the Women of the Bible*. St. Louis: Chalice, 2006.

de Jong, M. J. *Isaiah among the Ancient Near Eastern Prophets*. VTSup 117. Leiden: Brill, 2007.

———. "Ezekiel as a Literary Figure and the Quest for the Historical Prophet." Pages 1–16 in *The Book of Ezekiel and Its Influence*. Edited by Henk Jan de Jonge and Johannes Tromp. Aldershot: Ashgate, 2007.

de Moor, Johannes C., ed. *The Elusive Prophet. The Prophet as a Historical Person, Literary Character, and Anonymous Artist*. OTS 45. Leiden: Brill, 2001.
de Vries, Simon. "The Forms of Prophetic Address in Chronicles." *HAR* 10 (1986): 15–36.
Dearman, J. A. "My Servants the Scribes: Composition and Context in Jeremiah 36." *JBL* 109 (1990): 409.
Diamond, A. R. P. "Portraying Prophecy: Of Doubts, Variants, and Analogics in the Narrative Representatives of Jeremiah's Oracles—Reconstructing the Hermeneutics of Prophecy." *JSOT* 57 (1993): 99–119.
Dietrich, Walter. *David, Saul und die Propheten. Das Verhältnis von Religion und Politik nach den prophetischen Überlieferungen vom frühesten Königtum in Israel*. BWANT 122. Stuttgart: Kohlhammer, 1992.
———. Prophetie und Geschichte: Eine redaktionsgeschichtliche Untersuchung zum deuteronomistischen Geschichtswerk. FRLANT 108. Göttingen: Vandhoeck & Ruprecht, 1972.
Dillard, Raymond Bryan. *2 Chronicles*. WBC 15. Waco: Word Books, 1987.
———. "The Reign of Asa (2 Chronicles 14–16): An Example of the Chronicler's Theological Method." *JETS* 23 (1980): 207–18.
———. *The Garments of Torah*. Bloomington: Indiana University, 1988.
Dirksen, Piet B. "Prophecy and Temple Music: 1 Chron. 25,1–7." *Henoch* 19 (1997), 259–66.
Duguid, Iain M. *Ezekiel and the Leaders of Israel*. VTSup 163. Leiden: Brill, 1994.
Duhm, Bernhard. *Anmerkungen zu den zwölf Propheten*. Gießen: Töpelmann, 1911.
Edelman, Diana. "Huldah the Prophet—Of Yahweh or Asherah?" Pages 231–51 in *A Feminist Companion to Samuel and Kings*. Edited by Athalya Brenner. FCB 5. Sheffield: Sheffield Academic, 1994.
Eichrodt, Walter. *Theology of the Old Testament*. Translated by J. A. Baker. 2 vols.; Philadelphia: Westminster, 1961.
———. *Der Prophet Hesekiel*. ATD 22. Göttingen: Vandenhoeck & Ruprecht, 1966.
Eissfeldt, Otto. *Die Komposition der Samuelisbücher*. Leipzig: Hinrichs, 1931.
Engineer, Asghar Ali. *Islam in Contemporary World*. Elgin, Ill.: New Dawn, 2007.
Engnell, Ivan. *A Rigid Scrutiny: Critical Essays on the Old Testament*. Translated by John T. Willis. Nashville: Vanderbilt University, 1969.
Even-Shoshan, Abraham. *A New Concordance of the Bible*. Jerusalem: Kiryat Sefer, 1988.
Finkelberg, Margalit. and Guy G. Stroumsa, eds. *Homer, the Bible and Beyond: Literary and Religious Canons in the Ancient World*. JSHR 2. Leiden: Brill, 2003.
Firestone, Reuven. "The Qur'an and the Bible: Some Modern Studies of Their Relationship." Pages 1–22 in *Bible and Qur'an: Essays in Scriptural*

Intertextuality. Edited by John C. Reeves. Atlanta: Society of Biblical Literature, 2003.
Fishbane, Michael. *Biblical Interpretation in Ancient Israel*. Oxford: Clarendon, 1985.
———. *The Garments of Torah: Essays in Biblical Hermeneutics*. Bloomington: Indiana University, 1989.
Floyd, M. "The Nature of the Narrative and the Evidence of Redaction in Haggai." *VT* 45 (1995): 470-90.
———. "Traces of Tradition in Zechariah 1–8: A Case-Study." Pages 210–34 in *Tradition in Transition: Haggai and Zechariah 1–8 in the Trajectory of Hebrew Theology*. Edited by M. J. Boda and M. H. Floyd. New York: T&T Clark, 2008.
Floyd, M. and Robert D. Haak, eds. *Prophets, Prophecy, and Prophetic Texts in Second Temple Judaism*. LHBOTS 427. New York: T&T Clark, 2006).
Fohrer, Georg. *History of Israelite Religion*. Translated by D. E. Green. Nashville: Abingdon. London: SPCK, 1972) 237. ET of *Geschichte der israelitischen Religion*. Berlin: de Gruyter, 1968.
———. *Introduction to the Old Testament*. Nashville: Abingdon, 1968.
Frame, Grant and Andrew R. George. "The Royal Libraries of Nineveh: New Evidence for King Ashurbanipal's Tablet Collection." *Iraq* 67 (2005): 265–84.
Friebel, Kelvin G. *Jeremiah's and Ezekiel's Sign Acts: Rhetorical Nonverbal Communication*. JSOTS 283. Sheffield: Sheffield Academic, 1999.
Friedman, R. E. "The Deuteronomistic School." Pages 70-80 in *Fortunate the Eyes that See: Essays in Honor of David Noel Freedman in Celebration of his Seventieth Birthday*. Edited by A. B. Beck et al. Grand Rapids: Eerdmans, 1995.
Frolov, Serge. *The Turn of the Cycle: 1 Samuel 1–8 in Synchronic and Diachronic Perspectives*. BZAW 342. Berlin: de Gruyter, 2004.
Frymer-Kensky, Tikva. *In the Wake of the Goddesses: Women, Culture, and the Biblical Transformation of Pagan Myth*. New York: Fawcett Columbine, 1993.
Gafney, Wilda C. M. "A Black Feminist Approach to Biblical Studies." *Encounter* 64/4 (2006): 381–403.
———. *Daughters of Miriam: Women Prophets in Ancient Israel*. Minneapolis: Fortress, 2008.
Geoghegan, J. C. "Israelite Sheepshearing and David's Rise to Power," *Bib* 87 (2006): 55–63.
Gerstenberger, Erhard. *Psalms: Part 1 with an Introduction to Cultic Poetry*. FOTL XIV. Grand Rapids: Eerdmans, 1988.
Gese, Hartmut. "Zur Geschichte der Kultsänger am zweiten Tempel." Pages 222–34 in *Abraham unser Vater: Juden und Christen im Gespräch über die Bibel. Festschrift fur Otto Michel*. Edited by Otto Betz, Martin Hengel, and Peter Schmidt. Arbeiten zur Geschichte des Spätjudentums und Urchristentums 5. Leiden: Brill, 1963.

Giesebrecht, Friedrich. *Das Buch Jeremia*. HK III 2,1. Göttingen: Vandenhoeck & Ruprecht, 1894.
Ginzberg, Louis. *Bible Times and Characters from Joshua to Esther*. Vol. 4 of *The Legends of the Jews*. Baltimore: Johns Hopkins University Press, 1998.
Gitay, Yehoshua. "The Projection of the Prophet: A Rhetorical Presentation of the Prophet Jeremiah." Pages 41–55 in *Prophecy and Prophets: The Diversity and Contemporary Issues in Scholarship*. Edited by Y. Gitay. SBL Semeia Studies. Atlanta: Scholars Press, 1997.
Glatt-Gilead, David A. "The Root ינב and Historiographic Periodization in Chronicles." *CBQ* 64 (2002): 248–57.
Goldenberg, Robert. "Law and Spirit in Talmudic Religion." Pages 232–52 in *Jewish Spirituality: From the Bible Through the Middle Ages*. Edited by Arthur Green. New York: Crossroad, 1987.
Grabbe, Lester L. "Prophetic and Apocalyptic: Time for New Definitions—and New Thinking." Pages 107–33 in *Knowing the End from the Beginning: The Prophetic, the Apocalyptic, and their Relationships*. Edited by Lester L. Grabbe and Robert D. Haak. JSPSup 46. London: T&T Clark, 2003.
———. and Robert D. Haak, eds. Knowing the End from the Beginning: The Prophetic, the Apocalyptic, and their Relationships. JSPSup 46. London: T&T Clark, 2003.
———. *Judaic Religion in the Second Temple Period: Belief and Practice from the Exile to Yavneh*. London/New York: Routledge, 2000.
———. *Priests, Prophets, Diviners, Sages: A Socio-Historical Study of Religious Specialists in Ancient Israel*. Valley Forge, Pa.: Trinity, 1995.
Gunkel, H. *Die Propheten*. Göttingen: Vandenhoeck & Ruprecht, 1917.
———. *Creation and Chaos in the Primeval Era and the Eschaton: A Religiohistorical Study of Genesis 1 and Revelation 12*. 1895. Repr., translated by K. William Whitney, Jr.. The Biblical Resource Series. Grand Rapids: Eerdmans, 2006.
Halbertal, Moshe. *People of the Book: Canon, Meaning, and Authority*. Cambridge: Harvard University, 1997.
Halpern, B. "Brisker Pipes than Poetry: The Development of Monotheism in Ancient Israel." Pages 98–102 in *Judaic Perspectives on Ancient Israel*. Edited by J. Neusner et al. Minneapolis: Fortress, 1987.
———. "Why Manasseh Is Blamed for the Babylonian Exile: The Evolution of a Biblical Tradition." *VT* 48 (1998): 473–514.
Halpern, B. and David Vanderhooft. "The Editions of Kings in the 7–6 Centuries B.C.E." *HUCA* 62 (1991): 179–244.
Handy, Lowell K. "The Role of Huldah in Josiah's Cult Reform." *ZAW* 106 (1994): 40–53.
Hanson, P. D. *The Dawn of Apocalyptic*. Philadelphia: Fortress, 1975.

Hasson, Isaac. "David." Pages 495–7 in vol. 1 of *The Encyclopaedia of the Qur'an.* Edited by Jane Dammen McAuliffe. 5 vols. Leiden: Brill, 2001.

Hays, Richard B. *Echoes of Scripture in the Letters of Paul.* New Haven: Yale University, 1989.

Hazenbos, J. "Der Mensch denkt, Gott lenkt: Betrachtungen zum hethitischen Orakel personal." Pages 95–109 in *Das geistige Erfassen der Welt im Alten Orient: Sprache, Religion, Kultur und Gesellschaft.* Edited by C. Wilcke. Wiesbaden: Harrassowitz, 2007.

Hendel, Ronald. *Remembering Abraham: Culture, Memory, and History in the Hebrew Bible.* Oxford: Oxford University, 2005.

Hernando, Eusebio. "El Profetismo en los libros de las Crónicas." *Scriptorium Victoriense* 34 (1987): 45–66.

Hertzberg, H. W. "Sind die Propheten Fürbitter?" Pages 63–74 in *Tradition und Situation: Studien zur alttestamentlichen Prophetie. Artur Weiser zum 70. Geburtstag am 18.11.1963 dargebracht von Kollegen, Freunden und Schülern.* Edited by E. Würthwein and O. Kaiser. Göttingen: Vandenhoeck & Ruprecht, 1963.

Heschel, Abraham Joshua. *The Prophets.* New York: Harper & Row, 1962. Repr., New York: Perennial, 2001.

Hodgson, Marshall G. S. *The Classical Age of Islam. Vol. 1 of The Venture of Islam: Conscience and History in a World Civilization.* Chicago: University of Chicago Press, 1974.

Holladay, W. L. "Elusive Deuteronomists, Jeremiah and Proto-Deuteronomy." *CBQ* 66 (2004): 55–77.

———. "The Background of Jeremiah's Self-Understanding: Moses, Samuel and Psalm 22." *JBL* 83 (1964): 153–64.

———. *Jeremiah 1.* Hermeneia. Philadelphia: Fortress, 1986, 88–89.

———. *Jeremiah 2.* Hermeneia. Philadelphia: Fortress, 1989, 198.

Holm, Nils G. "Ecstasy Research in the 20th Century: An Introduction." Pages 7–26 in *Religious Ecstasy: Based on Papers Read at the Symposium on Religious Ecstasy Held at Åbo, Finland, on the 26th–28th of August 1981.* Edited by N. G. Holm. Stockholm: Almqvist and Wiksell, 1982.

House, P. *The Unity of the Twelve.* Sheffield: Sheffield University Press, 1990.

Hurowitz, V. A. *I Have Built You an Exalted House: Temple Building in the Bible in Light of Mesopotamian and Northwest Semitic Writings.* JSOTSup 115. Sheffield: JSOT, 1992), 271–7.

———. "'Proto-canonization' of the Torah: A Self-portrait of the Pentateuch in Light of Mesopotamian Writings." Pages 31–48 in *Study and Knowledge in Jewish Thought.* Edited by Howard Kreisel. The Goren-Goldstein Library of Jewish Thought 4. Beer Sheva: Ben-Gurion University of the Negev, 2006.

Irsigler, Hubert. *Gottesgericht und Jahwetag: Die Komposition Zef 1,1–2,3, untersucht auf der Grundlage der Literarkritik des Zefanjabuches.* Arbeiten zu Text und Sprache im Alten Testament 3. St. Ottilien: Eos, 1977.
Japhet, Sara. *1 and 2 Chronicles: A Commentary.* OTL. Louisville, Ky.: Westminster John Knox, 1993), 155–6.
———. *The Ideology of the Book of Chronicles and Its Place in Biblical Thought.* BEATAJ 9. Frankfurt a.M.: Peter Lang, 1989.
Jeremias, Jörg. *Der Prophet Hosea.* ATD 24. Göttingen: Vandenhoeck & Ruprecht, 1983), 62–63.
———. *The Book of Amos.* OTL. Translated by Douglas W. Stott. Louisville, Ky.: Westminster John Knox, 1998.
Jobling David et al., eds. "Feminist and Womanist Criticism." Pages 225–71 in *The Postmodern Bible.* New Haven: Yale University Press, 1995.
Johnstone, William. "Guilt and Atonement: The Theme of 1 and 2 Chronicles." Pages 113–38 in *A Word in Season: Essays in Honour of William McKane* (ed. J. D. Martin and P. R. Davies; JSOTSup 42. Sheffield: Sheffield Academic, 1986.
Joyce, Paul. *Ezekiel: A Commentary.* JSOTSup 482. London: T&T Clark, 2007.
Kaiser, Otto. *Das Buch des Propheten Jesaja: Kapitel 1–12.* ATD 17. 5th ed. Göttingen: Vandenhoeck & Ruprecht, 1981.
Kasher, Rimon. "The Saving of Jehosaphat: Extent, Parallels, Significance." *Beth Mikra* 31 (1985): 242–51.
Kegler, Jürgen. "Prophetengestalten im Deuteronomistischen Geschichtswerk und in den Chronikbüchern: Ein Beitrag zur Kompositions- und Redaktionsgeschichte der Chronikbücher." *ZAW* 105 (1993): 481–97.
Kelly, Brian E. *Retribution and Eschatology in Chronicles.* JSOTSup 211. Sheffield: Sheffield Academic, 1996.
Kessler, J. "Tradition, Continuity and Covenant in the Book of Haggai: An Alternative Voice from Early Persian Yehud." Pages 1–39 in *Tradition in Transition: Haggai and Zechariah 1–8 in the Trajectory of Hebrew Theology.* Edited by M. J. Boda and M. H. Floyd. New York: T&T Clark, 2008.
———. *The Book of Haggai: Prophecy and Society in Early Persian Yehud.* VTSup 91. Leiden: Brill, 2002.
Kleinig, John W. *The LORD's Song: The Basis, Function and Significance of Choral Music in Chronicles.* JSOTSup 156. Sheffield: Sheffield Academic, 1993.
Knoppers, Gary N. *1 Chronicles 10–29.* AB 12A. New York: Doubleday, 2004.
———. "Rethinking the Relationship between Deuteronomy and the Deuteronomistic History: The Case of Kings." *CBQ* 63 (2001): 393–415.
———. *Two Nations under God.* HSM 53. Atlanta: Scholars Press, 1994.

Koenen, K. *Ethik und Eschatologie im Tritojesaja buch: Eine literarkritische und redaktionsgeschichtliche Studie.* WMANT 62. Neukirchen-Vluyn: Neukirchener, 1990.

Kohn, Risa Levitt. "A Prophet Like Moses? Rethinking Ezekiel's Relationship to the Torah." *ZAW* 114 (2002): 236–54.

Kratz, R. G. "The Growth of the Old Testament." Pages 459–88 in *The Oxford Handbook of Biblical Studies.* Edited by J. W. Rogerson and J. M. Lieu. Oxford: Oxford University, 2006.

———. "Tritojesaja." *TRE* 34 (2002): 124-30.

———. *Die Propheten Israels.* Munich: C. H. Beck, 2003.

Kuntzmann, Raymond. "La fonction prophétique en 1–2 Chroniques: Du ministère de la parole au Service de l'institution communautaire." Pages 245–58 in *Ich bewirke das Heil und erschaffe das Unheil (Jesaja 45,7): Studien zur Botschaft der Propheten.* Edited by Friedrich Diedrich and Bernd Willmes. FzB 88. Würzburg: Echter, 1998.

Lafont, Bertrand. "Le Roi de Mari et les prophètes du dieu Adad." *RA* 78 (1984): 7–18.

Lambert, Wilfred G. "A Catalogue of Texts and Authors." *JCS* 16 (1962): 59–77.

Langohr, Guy. "Le livre de Sophonie et la critique d'autenticité." *ETL* 52 (1976): 1–27.

———. "Rédaction et composition du livre de Sophonie." *Museion* 89 (1976): 51–73.

Lapsley, Jacqueline E. *Can These Bones Live? The Problem of the Moral Self in the Book of Ezekiel.* BZAW 301. Berlin: de Gruyter, 2000.

Leuchter, M. "'The Levite in Your Gates': The Deuteronomic Redefinition of Levitical Authority." *JBL* 126 (2007): 429–32.

———. "The Manumission Laws in Leviticus and Deuteronomy: The Jeremiah Connection." *JBL* 127 (2008): 640–6.

———. "The Temple Sermon and the term מקום in the Jeremianic Corpus." *JSOT* 30 (2005): 107–9.

———. "Why is the Song of Moses in the Book of Deuteronomy?" *VT* 57 (2007): 314.

———. *The Polemics of Exile in Jeremiah 26–45.* New York: Cambridge University Press, 2008.

———. *Josiah's Reform and Jeremiah's Scroll: Historical Calamity and Prophetic Response.* HBM 6. Sheffield: Phoenix, 2006.

Levenson, Jon D. *The Death and Resurrection of the Beloved Son: The Transformation of Child Sacrifice in Judaism and Christianity.* New Haven: Yale, 1993.

———. *Theology of the Program of Restoration of Ezekiel 40–48.* HSM 10. Missoula, Montana: Scholars Press, 1976.

Levin, Christoph. "Das Amosbuch der Anawim." *ZTK* 94 (1997): 407–36. Repr., idem. Pages 265–90 in *Fortschreibungen: Gesammelte Studien zum Alten Testament*. BZAW 316. Berlin: de Gruyter, 2003.

———. "Josia im Deuteronomistischen Geschichtswerk." *ZAW* 96 (1984): 351–71. Repr., idem. Pages 198–216 in *Fortschreibungen*. Berlin: de Gruyter, 2003.

———. "Noch einmal: Die Anfänge des Propheten Jeremia." *VT* 31 (1981): 428–40. Repr., idem. Pages 217–26 in *Fortschreibungen*. Berlin: de Gruyter, 2003.

———. "The 'Word of Yhwh': A Theological Concept in the Book of Jeremiah." Pages 42–62 in *Prophets, Prophecy, and Prophetic Texts in Second Temple Judaism*. Edited by Michael H. Floyd and Robert D. Haak. LHBOTS 427. New York: T&T Clark, 2006.

———. "The Poor in the Old Testament: Some Observations." *R&T* 8 (2001): 253–73. Repr., idem. Pages 322–38 in *Fortschreibungen*. Berlin: de Gruyter, 2003.

———. *Der Jahwist*. FRLANT 157. Göttingen: Vandenhoeck & Ruprecht, 1993.

Levinson, Bernard M. "The Reconceptualization of Kingship in Deuteronomy and the Deuteronomistic History's Transformation of Torah." *VT* 51 (2001): 511–34.

———. *Deuteronomy and the Hermeneutics of Legal Innovation*. New York: Oxford University, 1997.

Lewis, I. M. *Ecstatic Religion: A Study of Shamanism and Spirit Possession*. 2d ed. London: Routledge, 1989.

Liebermann, Stephen J. "Canonical and Official Cuneiform Texts: Towards an Understanding of Assurbanipal's Personal Tablet Collection." Pages 305–36 in *Lingering Over Words: Studies in Ancient Near Eastern Literature in Honor of William L. Moran*. Edited by Tzvi Abusch et al. Atlanta: Scholars Press, 1990.

Livingstone, Alasdair. "Ashurbanipal—Literate or Not?" *ZA* 97 (2007): 98–118.

Lohfink, N. "Die Gattung der 'Historischen Kurzgeschichte' in den letzten Jahren von Juda und in der Zeit des Babylonischen Exils." *ZAW* 90 (1978): 333–42.

Lowery, R. H. *The Reforming Kings: Cults and Society in First Temple Judah*. JSOTSup 120. Sheffield: JSOT, 1991.

Lundbom, J. R. "The Inclusio and Other Framing Devices in Deuteronomy i–xxviii." *VT* 46 (1996): 309–312.

———. *Jeremiah 21–36*. New York: Doubleday, 2004.

Machinist, Peter and Hayim Tadmor. "Heavenly Wisdom." Pages 146–51 in *The Tablet and the Scroll: Near Eastern Studies in Honor of William W. Hallo*. Edited by Mark E. Cohen et al. Bethesda, Md: CDL, 1993.

Marinkovic, P. "Zechariah 1–8 and the Second Temple." Pages 88–103 in *Second Temple Studies 2, Temple Community in the Persian Period*. Edited by T. C. Eskenazi and K. H. Richards. JSOTSup 175. Sheffield: JSOT, 1994.

Marti, Karl. *Das Dodekapropheton*. KHC 13. Tübingen: Mohr Siebeck, 1904.

Mason, Rex. "The Prophets of the Restoration." Pages 137–54 in *Israel's Prophetic Tradition: Essays in Honor of Peter Ackroyd.* Edited by Richard Coggins, Anthony Phillips and Michael Knibb. Cambridge: Cambridge University, 1982.

———. "The Purpose of the Editorial Framework of the Book of Haggai." *VT* 27 (1997): 413–21.

———. *Preaching the Tradition: Homily and Hermeneutics after the Exile.* Cambridge: Cambridge University, 1990.

Mathias, Dietman. "'Levitische Predigt' und Deuteronomismus." *ZAW* 96 (1984): 23–49.

Maududi, S. Abul A'la. *The Meaning of the Qur'an.* Vol. 1. 16 ed. Lahore: Islamic Publications, 1997.

McCarter, P. Kyle *1 Samuel.* AB 8. Garden City: Doubleday, 1980.

McKane, William. "The Construction of Jeremiah Chapter xxi." *VT* 32 (1982): 59–73.

———. *A Critical and Exegetical Commentary on Jeremiah.* 2 vols. ICC. Edinburgh: T&T Clark, 1986 and 1996.

McKeating, H. "Ezekiel the 'Prophet like Moses'?" *JSOT* 61 (1994): 97–109.

Mein, Andrew. "Ezekiel as a Priest in Exile." Pages 199–213 in *The Elusive Prophet: The Prophet as a Historical Person, Literary Character, and Anonymous Artist.* Edited by J. C. De Moor. Oudtestamentische Studiën 45. Leiden: Brill, 2001.

Meyers, C. L. *Households and Holiness: The Religious Culture of Israelite Women.* Minneapolis: Fortress, 2005.

——— and E. M. Meyers. *Haggai, Zechariah 1–8.* AB 25B. New York: Doubleday, 1987.

Micheel, Rosemarie. *Die Seher- und Prophetenüberlieferungen in der Chronik.* BET 18. Frankfurt a.M.: Peter Lang 1983.

Middlemas, J. "Did Second Isaiah Write Lamentations 3?" *VT* 56 (2006): 505–35.

———. "Divine Reversal and the Role of the Temple in Trito-Isaiah." Pages 164–87 in *Temple and Worship in Biblical Israel.* Edited by John Day. LHBOTS 422. London: T&T Clark, 2005.

———. "The Violent Storm in Lamentations." *JSOT* 29 (2004): 81–97.

———. "Trito-Isaiah's Intra- and Internationalization: Identity Markers in the Second Temple Period." Pages 105–25 in *Judah and the Judeans in the Achaemenid Period: Negotiating Identity in an International Context.* Edited by Oded Lipschits, Gary N. Knoppers and Manfred Oeming. Winona Lake, Ind.: Eisenbrauns, 2011.

———. *The Templeless Age: An Introduction to the History, Literature, and Theology of the "Exile."* Louisville, Ky.: Westminster John Knox, 2007.

———. *The Troubles of Templeless Judah.* Oxford Theological Monographs. Oxford: Oxford University, 2005.

Milgrom, Jacob. *Leviticus 1–16.* AB 3. Garden City: Doubleday, 1991.

Miller, Patrick D. "Prayer and Divine Action." Pages 211–32 in *God in the Fray: A Tribute to Walter Brueggemann*. Edited by T. Linafelt and T. K. Beal. Minneapolis: Fortress, 1998.

———. *They Cried to the Lord: The Form and Theology of Biblical Prayer*. Minneapolis: Fortress, 1994.

Montgomery, James A. *A Critical and Exegetical Commentary on the Books of Kings*. ICC. Edinburgh: T&T Clark, 1951.

Mowinckel, Sigmund. *Psalmenstudien III. Kultprophetie und prophetische Psalmen*. Skrifter utgit av Videnskapsselskapets i Kristiania II: Hist.-Filos. Klasse. Oslo: Dybwad, 1923.

———. *The Spirit and the Word: Prophecy and Tradition in Ancient Israel*. Edited by K. C. Hanson, Minneapolis: Fortess, 2002.

Muff, Yochanan. *Love and Joy: Law, Language and Religion in Ancient Israel*. New York: Jewish Theological Association of America, 1992.

Muilenburg, J. "Form Criticism and Beyond." *JBL* 88 (1969): 1–18.

Müller, Reinhard. *Jahwe als Wettergott: Studien zur althebräischen Kultlyrik anhand ausgewählter Psalmen*. BZAW 387. Berlin: de Gruyter, 2008.

Na'aman, Nadav. "The King Leading Cult Reforms in His Kingdom: Josiah and Other Kings in the Ancient Near East." *ZABR* 12 (2006): 131–68.

Newby, Gordon Darnell. *The Making of the Last Prophet: A Reconstruction of the Earliest Biography of Muhammad*. Columbia: University of South Carolina Press, 1989.

Newsome, James D. "Toward a New Understanding of the Chronicler and his Purposes." *JBL* 94 (1975): 201–17.

———. *The Chronicler's View of Prophecy*. Nashville: Vanderbilt University, 1973.

Nissinen, Martti. "How Prophecy Became Literature." *SJOT* 10 (2005): 154–72.

———. *Prophets and Prophecy in the Ancient Near East*. Writings from the Ancient World 12. Atlanta: Society of Biblical Literature, 2003.

———. "Spoken, Written, Quoted and Invented: Orality and Writtenness in Ancient Near Eastern Prophecy." Pages 235–71 in *Writings and Speech in Israelite and Ancient Near Eastern Prophecy*. Edited by Ehud Ben Zvi and Michael H. Floyd. SBLSymS 10. Atlanta: Society of Biblical Literature, 2000.

———. ed. *Prophecy in Its Ancient Near Eastern Context: Mesopotamian, Biblical, and Arabian Perspectives*. SBLSymS 13. Atlanta: Society of Biblical Literature, 2000.

Nissinen, Martti and Matthias Köckert, eds., *Propheten in Mari, Assyrien und Israel*. FRLANT 201. Göttingen: Vandenhoeck & Ruprecht, 2003.

Nogalski, J. D. *Literary Precursors to the Book of the Twelve*. BZAW 217. Berlin: de Gruyter, 1993.

———. *Redactional Processes in the Book of the Twelve* BZAW 218. Berlin: de Gruyter, 1993.

Nogalski, J. D. and M. A. Sweeney, eds. *Reading and Hearing the Book of the Twelve*. SBLSymS 15. Atlanta: Society of Biblical Literature, 2000.

Noth, Martin *The Deuteronomistic History*. JSOTSup 15. Sheffield: JSOT, 1981.

O'Connor, K. M. "'Do Not Trim a Word': The Contribution of Chapter 26 to the Book of Jeremiah." *CBQ* 51 (1989): 625–7.

Odell, M. S. "You Are What You Eat: Ezekiel and the Scroll." *JBL* 117 (1998): 229–48,

———. "The Inversion of Shame and Forgiveness in Ezekiel 16:59–63." *JSOT* 56 (1992): 101–12.

Olyan, S. M. "Family Religion in Israel and the Wider Levant of the First Millennium BCE." Pages 113–126 in *Household and Family Religion in Antiquity*. Edited by J. Bodel and S. M. Olyan. Oxford: Blackwell Publishing, 2008.

———. "Some Neglected Aspects of Israelite Interment Ideology." *JBL* 124 (2005): 601–16.

Panetz, Raphael I. "Ephod." *ABD* 2 (1992): 550–1.

Parpola, Simo. "Mesopotamian Astrology and Astronomy as Domains of the Mesopotamian 'Wisdom.'" Pages 47–59 in *Die Rolle des Astronomie in den Kulturen Mesopotamiens*. Edited by Hannes D. Galter. Graz: Berger, 1993.

———. *Assyrian Prophecies*. SAA 9. Helsinki: Helsinki University Press, 1997.

Patton, Corrine L. "Layers of Meaning: Priesthood in Jeremiah MT." Pages 149–76 in *The Priests in the Prophets: The Portrayal of Priests, Prophets, and Other Religious Specialists in the Latter Prophets*. Edited by L. L. Grabbe and A. O. Bellis. JSOTS 408. London: T&T Clark, 2004.

———. "Priest, Prophet, and Exile: Ezekiel as a Literary Construct." Pages 73–89 in *Ezekiel's Hierarchical World: Wrestling with a Tiered Reality*. Edited by S. L. Cook and C. L. Patton. Atlanta: Society of Biblical Literature, 2004.

Paul, Shalom M. "Prophets and Prophecy." *EJ* 13 (2006): 1170–1.

Pauritsch, K. *Die neue Gemeinde: Gott sammelt Ausgestossene und Arme (Jesaja 56–66). Die Botschft des Tritojesaia-Buches literature-, form-, gattunskritische und redaktionsgeschichtliche untersucht*. AnBib 47. Rome: Biblical Institute, 1971.

Perlitt, Lothar. *Die Propheten Nahum, Habakuk, Zephanja*. ATD 25/1. Göttingen: Vandenhoeck & Ruprecht, 2004.

Person, Raymond F. *The Deuteronomic School: History, Social Setting, and Literature*. SBL Studies in Biblical Literature 2. Atlanta: Society of Biblical Literature, 2002.

Petersen, David L. *Haggai, Zechariah 1–8: A Commentary*. OTL. London: SCM Press, 1985.

———. *Late Israelite Prophecy: Studies in Deutero-Prophetic Literature and in Chronicles*. SBLMS 23. Missoula: Scholars Press, 1977.

———. *The Prophetic Literature: An Introduction*. Louisville, Ky.: Westminster John Knox, 2002.
———. *The Roles of Israel's Prophets*. JSOTSup 17. Sheffield: JSOT, 1981.
Pongratz-Leisten, Beate. *Herrschaftswissen in Mesopotamia*. SAAS 10. Helsinki: The Neo-Assyrian Text Corpus Project, 1999.
Potter, D. "The New Covenant in Jeremiah xxxi 31–34." *VT* 33 (1983): 349–50.
Press, Richard. "Der Prophet Samuel. Eine traditionsgeschichtliche Untersuchung." *ZAW* 56 (1938): 177–225.
Propp, William H. C. *Exodus 19–40*. AB 2A. Garden City: Doubleday, 2006.
Pucci, Joseph. *The Full-Knowing Reader: Allusion and the Power of the Reader in the Western Literary Tradition*. New Haven: Yale University Press, 1998.
Rahman, Fazlur. *Major Themes of the Qur'an*. 2d ed. Minneapolis: Bibliotheca Islamica, 1989.
Ramsey, George W. "Samuel." *ABD* 5 (1992): 954–7.
Redditt, P. L. "The Formation of the Book of the Twelve: A Review of Research." Pages 58-80 in *SBL Seminar Papers, 2001*. SBLSP 40. Atlanta: Society of Biblical Literature, 2001.
Renz, Thomas. *The Rhetorical Function of the Book of Ezekiel*. VTSup 298. Leiden: Brill, 1999.
Reventlow, Henning Graf. *Das Amt des Propheten bei Amos*. FRLANT 80. Göttingen, Vandenhoeck & Ruprecht, 1962.
———. *Gebet im Alten Testament*. Stuttgart: Kohlhammer, 1986.
———. *Liturgie und prophetisches Ich bei Jeremia*. Gütersloh: Gerd Mohn, 1963.
Rhodes, A. B. "Israel's Prophets as Intercessors, in Scripture in History and Theology." Pages 107–28 in *Essays in Honor of J. Coert Rylaarsdam*. Edited by A. L. Merrill and T. W. Overholt. Pittsburgh: Pickwick, 1977.
Riley, William. *King and Cultus in Chronicles: Worship and the Reinterpretation of History*. JSOTSup 160. Sheffield: JSOT, 1993.
Roberts, J. J. M. "Does God Lie? Divine Deceit as a Theological Problem in Israelite Prophetic Literature." Pages 211–20 in *Congress Volume: Jerusalem 1986*. VTSup 40. Edited by John A. Emerton. Leiden: Brill, 1988.
Rochberg-Halton, Francesca. "Canonicity in Cuneiform Texts." *JCS* 36 (1984): 127–144.
———. *The Heavenly Writing: Divination, Horoscopy, and Astronomy in Mesopotamian Culture*. Cambridge University, 2004.
Römer, Thomas. "Du Temple au Livre: L'idéologie de la centralization dans l'historiographie deutéronomiste." Pages 207–25 in *Rethinking the Foundations: Historiography in the Ancient world and in the Bible*. Edited by Thomas Römer and Steven L. McKenzie. BZAW 294. Berlin: de Gruyter, 2000.
———. "Transformations in Deuteronomistic and Biblical Historiography: On 'Book-finding' and other Literary Strategies." *ZAW* 109 (1997): 1–11.

Rost, Leonhard. *Die Überlieferung von der Thronnachfolge Davids*. BWANT 3/6. Stuttgart: W. Kohlhammer, 1926.
Roth, Martin. *Israel und die Völker im Zwölfprophetenbuch: Eine Untersuchung zu den Büchern Joel, Jona, Micha, und Nahum*. FRLANT 210. Göttingen: Vandenhoeck & Ruprecht, 2005.
Rudolph, Wilhelm. "Der Aufbau der Asa-Geschichte." *VT* 2 (1952): 367–71.
Sarna, Nahum M. *Exodus*. JPSTC. Philadelphia: Jewish Publication Society, 1991.
Sasson, Jack M. "The Posting of Letters with Divine Messages." Pages 299–316 in *Florilegium Marianum II: Recueil d'études à la mémoire de Maurice Birot*. Edited by Dominique Charpin and Jean-Marie Durand. Paris: N.A.B.U, 1994.
Schaeffer, G. E. "The Significance of Seeking God in the Purpose of the Chronicler." Th.D. diss., Southern Baptist Theological Seminary, 1972.
Schart, Aaron. "Combining Prophetic Oracles in Mari Letters and Jeremiah 36." *JANES* 23 (1995): 75–93.
Schaudig, Hanspeter. *Die Inschriften Nabonids von Babylon und Kyros' des Grossen, samt den in ihrem Umfeld enstandenen Tendenzschriften: Textausgabe und Grammatik*. AOAT 256. Münster: Ugarit, 2001.
Schmid, K. "The Late Persian Formation of the Torah: Observations on Deuteronomy 34." *Judah and Judeans in the Fourth Century B.C.E.* Edited by O. Lipschits, G. N. Knoppers and R. Albertz. Winona Lake: Eisenbrauns, 2007.
Schmitt, Armin. "Das prophetische Sondergut in 2 Chr 20,14–17." Pages 273–85 in *Künder des Wortes: Festschrift Josef Schreiner*. Edited by Lothar Ruppert et al. Würzburg: Echter, 1982.
Schniedewind, W. M. "Prophets and Prophecy in the Book of Chronicles." Pages 204–24 in *The Chronicler as Historian*. Edited by Matt Patrick Graham, Kenneth G. Hoglund and Steven L. McKenzie. JSOTSup 238. Sheffield: Sheffield Academic, 1997.

———. *How The Bible Became a Book: The Textualization of Ancient Israel*. New York: Cambridge University, 2004.

———. *The Word of God in Transition: From Prophet to Exegete in the Second Temple Period*. JSOTSup 197. Sheffield: Sheffield Academic, 1995.

Schökel, Luis Alonso. "Jeremías como anti-Moisés." Pages 245–54 in *De la Tôrah au Messe*. Edited by Maurice Carrez, Joseph Doré, Pierre Grelot. Paris: Desclée, 1981.
Schöpflin, Karin. *Theologie als Biographie im Ezechielbuch: Ein Beitrag zur Konzeption alttestamentlicher Prophetie*. FAT 36. Tübingen: Mohr, 2002.
Schwally, Friedrich. "Das Buch Sefanja, eine historisch-kritische Untersuchung." *ZAW* 10 (1890): 165–240.
Schwartz, Baruch J. "A Priest Out of Place: Reconsidering Ezekiel's Role in the History of the Israelite Priesthood." Pages 61–71 in *Ezekiel's Hierarchical World: Wrestling with a Tiered Reality*. Edited by S. L. Cook and C. L. Patton. SBLSymS 31. Atlanta: Society of Biblical Literature, 2004.

———. "Torah from Zion: Isaiah's Temple Vision (Isaiah 2:1–4)." Pages 11–26 in *Sanctity of Time and Space in Tradition and Modernity*. Edited by Alberdina Houtman et al. Leiden: Brill, 1998.
Seeligman, Isaac Leo. "Die Auffassung von der Prophetie in der deuteronomistischen und chronistischen Geschichtsschreibung." Pages 254–79 in *Congress Volume: Göttingen 1977*. Edited by John A. Emerton et al. VTSup 29. Leiden: Brill, 1978.
Seitz, Christopher R. "The Prophet Moses and the Canonical Shape of Jeremiah." *ZAW* 10 (1989): 3–27.
Sekine, S. *Die Tritojesajanische Sammlung (Jes 56-66) redaktionsgeschichtlich untersucht*. BZAW 175. Berlin: de Gruyter, 1989.
Seybold, Klaus. *Satirische Prophetie: Studien zum Buch Zefanja*. SBS 120. Stuttgart: Katholisches Bibelwerk, 1985.
Sharp, Carolyn J. *Prophecy and Ideology in Jeremiah: Struggles for Authority in the Deutero-Jeremianic Prose*. New York: T&T Clark, 2003.
Singer, Itamar. "Sin and Punishment in Hittite Prayers." Pages 557–67 in *An Experienced Scribe who Neglects Nothing: Ancient Near Eastern Studies in Honor of Jacob Klein*. Edited by Yitschak Sefati. Bethesda, Md.: CDL, 2005.
———. *Hittite Prayers*. SBLWAW 11. Atlanta: Society of Biblical Literature, 2002.
Smith, Mark S. *The Early History of God: Yahweh and the Other Deities in Ancient Israel*. 2d ed. Grand Rapids: Eerdmans, 2002.
———. "The Common Theology of the Ancient Near East." *JBL* 71 (1952): 135–147.
Smith, Morton. "Historical Method in the Study of Religion." Pages 3–11 in idem, *Studies in the Cult of Yahweh*. Vol. 1: *Studies in Historical Method, Ancient Israel, Ancient Judaism*. Edited by Shaye D. Cohen. Leiden: E. J. Brill, 1996.
Smith, Paul A. *Rhetoric and Redaction in Trito-Isaiah: The Structure, Growth and Authorship of Isaiah 56-66*. VTSup 62. Leiden: Brill, 1995.
Snyman, Gerrie. "'Tis a Vice to Know Him': Reader's Response-Ability and Responsibility in 2 Chronicles 14–16." *Semeia* 77 (1997): 91–113.
Sommer, Benjamin D. *A Prophet Reads Scripture: Allusion in Isaiah 40–66*. Stanford: Stanford University Press, 1998.
Sparks, Kent. "The Prophetic Speeches in Chronicles: Speculation, Revelation, and Ancient Historiography." *BBR* 9 (1999): 233–45.
Stager, L. E. "The Patrimonial Kingdom of Solomon." Pages 63–73 in *Symbiosis, Symbolism and the Power of the Past*. Edited by W. G. Dever and S. Gitin. Winona Lake: Eisenbrauns, 2003.
Stanton, Elizabeth Cady. *The Woman's Bible*. New York: European Pub. Co., 1895–1898. Repr., Boston: Northeastern University Press, 1993.
Steck, O. H. *Studien zu Tritojesaja*. BZAW 203. Berlin: de Gruyter, 1991.

Stoneman, Richard. *The Greek Alexander Romance*. Translated by Richard Stoneman. London: Penguin Classics, 1991.
Strübind, Kim. *Tradition als Interpretation in der Chronik: König Josaphat als Paradigma chronistischer Hermeneutik und Theologie*. BZAW 201. Berlin: De Gruyter, 1991.
Sweeney, Marvin A. *King Josiah of Judah: The Lost Messiah of Israel*. New York: Oxford University Press, 2001.
―――. *Zephaniah: A Commentary*. Hermeneia. Minneapolis: Fortress, 2003.
Swetnam, J. "Why Was Jeremiah's New Covenant New?" Pages 111–5 in G. W. Anderson et al, *Studies on Prophecy: A Collection of Twelve Papers*. VTSup 26. Leiden: Brill, 1974.
te Stroete, G. A. "Ezekiel 24,15–27: The Meaning of a Symbolic Act." *Bijdragen* 38 (1977): 163–75.
Then, Reinhold. *"Gibt es denn keinen mehr unter den Propheten?" Zum Fortgang der alttestamentlichen Prophetie in frühjüdischer Zeit*. BEATAJ 22. Frankfurt a.M.: Peter Lang, 1990.
Thiessen, M. "The Form and Function of the Song of Moses (Deuteronomy 32:1–43)." *JBL* 123 (2004): 401–24.
Tiemeyer, Lena-Sofia "God's Hidden Compassion." *TynBul* 57 (2006): 193–4.
―――. "The Watchman Metaphor in Isaiah lvi–lxvi." *VT* 55 (2005): 378–400.
Tollington, Janet E. *Tradition and Innovation in Haggai and Zechariah 1–8*. JSOTSup 150. Sheffield: Sheffield Academic, 1993.
Tromp, Nicholas J. "The Paradox of Ezekiel's Prophetic Mission: Towards a Semiotic Approach of Ezekiel 3,22–27." Pages 201–13 in *Ezekiel and His Book: Textual and Literary Criticism and Their Interrelation*. Edited by J. Lust. BETL: Leuven: Leuven University, 1986.
Tucker, G. M. "Prophecy and the Prophetic Literature." Pages 325–68 in *The Hebrew Bible and Its Modern Interpreters*. Edited by D. A. Knight and G. M. Tucker. Chico, Calif.: Scholars Press, 1985.
Uehlinger, Christoph. "Was There a Cult Reform under King Josiah? The Case for a Well-Grounded Minimum." Pages 279–316 in *Good Kings and Bad Kings*. Edited by Lester L. Grabbe. LHBOTS 393. New York: T&T Clark, 2005.
van der Kooij, Arie and Karel van der Toorn, eds. *Canonization and Decanonization: Papers Presented to the International Conference of the Leiden Institute for the Study of Religions*. SHR 82. Leiden: Brill, 1997.
van der Toorn, Karel. "From the Oral to the Written: The Case of Old Babylonian Prophecy." Pages 220–32 in *Writings and Speech in Israelite and Ancient Near Eastern Prophecy*. Edited by Ben Zvi and Michael Floyd. SBLSymS 10. Atlanta: Society of Biblical Literature, 2000. Reprint of *JNSL* 24 (1998): 55–70.
―――. "The Iconic Book: Analogies between the Babylonian Cult of Images and the Veneration of the Torah." Pages 229–48 in *The Image and the Book: Iconic*

Cults, Aniconism, and the Rise of Book Religion in Israel and the Ancient Near East. Edited by Karel van der Toorn. Leuven: Peeters, 1997.

———. *Scribal Culture and the Making of the Hebrew Bible*. Cambridge: Harvard University Press, 2007.

van der Woude, Adam S. *ṣābā'* / Heer. Pages 498–507 in *THAT* 2 (1967).

Van Rooy, Herculaas. "Prophet and Society in the Persian Period According to Chronicles." Pages 163–79 in *Second Temple Studies 2: Temple and Community in the Persian Period*. Edited by Tamara Cohn Eskenazi and K. H. Richards. JSOTSup 175. Sheffield: Sheffield Academic, 1994.

Veijola, Timo. *Die ewige Dynastie: David und die Entstehung seiner Dynastie nach der deuteronomistischen Darstellung*. AASF B/193. Helsinki: Suomalainen Tiedeakatemia, 1975.

von Rad, Gerhard. "Die levitische Predigt in den Büchern der Chronik." Pages 248–61 in *Gesammelte Studien zum Alten Testament*. ThB 8. Munich: Chr. Kaiser, 1965. Repr., *Festschrift für Otto Procksch*. Leipzig: A. Deichert & J. C. Hinrich, 1934.

Walker, Paul E. "Impeccability." Pages 505–7 in vol. 2 of *Encyclopaedia of the Qur'an*. Edited by Jane Dammen McAuliffe, 5 vols.; Leiden: Brill, 2001.

Walls, P. Dutcher. "The Social Location of the Deuteronomists: A Sociological Study of Factional Politics in Late Pre-Exilic Judah." *JSOT* 52 (1991): 77–94.

Watts, John D. W. "Prophetic Genre in the Book of the Twelve." Pages 123-33 in *Vision and Prophecy in Amos*. Expanded ed. Macon: Mercer University Press, 1997.

Watts, John D. and Paul R. House, eds. *Forming Prophetic Literature: Essays on Isaiah and the Twelve in Honor of John D. W. Watts*. JSOTSup 235. Sheffield: Sheffield Academic, 1996.

Weber, Max. "Charisma and its Transformation." Pages 1111–57 in vol. 2 of *Economy and Society*. Edited by G. Roth and C. Wittich. 2 vols. Berkeley: University of California Press, 1978.

———. "Charismatismus." Pages 753–78 in *Wirtschaft und Gesellschaft*. 2d ed. Tübingen: Mohr Siebeck, 1925.

———. "Religionssoziologie." Pages 227–363 in *Wirtschaft und Gesellschaft*. 2d ed. Tübingen: Mohr Siebeck, 1925.

———. *The Sociology of Religion*. 4th ed. Boston: Beacon Press, 1993.

Weinberg, Joel P. "Die 'Ausserkanonischen Prophezeiungen' in den Chronikbüchern." *Acta Antiqua* 26 (1978): 387–404.

Weinfeld, Moshe."Jeremiah and the Spiritual Metamorphosis of Israel," *ZAW* 88 (1976): 29–32.

———. *From Joshua to Josiah: Turning Points in the History of Israel from the Conquest of the Land until the Fall of Judah*. Jerusalem: Magnes,1992.

———. *Deuteronomy 1–11*. AB 5. New York: Doubleday, 1991.

Weippert, Helga. "Das Wort von neuen Bund in Jeremia xxxi 31–34." *VT* 29 (1979): 336–51.
Weippert, Manfred. "Assyrische Prophetien der Zeit Asarhaddons und Assurbanipals." Pages 71–115 in *Assyrian Royal Inscriptions: New Horizons in Literary, Ideological, and Historical Analysis*. Orientis Antiqui Collectio 17. Edited by Frederick Mario Fales. Rome: Istituto per l'Oriente, 1981.
Wellhausen, Julius. *Die kleinen Propheten*. 4 ed. Berlin: de Gruyter, 1963.
———. *Prolegomena to the History of Israel*. 1885. Repr., Atlanta: Scholars Press, 1994), 48.
Westermann, Claus. *Das Buch Jesaja: Kapitel 40–66*. ATD 19. Göttingen: Vandenhoeck & Ruprecht, 1966.
———. *Grundformen prophetischer Rede*. BEvT 31. Munich: Chr. Kaiser, 1960.
Wevers, John W. *Ezekiel*. NCB. London: Marshall, Morgan & Scott, 1969.
Widmer, Michael. *Moses, God, and the Dynamics of Intercessory Prayer*. FAT II/8. Tübingen: Mohr Siebeck, 2004.
Wildberger, Hans. *Isaiah 1–12: A Commentary*. Translated by Thomas H. Trapp. Continental Commentaries. Minneapolis: Fortress, 1991.
Willi, Thomas. *Die Chronik als Auslegung*. FRLANT 106. Göttingen: Vandenhoeck & Ruprecht, 1972.
Williams, James G. "The Social Location of Israelite Prophecy." *JAAR* 37 (1969): 153–165.
Williamson, Hugh G. M. *1 and 2 Chronicles*. NCB. Grand Rapids: Eerdmans, 1987.
Wilson, Robert R. "Prophecy in Crisis: The Call of Ezekiel." Pages 157–69 in *Interpreting the Prophets*. Edited by J. L. Mays and P. J. Achtemeier. Philadelphia: Fortress, 1987.
———. "An Interpretation of Ezekiel's Dumbness." *VT* 22 (1972): 98–101.
Wöhrle, Jakob. *Die frühen Sammlungen des Zwölfprophetenbuches: Entstehung und Komposition*. BZAW 360. Berlin: de Gruyter, 2006.
Wolff, Hans Walter. *Joel and Amos: A Commentary on the Books of the Prophets Joel and Amos*. Hermeneia. Translated by W. Janzen, S. D. McBride and C. A. Muenchow. Philadelphia: Fortress, 1977.
Wright, George Ernest. "Nations in Hebrew Prophecy." *Encounter* 26 (1965): 225–237.
Wright, Peter Matthews. "Modern Qur'anic Hermeneutics." Ph.D. diss. University of North Carolina at Chapel Hill, 2008.
Yee, Gale A. *Composition and Tradition in the Book of Hosea*. SBLDS 102. Atlanta: Scholars Press, 1987.
Zakovitch, Yair. *Through the Looking Glass: Reflection Stories in the Bible*. Tel-Aviv: ha-Kibbutz ha-Meuhad, 1995.
Zimmerli, Walther. *Ezekiel: A Commentary on the Book of the Prophet Ezekiel*. Vol. 1. Translated by Ronald E. Clements. Hermeneia. Philadelphia: Fortress, 1979.

Zuesse, Evan M. "Divination." Pages 375–82 in vol. 4 of *The Encyclopedia of Religion*. Edited by Mircea Eliade et al. New York: Macmillan, 1987.

AUTHOR INDEX

Abrams, M. H. 202
Abul A'la Maududi, S. 201
Abusch, Tzvi 58
Achtemeier, Paul J. 177
Ackerman, Susan A. 105, 106
Ackroyd, Peter 7, 32, 144
Albertz, Rainer 115, 163
Albright, William F. 67
Allen, Leslie C. 113
Alter, Robert 48, 198
Amit, Yairah 25
Anderson, Gary A. 169
Arbeitman, Yoel I. 106
Arneth, Martin 48
Ash, Paul S. 104
Astour, Michael C. 106
Aufrecht, Walter E. 154
Barrick, W. Boyd 109
Beal, Richard 53
Beck, Martin 130
Becker, Uwe...............................181
Beentjes, Pancratius.........2, 12, 14, 15, 16, 21, 22, 33, 37
Begg, Christopher 25, 31
Bellis, Alice O............................175
Ben Zvi, Ehud.....1, 44, 46, 56, 118, 120, 124, 125, 128, 129, 131, 142, 154
Bendavid, Abba...........................28
Ben-Dov, Jonathan.....3, 12, 14, 43, 46, 50, 52, 54
Berger, Peter L. 71
Berman, Joshua A. 101, 111
Beuken, Willem 7, 33, 143, 144
Bird, Phyllis 71
Blenkinsopp, Joseph............44, 165
Block, Daniel I..........177, 180, 189, 190, 193
Boda, Mark J. 142
Bodel, John 104
Bodi, Daniel 188, 191, 192

Bovati, Pietro.............................189
Brettler, Marc Z. 45
Brown, Norman O. 199
Bryan, Mark...............................180
Bynum, Carolyn 45
Campbell, Antony F. 80, 166
Carr, David M..... 43, 101, 105, 154
Carrez, Maurice 187
Carroll, Robert 91
Chavel, Simeon.........................115
Ciraolo, Leda 53
Cody, Aelred.................... 165, 171
Coggins, Richard 25
Cohen, Mark E............................58
Collins, John J. 87
Cook, Stephen L..............98, 100
Cook, Steve.......................... 4, 20
Crenshaw, James L. 80
Cross, Frank M. 96, 97
Curtis, Edward L. 32
Davies, Philip R. 48, 154
Davis, Ellen F. 194
Davison, Lisa Wilson 69
de Jong, Matthijs J.....56, 175, 180, 194
de Moor, Johannes C. 175
de Regt, Leonard J. 33
de Vries, Simon 25, 36
de Waard, Jan 33
Dearman, J. Andrew 109
Dever, William G. 105, 108
Diedrich, Friedrich......................25
Dietrich, Walter 166
Dillard, Ramond Bryan.........26, 29
Dirksen, Piet B......................38, 39
Doré, Joseph 187
Duguid, Iain M. 193
Duhm, Bernhard.......127, 129, 137, 141
Dutcher-Walls, Patricia 104
Eichrodt, Walter................. 72, 189
Eissfeldt, Otto 79

Elliger, Karl..............................129
Emerton, John A. 25
Engineer, Asghar Ali................197
Engnell, Ivan........................72, 141
Eskenazi, Tamara Cohn 25
Even-Shoshan, Abraham............78
Finkelberg, Margalit...................43
Firestone, Reuven.....................197
Fishbane, Michael..........29, 32, 57
Floyd, Michael...8, 13, 44, 56, 123, 142, 144, 148, 149, 150, 154
Fohrer, Georg.............................87
Fokkelman, Jan P. 33
Frame, Grant 58
Friebel, Kelvin G......................178
Friedman, Richard E. 98
Frolov, Serge.......4, 13, 18, 77, 79, 84, 85
Gauley, Steven W. 154
Geoghegan, Jeffrey C...............107
George, Andrew R. 58
Gerstenberger, Erhard 163
Gese, Hartmut 34
Giesebrecht, Friedrich..............126
Ginzberg, Louis........................202
Gitay, Yehoshua........................176
Gitin, Seymour.................105, 108
Glatt, David A. 28
Goldenberg, Robert....................57
Grabbe, Lester L......1, 5, 14, 16, 17, 18, 48, 87, 166, 175
Graham, M. Patrick 23
Green, D. E. 88
Grelot, Pierre............................187
Gunkel, Hermann......125, 141, 143
Haak, Robert D. 87, 123
Halbertal, Moshe.............43, 44, 57
Halpern, Baruch 47, 95, 107, 114
Handy, Lowell K........45, 46, 49, 53
Hanson, K. C............................204
Hanson, Paul D. 152
Hasson, Isaac............................200
Hays, Richard B. 197, 202

Hazenbos, Joost 53
Hendel, Ronald 198, 202
Hernando, Eusebio.....................25
Hertzberg, Hans Wilhelm.........181
Heschel, Abraham 72
Hodgson, Marshall G. S. ..199, 205
Hoffman, Hans D......................47
Hoglund, Kenneth G..................23
Holladay, William L....98, 101, 186
Hollander, John........................202
Holm, Nils G. 16
House, Paul R. 142
Hurowitz, Victor A. 58, 60, 107
Irsigler, Hubert . 118, 119, 129, 136
Janzen, W. 133
Japhet, Sara....... 22, 24, 29, 33, 171
Jeremias, Jörg ... 125, 153, 154, 187
Johnstone, William 30
Joyce, Paul...............................193
Kaiser, Otto...................... 136, 181
Kasher, Rimon 34
Kegler, Jürgen............................25
Kelly, Brian E...........................30
Kessler, John..... 144, 146, 147, 148
Kimḥi, R. David 171
Kleinig, John W...................38, 39
Knibb, Michael 25
Knight, Douglas A. 142
Knoppers, Gary N........38, 46, 103, 115, 153
Köckert, Matthias 54
Koenen, Klaus 152
Kohn, Risa Levitt.....................188
Kratz, Reinhard G..... 142, 153, 154
Kuntzmann, Raymond 25
Lafont, Bertrand.........................51
Lambert, Wilfred G. 60
Langohr, Guy...........................118
Lapsley, Jacqueline E.190, 194, 195
Leuchter, Mark..........6, 15, 18, 57, 78, 95, 96, 97, 98, 99, 100, 102, 106, 107, 108, 112, 113, 114

Levenson, Jon D. 173, 187
Levin, Christoph 7, 12, 117, 123, 124, 126, 130, 131, 137
Levinson, Bernard 50, 101, 103, 110
Lewis, Ivan M. 16, 17
Liebermann, Stephen J. 58
Lieu, Judith M. 154
Lipschits, Oded 115, 153
Livingstone, Alasdair 58
Lohfink, Norbert 103
Lowery, Richard H. 113
Lowth, Robert 141
Lundbom, Jack R. 100, 102, 112
Machinist, Peter 58, 59
Madsen, Albert A. 32
Marti, K. 129
Mason, Rex 25, 39, 144, 145, 146, 149, 151
Mathias, Dietman 34
Mays, James L. 177
McBride, S. D. 133
McCarter, P. Kyle 166
McKane, William M. ... 99, 108, 119
McKeating, Henry 188
McKenzie, Steven L. 23, 52
Mein, Andrew 177
Merrill, Arthur L. 181
Meyers, Carol 8, 13, 105, 146, 151
Meyers, Eric 8, 13, 146, 151
Micheel, Rosemarie 25, 34
Middlemas, Jill 7, 8, 13, 106, 141, 147, 153
Milgrom, Jacob 169
Miller, Patrick D. 181, 182, 192
Mirau, Neil A. 154
Montgomery, James A. 47
Mowinckel, Sigmund 18, 141, 204
Müller, Reinhard 133, 134
Muenchow, C. A. 133

Muff, Yochanan 182
Muilenburg, James 143
Na'aman, Nadav 49
Neusner, Jacob 107
Newby, Gordon Darnell 205
Newsome, James D. 25, 31
Nissinen, Martti 1, 2, 12, 16, 35, 54, 56, 74, 97, 154
Nogalski, James D. 142, 154
Noth, Martin 166
O'Connor, Kathleen M. 109
Odell, Margaret S. 189
Olyan, Saul M. 104, 108, 109
Overholt, Thomas W. 181
Panetz, Raphael I. 170
Parpola, Simo 54, 55, 59, 60
Patton, Corrine L. 175, 193
Pauritsch, Karl 152
Perlitt, Lothar 118, 119, 128, 129, 136
Person, Raymond F. 154
Petersen, David L. 8, 12, 25, 36, 117, 135, 144, 146, 157, 167, 184
Phillips, Anthony 25
Pongratz-Leisten, Beate ... 55, 56, 59
Potter, H. D. 100
Press, Richard 79
Propp, William H. C. 173
Pucci, Joseph 202
Rahman, Fazlur 197
Ramsey, George W. ... 165, 167, 168
Redditt, Paul L. 142
Reeves, John C. 197
Reventlow, Henning Graf 181, 184, 192
Rhodes, A. B. 181
Richards, Kent H. 25
Riley, William 24
Ritner, Robert K. 97
Roberts, J. J. M. 80
Rochberg-Halton, Francesca 60

Rodwell, J. M. 201
Rogerson, John W. 154
Römer, Thomas 47, 49, 52
Rost, Leonhard 80
Roth, Guenther 18
Roth, Martin 158
Rudolph, Wilhelm 29
Sarna, Nahum M. 181
Sasson, Jack M. 51, 72
Schaeffer, G. E. 31
Schmid, Konrad 115
Schmitt, Armin 36
Schniedewind, William M. 23, 25, 26, 28, 29, 39, 95, 145, 154, 203
Schökel, Luis Alonso 187, 188
Schöpflin, Karin 177, 194
Schwally, Friedrich 119
Schwartz, Baruch J. 51, 178
Seeligman, Isac Leo 25, 31
Sefati, Yitschak 54
Seidel, Jonathan 53
Seitz, Christopher R....186, 187, 190
Seow, C. L. 97
Seybold, Klaus 118, 128, 135
Sharp, Carolyn J. 112, 114
Singer, Itamar 52, 54
Smith, Mark S. 106
Smith, Michael J. 189
Smith, Morton 199, 206
Smith, Paul A. 152, 153
Sommer, Benjamin D. 197, 204
Sparks, Kent 34
Stager, Lawrence E. 108
Steck, Odil H. 153
Stoneman, Richard 205
Stroumsa, Guy G. 43
Strübind, Kim 25, 34, 39
Sweeney, Marvin A. 9, 19, 97, 99, 100, 110, 118, 120, 165
Tadmor, Hayim 58, 59
te Stroete, G. A. 189
Then, Reinhold 24, 25
Thiessen, Matthew 98

Tiemeyer, Lena-Sofia 10, 16, 19, 175, 182, 188, 190
Tollington, Janet 144
Trapp, Thomas H. 51
Tromp, Nicholas J. 194
Tucker, Gene M. 142
Uehlinger, Christoph 48
van der Kooij, Arie 43
van der Toorn, Karel 43, 44, 45, 50, 51, 52, 56, 58, 60, 61, 154
Van Rooy, Herculaas 25
Vanderhooft, David 47
Veijola, Timo 79
von Rad, Gerhard 34, 36
Walker, Paul E. 203
Watts, James W. 142, 145
Weinberg, Joel P. 25
Weinfeld, Moshe 3, 44, 52, 187
Weippert, Manfred 35
Wellhausen, Julius 67, 72, 122, 130
Westermann, Claus 22, 143, 152, 153
Wevers, John W. 189
Whitney, K. William Jr. 125
Widmer, Michael 181, 185, 186
Wildberger, Hans 51
Willi, Thomas 25, 36
Williams, James G. 71
Williamson, Hugh G. M. 32, 36
Willis, John T. 72
Willmes, Bernd 25
Wilson, Robert R. 177, 194
Wittich, Claus 18
Wöhrle, Jakob 118, 131
Wolff, Hans Walter 133, 141
Wright, George E. 161
Wright, Peter Matthews 11, 20, 197, 200
Würthwein, Ernst 181
Yee, Gale A. 125
Zakovitch, Yair 48
Zimmerli, Walther 119, 192

Zuesse, Evan M. 16, 93

INDEX OF SCRIPTURE CITATIONS

Genesis
- 6:5–8 124
- 6:6–7 182
- 6:7: 120, 124–5
- 6–8 .... 7, 125
- 7:4: 120, 124
- 7:23 125
- 15 172
- 18:16–33 184
- 18:22–33 185
- 20:7 .... 77, 184
- 20:17 184
- 22 173
- 28 .... 170, 172
- 31:54 128
- 38 106

Exodus
- 3:10–15 185
- 3:14–15 185
- 4:22 185
- 5:1 185
- 5:22 185
- 7:1 77
- 7:1–2 180
- 7:3 188
- 8:4–9 184
- 8:8 185
- 8:12 185
- 8:28 183
- 8:28–39 185
- 9:27–33 184
- 9:28 .... 183, 185
- 9:33 185
- 10:16–19 184
- 10:17 183
- 10:17–18 185
- 14 36
- 14:13–14 .... 3, 36
- 15:20 77
- 17:8–13 184
- 17:8–16 .... 168, 185
- 18 169
- 20:3 83
- 22:28–29 173
- 29:27 169
- 32:7–14 185
- 32:7–8 185
- 32:10 184
- 32:10–14 .... 185, 195
- 32:11–14 187
- 32:12 124
- 32:27 185
- 32:30–32 185
- 32:30–34 185
- 32:32 184
- 33 170
- 33:16 124
- 34:19–21 172–3

Leviticus
- 7:34 169
- 10:14–15 169
- 16:2 170
- 26:34–35, 43 22

Numbers
- 3 .... 10, 166
- 3:11–13 172–3
- 3:40–41 172
- 3:40–51 172–3
- 6:20 169
- 11 172
- 11:1–3 185
- 11:28–29 77
- 12:1–15 185
- 12:3 124
- 12:6–8 77
- 12:7 184
- 12:11–14 184
- 12:13–15 184
- 13–14 187

14:13–16 185
16:22–17 185
18:18 185
21:7 184
24:2 29

Deuteronomy
4:11 133
4:29–30 30
4:30 30
4:44 45
5:2–3 109
6:15 124
6:5–9 105
7:5 105
7:6 124
9:12–29 185
9:19 187
9:22–29 186
9:25–29 187
12 .... 6, 110–1
12:3 105
12–16 56
13:2–6 .... 77, 112
13:6 112
13:7–12 98
14:2 124
16:1–9 50
16:18–17:13 169
16:21 105
17:14–15 83
17:14–20 103
17:15 111
17:16 45
17:18 .... 4, 61
17:18–20 .... 104, 111
18 .... 4–5, 13, 78, 83, 85
18:6–8 99
18:9–22 186
18:15 .... 104, 184
18:15–18 .... 7, 111
18:15–22 .... 77, 82, 84, 112
18:18 .... 77, 79, 82, 104, 188

18:19 82
18:20 82
18:21–22 .... 112, 204
18:22 .... 5, 82
20:1–4 168
28 .... 5, 13, 56, 82–3
28:15–68 84
28:69 49
29–31 50
30:12 85
31 49
31:10 97
31:9–12 97
32 .... 6, 15
32:25–26 98
32:35–36 98
32:41–42 98
33:8–11 .... 6, 101
34:10 .... 77, 184–5
34:10–12 115

Joshua
8:31–32 61
9:17 83

Judges
2:1–3 81
3:10 29
4:1–9 35
4:4 77
4:4–16 70
6:34 29
6:8 77
8 170
11:29 29
13:1 80
18:30 .... 98, 100

1 Samuel
1–8 .... 5, 13, 83–85
1:1 .... 78, 171
2 80
2:4–6 79

2:4–8	79
2:7	79
2:8–10	79
2:8–9	79
2:10	79
2:11–26	98
2:11–36	100
2:12-17	80
2:12–17	83
2:19–20	79
2:27–36	78–9
2:34	81
2–4	84
3	4, 78, 81, 167, 171
3:1	78, 167, 174
3:11–14	78
3:15	80
3:20	184
3:20–1	166
3:20–21	9, 167–8, 174
4	5, 18, 82–3, 168
4–6	80, 167
4:1	4, 80–1, 167, 174
4:2	80
4:3–6	80
4:4	80
4:10	80
4:11	80, 81
5:2	80
6:21–7:2	83
7	83
7:2–17	168–9
7:3–4	83
7:6	10, 19, 168–9
7:9–10	83, 169
7:12	184
7:15	10, 19, 168, 184
7:17	10, 19, 168
8	5, 18, 81–3, 167
8:1–3	10, 19, 168
8:1–4	98, 100
8:4–6	81
8:5	84
8:7	18, 81
8:7–8	81, 83
8:9	81
8:10	81
8:18	81
8:22	82
9–10	9, 84
9:1–10:16	167–9, 171
9:5	78
9:9	19, 78, 167, 174
9:13	128, 169
9:22	128
10:5–6	15
10:10–11	15
10:13	15
10:17–27	167
13–14	167
13:8–14	170
13:13–14	167
15	167
15:2	167
15:10–11	168
15:11	182
15:17–19	168
15:20–23	168
15:28–29	168
15:35	182
16:3	128
16:5	128
16:15	170
17:47	36
18:10	15
19:20	16, 29
19:20–21	15
19:23	29
19:23–24	15
22:5	84

2 Samuel

6	170
6:15	135

7 84
7:1–17 22
11 200–1
12 ....84, 200
13 106
14:7 124
14:27 106
15:10 135
24:11–14 22

1 Kings 165
1:17 181
1:39 135
2:3 61
6:11–13 102
8:7–15 181
10:26–29 45
11:29–39 25
12–13 47
12:22–24 ....22, 27
12:24 27
13:34 124
14 181
14:25 27
14:26–28 27
15:9–24 28
17:18 194
21:19 84
21:28–29 84
22 ....38, 85
22:1–38 84
22:6–28 22
22:15–28 84
22:22 84
22:35–37 84
22:38 84
22:40 84

2 Kings 165
1:2–8 181
5:9 194
9 25
9:13 135

12:10–16 47
19:1–7 35
19:2–4 194
21:3 126
21:11-12 126
21:13–14 130
21:14: 121
22 ....48, 50–1, 57
22–23 ....46, 61, 103–4
22:3–15 47
22:3–7 47
22:4–15 48
22:8 ....38, 49, 51
22:10 38
22:11 49
22:12 38
22:12–20 131
22:13 54
22:14 131
22:14–20 70
22:15–20 22
22:16–20 46
22:18 38
22:20 47
23 ....7, 126, 138
23:1–2 44
23:1–3 ....47, 49
23:2 ....49, 104
23:4–5: 121, 126
23:5: 121, 127
23:12 126
23:13 127
23:15–20 47
23:21 49–50
23:21–23 ....44, 47, 49
23:25 ....52, 61, 103
23:26 126
24:3 126
24:9 103
25:18 123

Isaiah
2:12–17 136

2:3	51, 160
6	170
6:8	185
8:16–20	54
11:4	137
23:17	124
34:5	128
37:1–7	35
40–55	8, 153
42:19	146
44:26	146
51:1	127
56–59	152
56:1–8	152
56:9–57:21	152
56–66	8, 13, 152
58:1–59:20	152
60–62	8, 152–3
60:5–7	160
60:6	160
60:11	160
60:16	160
61:6	160
63:7–64:11	152
63:11–12	184
65:1–66:17	152
66:12	160
66:18	160
66:18–24	152

Jeremiah

1	170
1:1	95, 178
1:2:	120, 123
1:7	185
2–6	6, 98
2:7	115
2:8	101
6:1	131
6:17	78
7	73
7:(1–2)3–5	6

7:3	7, 111
7:3–15	95
7:4	111
7:5-6	111
7:7	111
7:8	111
7:11	107
7:1–15	110
7:16	181, 187
7:16–20	6, 105–7
7:25	24
8	57
8:1–3	6, 108–9
8:8	57
8:8–9	56, 95
11	99
11:14	181, 187
11:21–23	6, 15, 95, 97, 99
14:11	187
14:11–12	181
15:1	97, 184, 187
15:4	126
15:16	95
16:1–2	100
16:1–4	100
16:18	115
19	7, 126
19:3:	121
19:3–7	126
19:5:	121, 126
19:12	126
19:13:	121, 126
20:2	91
20:9	95, 179
20:14–18	95
21	108
21:1	123
22:15–16	95, 102–3
23:13–14	95
24	110, 170
24:1	103
24:5	103

24:5–7	109	38:7	123
25:4	24	38:10	123
25:11–12	22	38:12	123
25:26	124	38:20–21	194
26	109	39:14	123
26–45	114	39:16	123
26:8–9	91	42:2	186
26:18–19	185	42:4	186
27–29	112	44:15–19	106
27:18	186	46:10	128
28	112	48:3	131
28:2–4	113	51:25:	121
28:6	6, 110	51:54	131
28:16	124	51:59–64	113
29	12		
29:6–7	115	*Ezekiel*	
29:10–14	22	1–3	170, 179
29:13–14	30	1:1	177
29:14	30	1:1–2	126
29:19	24	1:3	177
29:25	123	1:4–28	179
29:29	123	1:14–28	178
30–31	6, 102, 110	1:28–2:2	178
30:1–2	12	2:1–2	180
31:6	33	2:2	17
31:16	33	2:3	185
31:31–34	6, 100, 102	2:4	188
31:33-34	101	2:5	188
32:6–15	95, 99	2:8	180
32:29	126	2:9–3:2	54
34	6, 97	2:9–3:3	189
34:8–9	108	2:10–3:3	188
35:15	24	3:12, 14, 22, 24	17
36	12, 109	3:14	179
36:5	91	3:15	179, 190
36:14	123	3:16–21	188
37	108	3:17	78
37–38	108	3:24–27	190
37:3	123, 194	3:26	189
37:11–16	91	3:26–27	188
37:17	194	4:12–15	193
38:1	123	6:14:	121, 126
38:6–13	91	8–10	170

8:1	190–2
8:1–8	178
8:2–3	192
8:3	178, 191
8:5	178
9:8	11, 19, 178, 190–1
11	11
11:1	191
11:1, 5, 24	17
11:4	191
11:5	16
11:13	178, 190–1
11:14–21	192
12:6	190
12:11	190
13:5	190, 192
14:1	190–2
14:2	192
14:3	192
14:8	126
14:9:	121, 126
14:13:	121, 126
14:17	126
16:27	126
20:1	190
20:1–3	191–2
20:2	192
20:3–4	192
20:32–44	187
21:6	178
21:8	126
21:9	126
22:30	11, 190, 192
22:30–31	192
24:15–27	178
24:24	190
24:27	189, 194
25:7	126
25:13:	121, 126
29:8	126
32:2	178
32:18	178
33:2	78
33:6	78
33:6–7	78
33:7–20	188
33:10	57
33:22	189
33:24	57
33:25	57
35:3:	121, 126
35:7	126
37	187
37:1	17
37:1–14	179
37:3	179
37:9–10	179
37:11b	57
37:12	57
38:20	124
39:17	128
40–48	11, 170, 179, 187, 193
40:1	17
40:4	179
43:10–11	179
44:4	178
44:5	179
47:6	179

Hosea
3:4	32–3
3:5	33
4:3	125
9:8	78
10:5	127
11:8	195

Joel
2:2	133
2:28	68
3–4	157
4:2	158
4:6	159
4:11–12	160

4:19 159

Amos 93
  1–2 .... 88, 161
  2:14–16 132
  3–6 89
  3:4 124
  3:7 .... 5, 90
  3:8 124
  3:9 32
  4:1–3 88
  4:4–5 134
  5 7
  5:11: 122, 130
  5:18 ... 120, 122, 132–3, 135, 138
  5:18–20 .... 132, 137
  5:20: 120, 122, 132, 135, 138
  5:21 88
  5:22 133
  7 185
  7–9 .... 89, 170
  7:1–3 89
  7:1–6 .... 185, 195
  7:1–9 186
  7:1–8:3 .... 181, 187
  7:4–6 89
  7:7–8 89
  7:7–9 89
  7:9 89
  7:10 89
  7:10–17 .... 89, 149
  7:16 89
  7:17 89
  8:1–3 186
  8:4 137
  8:8 125
  9:5 125
  9:8 124

Obadiah
  15–16 158

Micah
  4:1–2 160
  4:1–3 158
  4:11 160
  5:7–9 158
  6:4 184
  7:17 162

Nahum 8, 12

Habakkuk 8, 12, 182
  1:6 158
  2–3 170
  2:20: 120, 128
  2:2–3 54

Zephaniah 8, 12
  1 .... 7, 119
  1:1 .... 7, 123
  1:1–2:3 .... 7, 117, 119–20
  1:2–3 ... 7, 124–6, 130, 136, 138
  1:3 125
  1:4 125–7
  1:4–5 126
  1:4–6 .... 7, 126
  1:5 126–7
  1:6 .... 7, 125, 127, 137
  1:7, 14, 15 7
  1:7 ... 7, 127–8, 130–2, 134, 137
  1:7a 132
  1:8 .... 130, 136
  1:8–13 .... 7, 129
  1:8–9 .... 129, 130–1
  1:9 .... 130, 136
  1:10 .... 7, 129, 131
  1:10–11 129–31
  1:12 129
  1:12–13 .... 130–1, 136
  1:13 .... 7, 130
  1:14 .... 128, 131, 132, 137–8
  1:14–16 131
  1:14–16a 7, 135
  1:15 .... 7, 132–6

1:15–16	132, 137
1:16	135–6
1:16–2:3	136
1:16b–2:3	7
1:17	125, 136
1:17–18	136, 138
1:18	130, 136–7
2	163
2–3	119
2:1	122
2:1–2	137
2:1–3	138
2:15–3:5	119
2:3	125, 127, 130, 137
2:4–14	119
2:4–3:20	119
2:5–15	158–9
2:7	119
2:8	158
2:11	160
2:12	124, 158
3:6	119
3:8	119, 137, 159
3:9	160
3:9–20	119
3:12	130, 137, 139
3:13	139
3:16	32–3

Haggai 8, 12–3, 143, 155
1:1	144–5
1:12	144, 148
1:1–2	8
1:1–2	147
1:13	144, 146
1:14	148
1:14–15	144
1:15	146
1:3	144–5
1–2	8
2:1	8, 145, 147
2:10	144–5
2:1–2	144
2:1–3	147
2:2	144
2:4–5	144
2:5	144
2:7	160
2:13–14	144
2:20	144–5

Zechariah
1:1	145, 147, 151
1:1–6	151–2
1:7	145, 147, 151
1:7–6:25	151
1:9–14	146
1:15	160
1–6	170
1–8	7–8, 13, 143, 148, 152–3, 155
2:3	146
2:4	160
2:7	159
2:12	160
2:15	160
2:17:	120, 128
3:6–10	8, 145, 148
4:1	146
4:6–10	148
4:8	146
5:5	146
5:11	159
6:4	146
6:8	159
6:9	146
6:9–15	148
7	149
7–8	148, 152
7:1	145, 147, 151
7:1–3	8, 145, 147
7:1–8:23	151
7:8	145, 151
8:7	159

8:10	32, 33
8:22	160
8:23	160
9	163
9:1–8	159
9:7	159
9:13	159
10:11	159
11:1	159
12:2–4	160
12:9	160
14:2	160
14:14	160
14:16	160
14:18–19	159
14:19	159

Malachi

1:1	146
1:4	159
1:11	160
1:14	160
2:7	146
3:1	146
3:22	61
4:5–6	184

Psalms

9:11	127
19:11	78
22:2	162
22:29	163
29	134
34:11	127
37:11	137
37:32	78
47:6:	120, 135
67:3–4	162
67:4	163
68:32	162
72:10	160
72:17	162
76:10	137
86:9	162–3
93	134
97	7, 133
97:2	133
97:2–5:	120
98:4–6	134
98:6	134
99:6	184
100	134
102:16	162
105:3–4	127
105:4	127
117:1	162
117:2	163

Proverbs

28:5	127
30:14	137

Job ... 182

24:4	137

Daniel ... 94

2	89, 91
3	91
6	91
7	89
8	89
9	91
9:11	61
9:13	61
10–12	91
11	89

Ezra

1:1	115
6:21	127
9:11	115
9:12	115

Nehemiah

3:3	131

6:12 37
6:14 70
6:16 161
8:1 61
11:9 131
12:27 163
12:39 131

1 Chronicles
2:7 27
5:25–26 27
6 165
6:7–13 .... 168, 171
9:1 27
9:22 168
10:13 27
12:19 .... 16, 23, 29, 34
15:16–17 39
16:4–6 39
16:10 127
16:11 127
16:37–42 39
17:1–15 22
20 .... 11, 201
21:1 202
21:9–13 22
22:18 30
22:19 127
25:1–3 .... 3, 15, 38–9
25:1–6 38
25:3–6 15
25:5 38
26:28 168
28:9 .... 27, 30–1, 127
28:20 27
29:29 .... 14, 37, 168

2 Chronicles
5:12 39
7:14 24
7:19 27
8:14 31

9:29 .... 3, 14, 37
11:2 28
11:2–4 .... 22, 27
11:3 27
11:11–12 27
11:17 27
12:1 27–8
12:2 27
12:2–8 27
12:5 27–8
12:5–8 .... 2, 26–7
12:6–7 28
12:7 24
12:9–11 27
12:12 28
12:14 127
12:15 .... 14, 37
13:10–11 27
13:22 .... 14, 37
14–15 30
14:2–15:15 28
14:3 .... 31, 127
14:5–6 31
14:6 .... 31, 127
14:11–12 28
14:15 28
15:1 .... 16, 23, 28, 30, 34
15:1–7 .... 3, 26, 28
15:2 27–31
15:3 32–3
15:3–6 .... 29, 31–2
15:3–7 33
15:4 .... 30–1, 33
15:5 32–3
15:7 .... 29, 32–3
15:8 37
15:9 30
15:12 30
15:12–13 .... 30, 127
15:15 .... 30, 31
16:7–10 .... 26, 28
16:12 127

18	38
18:5–27	22
18:7	38
18:9	38
18:11	38
18:17	38
19:1–3	26
20	36
20:3	127
20:14	16, 23, 30, 34
20:14–17	3, 26, 34–6
20:15	34–6
20:17	30, 35–6
20:20	37
20:21	36
20:37	26, 39
21:10	27
21:12	14, 37
21:12–15	26
22:9	127
23:18	61
24:18	27
24:20	16, 23, 27–9, 31, 34
24:20–21	26
24:24	27
25:7–9	26
25:15–16	26
26:5	127
26:16	27
26:18	27
26:22	37
28:6	27
28:9	24
28:9–11	26
28:19	27
28:22	27
29:6	27
29:19	27
29:30	38
30:7	27
32:31	27
32:32	14, 37
33:14	131
33:19	27
34:21	24
34:22	131
34:23–28	22
34:25	24
35:15	38, 184
35:18	168
35:21	16, 23
35:25	115
36:12b	23
36:14	27
36:15–16	23, 146
36:15a	24
36:16	24
36:21–22	22
36:22–23	115

4 Ezra 5
   14:37–47 54

2 Baruch
   53–76 89

1 Enoch 93

Matthew
   24:15 91

Mark
   13:14 91

Qur'an
   2:42 198
   2:89 198
   2:91 198
   2:97 198
   2:101 198
   2:251 200
   3:3 198
   3:81 198
   4:163 200
   4:47 198
   5:19 203

5:48	198
6:84	200
6:92	198
18:83–101	206
21:78	200
35:31	198
38:18	200
38:21–25	200
46:12	198
46:30	198

www.ingramcontent.com/pod-product-compliance
Lightning Source LLC
Chambersburg PA
CBHW021139230426
43667CB00005B/184